PEACEKEEPING INTELLIGENCE

Peacekeeping Intelligence offers a new evaluation of the role, dynamics, and challenges of intelligence in peacekeeping activities and places it in a wider social, economic, and political context.

This work assesses the role of coalition forces, law enforcement agencies, development institutions, and non-governmental organizations that have become partners in peace-support activities.

Peacekeeping intelligence (PKI) is a new form of intelligence that brings together predominantly open sources of information, or open-source intelligence (OSINT), and synthesizes it with human and technical sources to create a holistic perspective at the strategic, tactical, and operational levels, while emphasizing a wide sharing of information. Unlike national intelligence, which emphasizes spies, satellites, and secrecy, PKI brings together many aspects of intelligence gathering including the media and non-governmental organizations. It seeks to establish standards in open-source collection, analysis, security, and counter-intelligence and training, and produces unclassified intelligence useful to the public. The challenges facing PKI are increasingly intertwined with questions of arms control, commercial interests, international crime, and ethnic conflict.

This book will be of great interest to all students and scholars of military and security studies, intelligence, and peacekeeping.

David Carment is Professor of International Affairs and Director of the Centre for Security and Defence Studies at the Norman Paterson School of International Affairs, Carleton University. His most recent books include *Using Force to Prevent Ethnic Violence: An Evaluation of Theory and Evidence.*

Martin Rudner is Professor at the Norman Paterson School of International Affairs, Carleton University, and founding Director of its Canadian Centre of Intelligence and Security Studies. He is the author of more than seventy scholarly articles and books on Intelligence and Security Studies and International Affairs.

STUDIES IN INTELLIGENCE SERIES
General Editors: Richard J. Aldrich and Christopher Andrew

Richard Aldrich is Professor at the Department of Politics, University of Nottingham

Christopher Andrew is Professor of Modern and Contemporary History at Corpus Christi College, University of Cambridge.

OUR MAN IN YUGOSLAVIA:
THE STORY OF A SECRET
SERVICE OPERATIVE
Sebastian Ritchie

UNDERSTANDING
INTELLIGENCE IN THE
TWENTY-FIRST CENTURY:
JOURNEYS IN SHADOWS
Len Scott and Peter Jackson

MI6 AND THE MACHINERY
OF SPYING
Philip H.J. Davies

TWENTY-FIRST CENTURY
INTELLIGENCE
Edited by Wesley Wark

INTELLIGENCE AND
STRATEGY: SELECTED
ESSAYS
John Robert Ferris

THE US GOVERNMENT,
CITIZEN GROUPS AND THE
COLD WAR: THE
STATE–PRIVATE NETWORK
*Edited by Helen Laville and
Hugh Wilford*

PEACEKEEPING
INTELLIGENCE: NEW
PLAYERS, EXTENDED
BOUNDARIES,
*Edited by David Carment and
Martin Rudner*

PEACEKEEPING INTELLIGENCE

New players, extended boundaries

Edited by David Carment and Martin Rudner

Routledge
Taylor & Francis Group

LONDON AND NEW YORK

First published 2006
by Routledge
2 Park Square, Milton Park, Abingdon, Oxon, OX14 4RN

Simultaneously published in the USA and Canada
by Routledge
270 Madison Ave, New York NY 10016

Routledge is an imprint of the Taylor & Francis Group, an informa business

Transferred to Digital Printing 2009

© 2006 David Carment and Martin Rudner

Typeset in Sabon by Taylor & Francis

British Library Cataloguing in Publication Data
A catalogue record for this book is available from the British Library

Library of Congress Cataloging in Publication Data
A catalog record for this book has been requested

ISBN10: 0-415-37489-8 (hbk)
ISBN10: 0-415-54497-1 (pbk)
ISBN10: 0-203-08747-X (ebk)

ISBN13: 978-0-415-37489-7 (hbk)
ISBN13: 978-0-415-54497-9 (pbk)
ISBN13: 978-0-203-08747-3 (ebk)

FOR
DAVID WILLIAM CARMENT, 1928–2004
ESTHER RUDNER 1911–1992
RYAN NEIL

CONTENTS

CONTENTS

CONTENTS

LIST OF ILLUSTRATIONS

LIST OF CONTRIBUTORS

Matthew M. Aid is a native of New York City and holds a Bachelor's degree in International Relations from Beloit College in Beloit, Wisconsin. He has served as a senior executive with several large international financial research and investigative companies for more than fifteen years. Mr. Aid was the co-editor with Dr. Cees Wiebes of *Secrets of Signals Intelligence During the Cold War and Beyond* (London: Frank Cass, 2001), and is currently completing a history of the National Security Agency and its predecessor organizations covering the period 1945 to the present. He is also the author of a chapter about the National Security Agency in *A Culture of Secrecy: The Government Versus the People's Right to Know* (University of Kansas Press, 1998), as well as a number of articles on intelligence issues in the journal *Intelligence and National Security* focusing primarily on issues relating to signals intelligence (SIGINT).

Christopher Ankersen is Security and Defence Forum Fellow at the Centre for Security and Defence Studies at Carleton University's Norman Paterson School of International Affairs. His research interests include civil–military relations, civil–military cooperation in post-conflict scenarios, and Canadian defence policy. Since 2001 he has acted as a consultant for government, the military, and firms in the private sector on strategic policy and management issues in Canada and the UK. He is editor of *Terrorism* (Cambridge: Polity Press, 2005) and has written a number of articles and book chapters on a wide array of defense and security topics, including disarmament, defense management, European defense policy, and peace-building. Christopher's work has earned him awards from the Canadian Defence Associations Institute, the British Ministry of Defence, the United States Naval Institute, and the Royal United Services Institute of Defence Studies. Christopher received his undergraduate education in Military and Strategic Studies at Royal Roads Military College, and his graduate education in International

Relations at the London School of Economics and Political Science. Christopher was in the Canadian Forces for twelve years, serving as an officer in Princess Patricia's Canadian Light Infantry. He has held a number of appointments within the First and Third Battalions and deployed to Croatia in 1992–93 and Kosovo in 1999.

Eric G. Berman was a Visiting Fellow at the Thomas J. Watson Jr. Institute for International Studies at Brown University and a Consultant for the Geneva-based Small Arms Survey. He joined the United Nations (UN) in 1990 in the Department for Disarmament Affairs and subsequently served as the Assistant Spokesman for the UN Transitional Authority in Cambodia, the Special Assistant to the Director-General of the UN Office at Geneva, and the Political Affairs Officer for the UN International Commission of Inquiry (Rwanda). He has published widely on UN and African security issues, including "The Security Council's Increasing Reliance on Burden-Sharing: Collaboration of Abrogation? (*International Peacekeeping*, Vol. 4, No. 1, Spring 1998), (with Katie E. Sams) *Peacekeeping in Africa: Capabilities and Culpabilities* (Geneva: UN Institute for Disarmament Research, 2000), "Re-armament in Sierra Leone: One Year After the Lomé Peace Agreement" (*SAS Occasional Paper Series: Number 1*, Geneva: Small Arms Survey, 2000), and "The Provision of Lethal Military Equipment: French, UK, and US Peacekeeping Policies Toward Africa" (*Security Dialogue*, Vol. 34, No. 2, 2003). He is currently undertaking a study on small arms in the Central African Republic.

Tamal Bhattacharya enlisted in the US Air Force Reserve in 2000 where he presently holds the rank of Senior Airman. In 2002 he enrolled into the Research Intelligence Analyst Program (presently Mercyhurst College Institute of Intelligence Studies), Erie, PA. During his two years at Mercyhurst College, Tamal worked on various government-sponsored projects for his department. Also during this period he interned as an intelligence analyst with the US Government and Booz Allen Hamilton Inc. Tamal holds a Bachelor of Commerce from the University of Calcutta and a Bachelor of Arts in Intelligence Studies from Mercyhurst College. He is an intelligence analyst by training and an avid reader of history. His primary fields of interest are history of intelligence, terrorism, counter-intelligence, and denial and deception. His region of specialization is South Asia.

Douglas Bond has a PhD from the University of Hawaii at Manoa and serves as Associate Director of the Program on Nonviolent Sanctions and Cultural Survival, Center for International Affairs, Harvard University. Since 1988 he has led the development of a Protocol for the Assessment of Nonviolent Direct Action (PANDA) at Harvard to assess this pre-violent contentious struggle, initially using manual, and since 1992 automated, event-data development systems. The PANDA project's protocol facilitates the identification and tracking of conflict situations before they erupt into violence. The project currently monitors global news wire reports using automated event-coding technology guided by the project's recently developed events data protocol, dubbed IDEA (Integrated Events Data Analysis). Dr. Bond's recent publications include two articles on automated events-data development published in the *Journal of Conflict Resolution* (August 1997 and January 2001) and an article on the IDEA protocol in the *Journal of Peace Research* (November 2003).

Patrick Cammaert is Military Advisor in the UN Department of Peacekeeping Operations. He was Force Commander of the UN Mission in Ethiopia and Eritrea (UNMEE) and has served previously as Commander of the Multinational UN Stand-by Forces High Readiness Brigade (SHIRBRIG). He also served as Battalion Commander in the UN Transitional Authority in Cambodia (UNTAC) and Assistant Chief of Staff of the Multinational Brigade of the Rapid Reaction Forces of the UN Protection Force (UNPROFOR).

David Carment is Professor of International Affairs and Director of the Centre for Security and Defence Studies at the Norman Paterson School of International Affairs, Carleton University. His most recent books include *Using Force to Prevent Ethnic Violence: An Evaluation of Theory and Evidence.*

Walter Dorn is an Associate Professor at the Canadian Forces College and is cross-appointed to the Royal Military College. He is also an Adjunct Research Professor with the Norman Paterson School of International Affairs at Carleton University and a faculty member of the Pearson Peacekeeping Centre. Since 1983 he has served as the UN Representative of Science for Peace, a Canadian non-governmental organization, and addressed the UN General Assembly in 1988 at the Second UN Special Session on Disarmament. In the US, he was a Senior Research Fellow at Cornell University (Mario Einaudi Centre for International Studies, 1998–2000), a consultant to Yale University (UN Studies, 1996), a visiting scholar at the Cooperative Monitoring Centre (Sandia National Laboratories, NM, 1999), and advisor to the Federation of American Scientists (Biological Weapons Control Expert Group, 1990).

Angela Gendron is a Senior Fellow at the Canadian Centre of Intelligence and Security Studies, Norman Paterson School of International Affairs, Carleton University, and a Research Fellow at the Centre for Intelligence and Security Studies at Brunel University in the UK. She has consulted and lectured on security and intelligence issues to Canadian government departments and agencies, as well as for British government departments where she contributes to training programs. Prior to this she worked for the UK Ministry of Defence, including an assignment as First Secretary, Political, at the British High Commission in Ottawa.

Robert Grossman-Vermaas is a strategic analyst with the Department of National Defence (Canada). His current position is with Advanced Concept Development—Directorate of Defence Analysis (DDA) and Canadian Forces Experimentation Centre. He is the Canadian concept lead for the multinational and national effects-based concept and has presented and published extensively on the topic. He is Canadian effects-based concept liaison to the US Joint Forces Command (JFCOM), Joint Experimentation (J9), and is a core concept development contributor to the Multinational Experimentation (MNE) series. Previous assignments have included the US Department of Defense and the UK Defence Science and Technology Laboratory (DSTL). He has been awarded a MacArthur Fellowship and is a PhD candidate at the Department of War Studies, King's College, London.

Robert Heibel is a twenty-five-year veteran of the FBI, where he served as Deputy Chief of Counter-terrorism. He holds a Masters Degree from Georgetown University and is the Director of the Research/Intelligence Analyst Program (R/IAP) at Mercyhurst College, Erie, PA. The award-winning R/IAP, which he designed, is the only four-year college undergraduate program designed to generate a qualified entry-level analyst for government and the private sector. Heibel is also Director of the Center for Information Research, Analysis and Training (CIRAT), a non-profit organization created at Mercyhurst to capitalize on the talent, expertise, and technical capability of R/IAP. CIRAT is an academic pioneer in the application of computerized analytical tools and techniques to open-source intelligence (OSINT). He also serves on the board of directors of the Association of Former Intelligence Officers (AFIO) and was the 2001 recipient of the Society of Competitive Intelligence Professionals (SCIP) Meritorious Award.

Rachel Lea Heide is a Doctoral Candidate with the Department of History at Carleton University. Her dissertation investigates civil–military relations, leadership, and organizational culture in the Royal Canadian Air Force during the 1930s, 1940s, and 1950s. The particular area of interest for both her Masters thesis and Bachelors thesis research has been Canada's participation in the British Commonwealth Air Training Plan. Her publications and conference presentations have covered topics spanning from the First World War, the Second World War, and into the Cold War period. In addition to being a Pre-Doctoral Fellow with the

Centre for Security and Defence Studies, she is also an Associate Air Force Historian with the Office of Air Force Heritage and History (1 Canadian Air Division, Winnipeg, Manitoba), a teaching assistant in the Department of History at Carleton University, and a part-time professor at Algonquin College (Ottawa, Ontario).

Michael A. Hennessy is an Associate Professor of History and War Studies at the Royal Military College of Canada, Kingston and Chair of the Department of History. Dr. Hennessy served as the founding editor of the *Canadian Military Journal/Revue militaire canadienne*, and remains a member of its editorial and advisory boards. He is also a member of the editorial board of *Defence Studies. The Journal of the Joint Services Command and Staff College* (UK). He has authored numerous scholarly articles on Canadian naval and maritime history, intelligence and strategy during the Vietnam War, and Canadian foreign and defence policy. Recent publications include *Strategy In Vietnam: The Marines and Revolutionary War in I Corps, 1965–1971* (Praeger, 1997), and "Operation Assurance: Planning a multinational operation for Rwanda/Zaire" (*Canadian Military Journal*, Spring 2001). Dr. Hennessy designed the five-course Master of Arts Intelligence degree stream of the War Studies program for which he created the courses on Asymmetric Threats and Regional Strategic Analysis methodology. He is the former Deputy Project Director for the Canadian Forces Leadership Institute and is a Senior Research Fellow of the Institute.

George Kolisnek is Director of Strategic Intelligence at J2, Defence Intelligence, National Defence Headquarters, Ottawa. Earlier in his career he served in the Royal Canadian Navy, on ships and submarines, and also in staff positions abroad, including Commander Second Fleet staff in Norfolk Virginia and CINCEASTLANT/CINCHAN staff at *HMS Warrior* in the UK. Since retiring from the navy he has been with National Defence, Directorate General Intelligence.

Robert Martyn has a twenty-five-year military career including service in the Canadian Airborne Regiment, Search & Rescue, and Intelligence, with peace support tours in Cyprus, Bosnia, and Kosovo. Foreign military qualifications include psychological operations, information operations, and counter-terrorism intelligence. His History PhD from Queen's University examined problems of peacekeeping intelligence. He is currently a post-doctoral fellow at the Canadian Centre of Intelligence and Security Studies within Carleton University's Norman Paterson School of International Affairs, where his current research addresses issues of intelligence, terrorism, and special operations.

Patrick Meier is a fellow at Columbia University's Center for International Conflict Resolution (CICR) and an affiliate of Harvard University's

Program on Nonviolent Sanctions and Cultural Survival. Mr. Meier serves as a conflict prevention consultant to International/Regional organizations, non-governmental organizations, and research institutes. He is the co-founder of the American Council on Africa (ACA) and an active member of the Alliance for International Conflict Prevention and Resolution (AICPR). He has also worked as special assistant to Dr. David Hamburg, co-chair of the Carnegie Commission on Preventing Deadly Conflict. Mr. Meier's present work focuses on the application of geographic information systems for early warning and sustainable development. He is the author of more than seventy scholarly articles and books on Intelligence and Security Studies and International Affairs. Mr. Meier graduated magna cum laude from Columbia University's School of International and Public Affairs (SIPA) and holds an MA in Conflict Prevention.

Paul T. Mitchell His academic research has largely revolved around naval issues. As a post-doctoral fellow with the Centre for Foreign Policy Studies at Dalhousie University, he conducted research into the proliferation of naval arms in small navies. In 1998 Dr. Mitchell joined the staff of the Canadian Forces College in Toronto. He has had articles published in the *Journal of Strategic Studies, Armed Forces and Society,* the electronic *Journal of Military and Strategic Studies,* as well as *International Insights,* and is the co-author of *Multinational Naval Co-operation and Foreign Policy in the 21st Century,* (London: Ashgate, 1998), in addition to articles published in several books and trade magazines.

Christopher K. Penny is Assistant Professor of International Affairs at the Norman Paterson School of International Affairs, Carleton University, Ottawa.

Martin Rudner is Professor at the Norman Paterson School of International Affairs, Carleton University, and founding Director of its Canadian Centre of Intelligence and Security Studies. He is the author of more than seventy scholarly articles and books on Intelligence and Security Studies.

Kristan J. Wheaton is an Assistant Professor in the Department of Intelligence Studies at Mercyhurst College, Erie, PA. He spent twenty years in the US Army in a variety of intelligence and intelligence-related billets and participated in or supported every peacekeeping operation in the Balkans from 1994–2003. He is the author of *The Warning Solution: Intelligence Analysis In The Age Of Information Overload.*

FOREWORD

Introduction

The principles of war remain the basic tenets of military planning and action—whether in a peacekeeping or a peace-enforcement operation. First, you must have the right force, with the right equipment and training, in the right place and at the right time, in order to conduct operations. Then you have to apply those principles within a doctrinal framework to execute the operation. In order to accomplish all of this in a peacekeeping environment, you need to plan correctly, plan on the realities of the situation, and plan for possible escalation in the expected levels of conflict and destabilization that may be encountered. This planning needs an accurate information base and specific intelligence products.

It has been my experience, however, that the successful execution of operations and managing to remain within the decision cycle of belligerent forces in a complex, multidimensional peacekeeping environment is inevitably problematic, as there is rarely adequate operational and tactical-level intelligence available.

Peacekeeping, like intelligence, is booming business these days. Multidimensional UN peacekeeping operations in Sierra Leone and East Timor continue to downsize according to plan, and meanwhile operations in Kosovo, Georgia, Eritrea/Ethiopia, and Afghanistan continue to play a leading and demanding role in helping to facilitate complex and fragile peace processes.

In 2003 two new missions in Côte d'Ivoire and Liberia were launched. Two assessment missions are also underway, one for expansion of the Mission des Nations Unies en Côte d'Ivoire (MINUCI) and one for establishing a new operation in the Sudan. At the same time, the United Nations (UN) has expanded its Mission in the Democratic Republic of Congo, increasing MONUC's military strength to almost 11,000 troops and authorizing MONUC to use all necessary means to fulfill its mandate in Ituri and North and South Kivu.

On August 14, 2003, the Security Council authorized the establishment of the UN Assistance Mission for Iraq—UNAMI—just four days prior to the devastating attack on UN Headquarters in Baghdad, which claimed the lives of 22 colleagues and friends, and injured over 100 personnel. The events of August 19 in Baghdad were unprecedented. Never before have UN unarmed personnel been so viciously and deliberately targeted, with such devastating effect.

Before I define what is needed to mount a successful UN mission, let's have a sense of under what circumstances we deploy our troops today.

What can be expected in a complicated operational environment, where consent is only partial or limited to one or two of the parties to the conflict? Political developments may have improved the security situation, but a country remains very unstable as armed groups, militia, and criminal elements may be present throughout. More likely than not, exact figures regarding the strength of the various armed groups, which may include large numbers of child soldiers and paramilitary personnel, are not available.

Intelligence issues

From force generation down to the utilization of a section on the ground in a UN peacekeeping mission, you need information—accurate, timely information—specifically, the analyzed product that we call intelligence. This need is becoming more and more critical due to the change from traditional peacekeeping operations, or PKOs, to more complex multidimensional operations in much more volatile circumstances—particularly in Africa.

Of the types of intelligence needed for a mission, much is already available in the UN system through open-source information (OSINT) and the various departments, organs, and associated organizations that have the same ultimate aim. You do not need to meet Mr. Bond at the Hard Rock Cafe to receive a thick, red dossier under the table in order to have an accurate intelligence product. The trick is to develop a system of "data mining," and to have the expertise available for this information to analyze and assess within the framework of politico-military strategic objectives to produce an intelligence product on which decisions can be made and operational campaigns planned.

The lessons of Rwanda have been clear—the failures there go back to the absence of a strong mandate. However, we can take this back one step further. Had there been a more detailed intelligence assessment considering historical tendencies, the political will and military capability of the belligerents, and looking at all escalation scenarios, we could have seen a stronger mandate. This, together with a broader, multi-source and credible intelligence capability on the ground, could have prevented the genocide and atrocities that followed.

Sadly, despite the increasing paradigm shift that UN member states are making toward recognizing the need for intelligence, the Brahimi Report recommendations relating to peacekeeping and intelligence have not yet been fully implemented. This is due to a reluctance on the part of the member states to take action. Call it political, military, humanitarian, socio economic or security information—the UN needs processed intelligence product and analysis on all of those fields to function effectively. In order to achieve this we need the posts and the expertise—specifically in the Department of Peacekeeping Operations (DPKO), where I would have liked to have seen our situational awareness and general "intelligence analysis" capacity increased with the creation of more posts and the development of specialized capacity. Unfortunately, things are dependent on an overstretched budget and possibly influenced by misperceptions that the word "intelligence" conjures up! Member states are recognizing that on an operational and tactical level, a Force Commander needs accurate information and intelligence on armed groups and former warring factions in order to be pre-emptive and neutralize destabilizing influences and "spoilers" in a PKO.

The growing operational requirement for intelligence can be evident on the ground in relation to basic force-protection issues. The tragic loss of the Special Representative and the other UN personnel killed in the bomb attack on the UN HQ in Baghdad brought home the lesson of the lack of intelligence structures in the UN and the resultant poor situational and threat awareness as well as a failure to plan for the worst-case scenario on both tactical force protection and operational levels.

A conceptual issue that the UN faces is the need for a transition in thinking. Specifically, the need for member states to accept that peacekeeping and peace enforcement operations need to be planned on sound military assessment and not around present political sensitivities, with the mindset that the military contribution can be upgraded later. Another conceptual issue is the critical need for the member states to recognize that intelligence in the twenty-first century must focus on OSINT, on many smart analysts working together, and on analytic tools. Member states need to empower the technical and analytic capability of the UN by creating the structures, posts, and process for information liaison and analysis. The challenges of the intelligence community, on the other hand, are that instead of stealing a few secrets, they must make sense of vast, overwhelming quantities of non-secret information.

A critical challenge that the UN faces remains the issue of secret intelligence; that small percentage of sensitive information that member states have and which can have a critical impact on the operational and tactical level in a complex peacekeeping operation. Secret-level intelligence is after all a commodity. There is always a price to pay for a commodity that has to be bartered for or paid for in kind. It can however be obtained for free from member states if it is perceived that, firstly, it will be kept in confidence, and secondly, it will be used in such a way as to contribute to collective security or regional stability in some form. Secret member-state intelligence can be extremely valuable and intelligence contributions from member states are critical to the success of any mission. The sticky question has always been how, in an organization designed to be transparent, will confidences be held.

One answer would be for troop-contributing countries to ensure an enhanced intelligence capability of a mission by providing their contingent contribution to that mission directly with available intelligence and thereby also enhancing force security.

Another method would be for intelligence, specifically from the P5 (namely China, France, Russia, the United Kingdom and the United States, the five permanent members of the UN Security Council), to be provided directly to a mission via their embassies. Regional member states that have a vested interest in the stabilization effect of a UN-mandated peacekeeping mission should also utilize official intelligence-sharing fora and regional structures to ensure the availability of sufficient intelligence either to monitor a situation or plan a peacekeeping mission using regional "high readiness" forces—from the Standby High Readiness Brigade (SHIRBRIG) deployed in the Sudan to the envisaged "African Standby Force."

If we look at operational-level issues, at present, the United Nations Missions in the Congo, East Timor, Sierra Leone, and Liberia (MONUC, UNMISET, UNAMSIL, and UNMIL respectively) are prime examples of where there is a strong requirement for a broad spectrum of military information and intelligence products. These missions require a mixture of peace-enforcement and peacekeeping-intelligence capabilities in order that worst-case scenarios can be planned for. The biggest challenge that the Force Commanders in these missions face is getting the type of intelligence to enable force multiplication by remaining ahead of the power curve of the "armed groups" and "warring factions."

The big question is how to achieve this without relying on DPKO HQ in New York, which is still developing the cooperation and capacity to be able to provide operational-level intelligence because they simply do not have the posts to cater for this. We can plan a strong intelligence analysis capability on mission HQ-level during the force generation phase, but are largely dependent on the capabilities of the troop contributing contingents. To increase the military information and intelligence product capacity at mission level, we need to organize the structure, and most importantly the way we do things, in a different way.

There are two facets to this problem that I have tried to address. At the mission HQ-level there has long been a challenge in coordinating the availability and analysis of information from all role players. A mission is after all a complex mixture of political, military, humanitarian, and other components. Each has its own sources of information, analytical process, and operational objectives, with related intelligence requirements and planning cycles. What we need is the formation of a Joint Mission Analysis Cell (JMAC) as a central location for information to be received, analyzed, evaluated, and appropriately disseminated. Contributing role players would include military, political, and humanitarian organizations. This structure enables a broader spectrum of information contributions and for information to be analyzed in terms of its impact across a much broader scope of the mission as well as enable analysis of the impact of different factors on each other, e.g. political developments on the military situation. We have started implementing this concept in several of the missions and it has definitely enhanced their intelligence capability.

The analytic process and quality of intelligence product is however dependent on the information available on the tactical level, where we find that some contingents are strong in technological intelligence-gathering capability, others in low-tech, on the ground human intelligence (HUMINT) ability—gained through experience in operating in similar environments or on peacekeeping missions. Unfortunately, much of this organic intelligence capability is designed only to satisfy the tactical "force security" requirement of the contingent, and seldom provides the scope and quality of intelligence required by Contingent and Force Commanders in a dynamic peacekeeping environment, where limited resources mean you need the force multiplier effect of accurate, timely intelligence to achieve your mission objectives.

In the continuum of war, the C4I paradigm has become the basic tenet of operational planning; however, the new paradigm is network-centric warfare, which has information superiority and the ability to make sense of that information as its foundation. The idea is to increase combat power by utilizing all assets in the field and at HQ, to link decision-makers and shooters electronically. With access to the same information at the same time, they achieve shared awareness, increased speed of command, higher tempo of operations, greater lethality, increased survivability, and a degree of self-synchronization. In short, the net-centric approach provides situational awareness on the tactical level and is a definite force multiplier. It is however dependent on that information being available—largely from sensors and technical means. In a PKO things are a bit different, but this concept is still valid, though largely dependent on the mark-1 eyeball of the personnel deployed in a mission as the sensor platform. However, introduce better HUMINT capability and general intelligence awareness to the man on the ground, add a cheap digital camera to every section and the technical communication capability, some aerial photo surveillance and defensive electronic warfare capability and you have a net-centric capability when processed through a JMAC structure.

To improve the tactical intelligence support to UN forces, we need to improve capability and here we need to go back to UN member states. Specifically the capability of troop contributing countries begins with the selection of the right "profile" personnel, especially for leadership and key staff posts. Capability is enhanced by the quality of the training and the type of equipment and resources allocated to a contingent by the member state. Finally, tactical intelligence support is entirely dependent on the degree to which each and every soldier in a contingent is utilized as a collector of information. The effectiveness of this process is also dependent on there being sufficient intelligence specialists to collect, analyze, and utilize this information. For instance, a reconnaissance company with the right equipment and operational application can be far more effective than a battalion of infantry.

We need to move away from the traditional UN peacekeeping "security guard" mentality of manning a checkpoint or just showing a presence by "being there," to a more interactive approach. Here is often where the problem lies: language capability is essential, to communicate both with the local population and belligerents in a mission area. You need some very basic "intelligence 101" orientation at the lowest level so that peacekeepers know how to approach someone, speak to them, ask questions that include the basic "Ws" (Who, What, Where, Why, How), how to write the information down with an on-the-spot assessment, and have the means to send this, possibly accompanied by a photo from a cheap digital camera, over a radio channel to an HQ within minutes instead of days.

Imagine 80 per cent of a force with this basic capability and having made the "mind shift" to utilize it instead of the maybe 5 per cent we have sometimes seen in the past.

Lastly, to avoid what we term "command paralysis," member states should give the political mandate and intelligence support to their contingents so that they can go out there and use their leadership in the information-warfare peacekeeping game with activities that produce results! Fortunately in the UN recently the taboo has been broken that we can't speak about intelligence. There has always been a tradition within the UN system that intelligence gathering is contrary to the open nature of the system itself and is therefore absolutely forbidden. In addition it was not considered necessary for traditional peacekeeping operations where consent of all parties involved was a leading principle. However member states have come to the conclusion that the nature of conflict has changed and threats to missions have changed. Force protection is now the main factor when approving the gathering of military information. However we have to operate carefully since it is still a sensitive issue. In the UN HQ we have started the discussion on how to improve the analyzing capability on the strategic level.

In the post-September 11 period, American law enforcement and intelligence organizations soon realized that they held a lot of useful information. But systems and structures failed to share that information properly. The left hand did not know what the right hand knew. Suddenly the concepts of "net-centric information warfare" and "data mining" became very popular. Unfortunately, the UN has hundreds of hands, but the 9/11 lessons are valuable nonetheless. I think more information gets passed in casual conversation in the corridors of the UN than what the KGB could ever have aspired to collect when at the height of its power. The difference is that the puzzle pieces are not brought together in one central place to form a dossier of "usable intelligence." This is essentially operational- and strategic-level information—exactly what we need at this level for mission planning.

The strength of the UN's intelligence capacity is often based on those individuals in the system that have become regional experts on a theater of operation or problem area through their own "networking" and "data mining." They build up contacts across agencies and organizations and down to the tactical field-worker level in order to be able to see the "bigger picture" and do their specific job better. They gather some of the puzzle pieces together, add a bit of OSINT and "Hey Presto"—they are both the local expert and the holder of what some would refer to as "secret intelligence." These reservoirs of knowledge are often our strength and our greatest untapped resource. At the mission-planning level, if we were able to "data mine" this resource, include some commercial intelligence or OSINT from satellite imagery, geographical information systems or CNN and other sources, add in selective operational-level and perhaps tactical intelligence from concerned member states with a vested interest in stability in their region, then we could have a very successful formulae.

We do not need a massive intelligence organization, only a few more specialists and the freedom to coordinate and data mine the "information knowledge" of our many left and right hands, and, critically, we need the confidence of member states—especially troop contributing countries who would be willing to empower their contingents with all the available intelligence resources and information needed to win the information war when employed in PKOs—from appreciation to mission planning, mission control down to tactical deployment!

The collection and analysis of information on all levels of PKOs in the UN needs critical attention. We need to develop an information "road map" with the structures, strategies, and specialist personnel to handle the analysis. Without the personnel and posts to do this we face many challenges, but by formalizing the informal networking process that often provides much of the expertise and knowledge in missions and at the HQ level, we can make significant progress in enhancing our intelligence capability.

By preparing for possible robust tasking and not just traditional peace-keeping missions, member states are also starting to provide more capable and better equipped contingents that realize the role and importance of intelligence. Progress is slow, and happening more in the field than at New York HQ, but the bottom line is that we are making progress.

Major-General Patrick Cammaert[1]

Notes

1 Originally presented as the keynote at the Peacekeeping Intelligence Conference in Ottawa, December 4–5, 2003.

ACKNOWLEDGMENTS

This book had its origins in the Conference on Peacekeeping Intelligence: New Players, Extended Boundaries, which took place in Ottawa, December 4–5, 2003. The conference took place under the joint aegis of the Canadian Centre of Intelligence and Security Studies (CCISS) at Carleton University, the Centre for Security and Defence Studies (CSDS), also at Carleton, and the War Studies Program at the Royal Military College of Canada. This was the second in what is now an annual series of international conferences on peacekeeping intelligence which were initiated and inspired by Robert David Steele. The Ottawa conference brought together military and civilian experts from around the world to draw lessons from recent peacekeeping operations, and to examine the role of new players and their work across organizational, disciplinary, and analytical boundaries in relation to international peacekeeping, peace support and peace-enforcement missions. A selection of papers from that conference is presented in this volume, together with some additional contributions that were invited by the editors to address pertinent issues.

A project of this magnitude depends on the support and encouragement of many individuals and institutions. The editors would like to acknowledge the invaluable support of our fellow member of the conference-organizing committee, Dr. David Last, and the War Studies Program at the Royal Military College of Canada, which co-sponsored the conference, as well the backing provided by our own institution, the Norman Paterson School of International Affairs at Carleton University.

The conference benefited from financial assistance and the goodwill of a number of external organizations: the Belgian Ministry of Defence; Cranfield University, the Royal Military College of Science in the United Kingdom; the Royal Netherlands Embassy in Ottawa; the Norwegian Ministry of Foreign Affairs; the government and embassy of Romania in Ottawa; and the Swedish Armed Forces Intelligence and Security Centre. All of these institutions helped bring speakers from their respective countries to participate in the Conference. The Canadian Forces, Pearson

ACKNOWLEDGMENTS

Peacekeeping Centre, the Royal Military College, and the Royal Canadian Mounted Police covered costs for speakers from their own organizations while Canada's Department of National Defence, through the Security and Defence Forum Special Projects fund, and the Department of Foreign Affairs and International Trade, through the John Holmes Fund, both provided funding for scholarships that enabled students from across Canada to attend this important event. The generous support of all these benefactors is gratefully acknowledged.

We would also like to recognize the ongoing support from the Security Defence Forum to the Centre for Security and Defence Studies at Carleton and the Operational Research Division of the Department of National Defence who agreed to publication of Robert Grossman-Vermaas' research on effects based operations.

The preparation of this volume was expedited and facilitated by the efforts of many individuals. We are grateful to the contributing authors for their unstinting support for this initiative, for their exceptional contributions, and for meeting exacting deadlines. We are heavily indebted to Rachel Lea Heide for her assistance in transcribing conference presentations and her contribution to the introduction, and to Aleisha Arnusch for her excellent assistance with the editorial work. We thank our publishers, Taylor & Francis and their staff, Marjorie Francois and Andrew Humphrys, for their congenial efficiency in working together to bring this volume into print so expeditiously.

Through the conference and this volume, CCISS and CSDS seek to contribute to a better understanding of the value and role of intelligence in support of the vital missions of international peacekeeping, peace support, and peace-enforcement that our contemporary world embraces.

LIST OF ABBREVIATIONS

ABCA nations	American, British, Canadian, and Australian
C4ISR	Command, Control, Communications, Computers, Intelligence, Surveillance, and Reconnaissance
CAR	Central African Republic
CEWARN	Conflict Early Warning and Response Mechanism
CIMIC	civil–military cooperation
CJTL	Canadian Joint Task List
CSO	civil society organizations
DDR	disarmament, demobilization, and reintegration
DND	Department of National Defence (Canada)
DSD	Defence Signals Directorate
EBO	effects-based operation
EBP	effects-based planning
EUCOM	US European Command
FIDO	Fundamental Investigation of Defence Options
GIS	Geographic Information System
HEWS	Humanitarian Early Warning System
HUMINT	human intelligence
ICC	International Criminal Court
IMINT	imagery intelligence
INTERFET	UN Sanctioned International Force in East Timor
JETL	Joint Essential Task List
JMACs	Joint Mission Analysis Cells
JMTEL	Joint Mission Essential Task List
MISAB	Mission interafricaine de surveillance des accords de Bangui
MND	Multinational Division
MNE	Multinational Experiment
MONUC	UN Mission in the Congo
NATO	North Atlantic Treaty Organization
NCW	network-centric warfare

NGO	non-governmental organization
OIVC	Operational Signals Intelligence Center
ONUMOZ	United Nations Operation in Mozambique
ORCI	Office for Research and Collection of Information
OSINT	open-source intelligence
PKI	peacekeeping intelligence
PSO	peace support operations
RENAMO	Resistência Nacional Moçambicana
SABA	small arms baseline assessment
SALW	small arms and light weapons
SAS	Small Arms Survey
SIGINT	signals intelligence
SOCRAM	Scenario Operational Capability Risk Assessment Model
UAV	unmanned aerial vehicles
UN	United Nations
UNAVEM	United Nations Angola Verification Mission
UNDP	United Nations Development Program
UNITA	União Nacional para a Independência Total de Angola
UNMEE	UN Mission in Ethiopia and Eritrea
UNPROFOR	United Nations Protection Force

1

PEACEKEEPING INTELLIGENCE

Extending partnerships and boundaries for peacekeeping

David Carment, Martin Rudner, and Rachel Lea Heide

Peacekeeping intelligence, or PKI, is the emerging term for a new form of intelligence that emphasizes open sources of information, multilateral sharing of intelligence at all levels, the use of intelligence to ensure force protection, and interoperability and commonality with coalition partners and non-governmental organizations (NGOs). Unlike national intelligence efforts, which tend to be intensely focused on designated tasks and perceived threats, PKI covers a broad array of information gathering, partners, and objectives.[1]

PKI is fundamental because, for the past five decades, peacekeeping and peace enforcement operations have represented the predominant international deployment of most armed forces. Experience indicates that the information and intelligence requirements and capabilities for these kinds of PSOs can differ in significant respects from those enjoined by traditional operational doctrine. Information and intelligence capabilities for peace support missions relate to operational situations of far greater complexity and ambiguity, as compared to the traditional combat operations for which these systems were designed. For one thing, in peace support missions, the identities and capabilities of potential adversaries (and their forces) are often cloaked in obscurity. For another, the intentions of belligerents are typically ambiguous and volatile and may not always be indicated by the positioning and activity of military or paramilitary forces. The familiar principles of offensive, target-oriented combat intelligence has to be modified in order to yield an accurate and nuanced assessment of complex, elusive, and ambiguous situations.

Peacekeeping and peace support missions can involve different participating countries and can vary significantly in scope and purpose, yet they appear to demonstrate some common operational requirements apropos information and intelligence. Historically, United Nations (UN) peace missions eschewed intelligence capabilities. Inasmuch as the UN considered itself an essentially neutral, multilateral organization, "intelligence systems" were not countenanced as part of UN-mandated peace operations, ostensibly due to their covert and ominous connotations (International Peace Academy, 1984). "Information-gathering" efforts that were attempted within the UN in the 1980s and 1990s, such as ORCI (Office for Research and Collection of Information) and HEWS (Humanitarian Early Warning System), contributed to the advancement of the concept of a UN-based and centralized early warning system but foundered for a number of reasons, both external and internal. In their place, the process of sharing information and analysis across UN agencies and departments has led to a more comprehensive and qualitative understanding of a broader range of actions that can be employed to prevent conflict and reduce its impact through peacekeeping. Nonetheless, these efforts still require the specific authorization and support of governments and intergovernmental bodies.

For most UN missions conducted during the 1990s, the operational consequences of this aversion to intelligence has proven problematic. The PSO in the former Yugoslavia is a case in point. The United Nations Protection Force's (UNPROFOR's) tasks began to multiply in response to a rapidly deteriorating situation in Bosnia and Herzegovina, and its intelligence resources lagged behind its needs as the political process upon which intelligence-sharing relied for direction proved insufficient. Mandates, tasks, and responsibilities were changed and upgraded in an ad hoc fashion, indicating that comprehensive analysis and intelligence had not been carried out during the planning stages. Further, the peacekeepers deployed were sent to keep a peace that was fragile at best, and to support a peace plan that was never fully accepted by the local population. The frequent absence of unambiguous consent, on the part of the parties in the conflict, to the deployment of external forces made the operation increasingly dangerous and the need for tactical intelligence increasingly evident. In the aftermath of Bosnia, as well as Rwanda and Somalia, it is obvious that today's PSOs demand a level of intelligence capability, coherence, and coordination that is unparalleled.

The Report of the Brahimi panel, a review of UN peacekeeping doctrine undertaken at the behest of the Secretary-General and published in August 2000, recommended that UN peace operations require a more robust and realistic mandate to achieve their objectives. (UN, 2000). As a result, the UN established an Information and Strategic Analysis Secretariat within the Department of Political Affairs to collect and manage "strategic information," an acceptable euphemism for intelligence (UN, 2000). It remains to be seen whether, and how, this new-found acceptability of information and analysis at the strategic policy level will percolate down to the intelligence requirements at the tactical and operational levels of UN peace support missions. Despite the obvious need for political, military, humanitarian, socio-economic, and security information, member states of the UN have been reluctant to implement changes to intelligence gathering and sharing for these missions.

To be sure, the UN is not the only peacekeeping player in today's conflict environment, and few operations now follow the template of missions that were the norm during the Cold War. Both the military and civil requirements for modern, multidisciplinary PSOs far exceed those of traditional missions. Conflict situations have now come to include non-state actors, cyberspace, the nano-dimension, space, and the biological and chemical environments. The wider range of military tasks can include, but are not limited to, assisting in disarmament and demobilization, monitoring of elections, de-mining assistance, restoration of infrastructure, and conducting concurrent enforcement operations. Maritime and air forces may have particular diplomatic, deterrent, enforcement or intelligence-gathering functions, while land forces will generally conduct the detailed control of the operation at the tactical level. Maritime and air forces will thus help to create the conditions for the conduct of land operations, and their joint efforts will be designed to create an environment that assists the civilian agencies to achieve their mission (DND (Canada), 2002). The recent deployment of international naval, air, and army units to assist and support disaster relief in the aftermath of the Indian Ocean tsunami of December 2004 represents a telling example of military aid to human security.

Intelligence gathering and deciphering are needed at all levels, from the strategic planning stages to tactical implementation on the ground. Effective operations are now considered to have a clear definition of what success is, and a strategy to achieve it; this includes a focus on the end-state and recognition that, as things change on the ground, the strategy and its personnel must be adaptable, with the appropriate and flexible mandate and resources to respond to such changes. Accordingly, detailed intelligence assessments consider the historical tendencies, the political will, and the structure of the current government as well as the military capability of the belligerents.

Intelligence gathering is also crucial for determining mission capabilities, and is as crucial at the latter stages of a PSO as it is at the onset.[2] Intelligence must be able to address the effectiveness of the campaign, particularly the number of militia or guerrilla groups still active. Intelligence often focuses on battle damage assessments using surveillance reconnaissance to determine hard or physical damage, but just as much must be done to assess behavioral indicators.

The North Atlantic Treaty Organization (NATO) peacekeeping and peace enforcement operations display their own ambiguities and complexities apropos intelligence cooperation, even among allies. NATO does not possess an intelligence collection capability of its own, except in certain particular domains of military intelligence, but it does have a limited capacity for intelligence analysis. NATO's intelligence requirements are met, for the most part, from input supplied by member countries for the exclusive use of the Alliance itself and for its constituent governments. Since the end of the Cold War, NATO has taken upon itself "peace support" missions that were not only "out of theater," but also involved NATO in new kinds of quasi-military operations aimed at conflict prevention, peace-making, peacekeeping, humanitarian aid, peace enforcement, and peace-building. These experiences, which sometimes entailed tragic losses, encouraged the Alliance to recognize that peace support missions require robust information and intelligence capabilities at the strategic as well as operational levels (Nomikos, 2000). However, this perceived need for enhanced capabilities challenged, in effect, the core principles of NATO's intelligence-sharing system.

NATO also has a Special Committee charged with facilitating the sharing of security intelligence (as distinct from military intelligence) among Alliance members (see Rudner, 2002: 141–171, 2001: 97–128). This Special Committee was initially composed of representatives of member countries' security intelligence services. Following the attacks of September 11, 2001, the NATO Special Committee augmented its staffing and capabilities in order to provide the North Atlantic Council with regular assessments of threats to Alliance security and the national security of member countries from militant Islamic organizations, based on intelligence received from member-country security services (BVD, 2002).

NATO intelligence cooperation is grounded on a precept of absolute exclusivity, so that none of the intelligence supplied to the Alliance could ever be shared with non-member countries or with any international organization composed of non-member countries (BVD, 2002). This precept applied *passi passu* to peace support missions involving NATO in coalition with other countries or international organizations. Thus, NATO intelligence could not be made available to non-Alliance partners or international organizations involved in peace support missions even in circumstances and situations where there were operational requirements for such sharing (Berlin Information Center for Transatlantic Security, 1994). Some of the high value intelligence products collected by the United States, using its sophisticated surveillance and sensor technologies, were not shared even with some other Alliance-member countries who were partners in NATO-led peace support missions.

These operational precepts shape the intelligence architecture for NATO-led peace support missions into a compartmentalized, three-tier, differentiated-access sharing arrangement for operational information and intelligence. The top tier is restricted to US forces and their most intimate allies, notably Canada and the United Kingdom, who share access to US

4

intelligence, surveillance, and reconnaissance capabilities, as well as NATO resources. A second tier consists of other NATO allies who may acquire intelligence products made available through the Alliance mechanism, but without having access to reserved American products generated from the high-technology assets. A third tier is composed of all other countries or international components that are denied access to either NATO or US intelligence resources.

All of this translates to a broader purview for PKI than was hitherto acknowledged. Since the end of the Cold War, the uncertainties arising from the changing context, and the scope of international conflicts, pose new and heightened challenges for the international community, for peace-keeping, and for PKI in particular. It is for PKI to light the way for international efforts to maintain, support, and enforce peaceable solutions in this era of multiple uncertainties.

Accordingly, this volume examines the role of intelligence within coalition forces, multilateral institutions, and NGOs that have become partners in peace support activities. The overarching theme of the volume is that there is a widening range of organizations that are being called upon to "do" PKI. These actors range from NGOs to multilateral economic and political organizations whose mandates were developed in very different times, historically speaking, and whose objectives and interests are quite different. The ways in which one can reasonably expect this range of actors to become involved in intelligence gathering, coordination, and dissemination needs to be informed by an understanding of their diverse mandates, leadership, experiences, and operational activities.

Complex PSOs now demand increased cooperation between governments of member states; nonetheless, regional organizations, as well as a number of civilian organizations and non-governmental humanitarian agencies, are also involved. Coordination is complicated at the strategic, operational, and tactical levels. At the strategic planning level, if leaders of NGOs, governments, and international organizations are unclear on exactly how a mission is to accomplish its goals, the operation may suffer from lack of clarity. The relationship between external military and civilian actors has also begun to change from detachment and suspicion toward an institutionalization of civil–military cooperation (CIMIC).

A secondary theme throughout the volume is identification of how to transform the role and functions of intelligence in peacekeeping and peace support missions. This transformation would seem to involve a three-tier fusion of PKI capabilities (Arrol, 1996). The first tier of fusion would aim to enhance the operational capabilities of PKI, including its HUMINT (human intelligence), SIGINT (signals intelligence), IMINT (imagery intelligence), OSINT (open-source intelligence), counter-intelligence, and other related intelligence disciplines, while integrating these into an all-sources synthesis of actionable intelligence. Among the interdisciplinary spheres of knowledge that should be tapped are the vast quantum of experiential and conceptual information on international area and country studies, and on their political, economic, sociological, and cultural attributes; this is vested in various government departments and agencies, universities, and research institutions, NGOs, and consulting enterprises. The achievement of fusion between technical and HUMINT capabilities and interdisciplinary knowledge would pave the way to a transformative revolution in PKI.

A second tier of fusion would aim at integrating the strategic, tactical, and operational levels of PKI into a vertically integrated, holistic, interoperable Information and Intelligence system. During the 1990s, considerable emphasis was placed on interoperability and dissemination issues. Projected future roles for peace support and peace enforcement point to an increasing requirement for strategic, tactical, and operational intelligence support for force protection as well as for realizing mission objectives. Vertical interoperability should build on a fusion of technical and HUMINT assets while ensuring the relevance and responsiveness of the Information and Intelligence system to the requirements of peacekeeping and peace support forces.

A third tier of capabilities should focus on ensuring that the emergent architecture for Strategic Information and Analysis remains horizontally compatible among allies and other coalition partners, and with the PKI systems of other international stakeholders on peace and humanitarian missions. While respecting the need to protect the classified elements of intelligence, a particular effort could be made to find ways to achieve a functional horizontal interoperability for the dissemination of Information and Intelligence products, duly "sanitized," between NATO and other non-member coalition partners on PSOs.

Volume outline

The first part of the volume is devoted to understanding "Peacekeeping and its intelligence requirements" in the pre- and post-9/11 conflict environment. Chapter 2, by Robert Martyn, delineates the trends that are clearly appreciable in the future security environment, in multinational coalitions, and in intelligence collection. With an increasing number of internal conflicts, ethnic-religious wars, and failed or failing states, and with the predictable humanitarian crises stemming from diminishing natural resources and rising population numbers, the impetus to intervene in the name of protecting human rights will only grow. Nonetheless, intervention forces will be facing asymmetric threats that are not the once predictable and readily "templated" enemy forces. Though it is very likely that the UN will continue as an international player, Martyn predicts that its history of inaction and corruption, and its lack of a proper military command structure, means that, in the future, the more demanding missions will fall to lead-nation coalitions of the willing, which will undertake interventions regardless of UN sanction. In this new security environment, haphazard intelligence collection and inadequate leadership can no longer be tolerated. Intelligence operations must be directed toward a specific end; missions require forceful, intelligence-savvy commanders; and adequate information needs to be collected to support the decision-makers. Hence, Martyn argues that a proper balance of OSINT, HUMINT, IMINT, and SIGINT needs to be a priority, as does the training of adequate numbers of intelligence analysts and the development of systems of dissemination.

Michael Hennessy's chapter focuses on the important role of HUMINT in four recent peacekeeping missions (Zaire, Haiti, Bosnia, and East Timor). To make his point, Hennessy argues that though each mission was unique, all four provide important lessons learned for tactical-level intelligence gathering. The 1996 Operation Assurance in Zaire was an intelligence failure, whereas the 1997 Operation CONSTABLE in Haiti was more successful. Among other important lessons, the experience in Haiti demonstrated the value of intelligence passed down from previous missions and the importance of knowing the local language. Intelligence sharing and collection coordination were the challenges faced by NATO allies France, the United States, and Great Britain in the 1997 SFOR nation-building stabilization campaign in Bosnia. Because each participant was reluctant to share and plan intelligence together, each national sector conducted its intelligence, psyops, CIMIC, and espionage differently—sometimes with negative consequences. Australia's mission to East Timor (INTERFET) in 1999–2000 reinforced the benefits of having intelligence—both before and during an operation—and being able to converse in the local language. Hennessey recommends that individual nations within the UN system need to increase their intelligence capabilities, to share this information with their peacekeeping partners, and to contribute to the development of an intelligence component within the UN itself.

The fourth chapter, by Matthew Aid, focuses specifically on the role of SIGINT in peacekeeping and peace support missions. International peacekeeping needs reliable, timely, fact-based intelligence information—hard facts, not best-guesses. Aid argues cogently that SIGINT can be of high value when its product is merged with the materials being produced by other intelligence sources, such as IMINT, HUMINT, and even OSINT. Aid also points out that there is a clear and direct correlation between the relative value of SIGINT and the level of military activity in the geographic region where the peacekeeping operation is set to take place. The higher the level of violence endemic to the region, the greater the value of SIGINT for providing peacekeepers with timely and accurate intelligence about military activities and movements. Nonetheless, SIGINT's value and import in peacekeeping is also largely determined by the level of technological sophistication of the region where the operation in question is taking place. At present, according to Aid, the process of selecting intelligence resources for specific peacekeeping missions is accomplished in reverse of how it should be done. Senior military and intelligence planners in New York, and in various world capitals, determine what national collection resources will be contributed to specific peacekeeping missions based upon case-by-case political considerations and pre-formatted plans that are generic templates rather than country-specific. Aid argues that the process should be turned on its head to enable peacekeeping force commanders to determine what intelligence collection assets they need based upon their first-hand assessments of what is required for them to perform their missions.

The fifth and last chapter in this section, by George Kolisnek, examines how the Command, Control, Communications, Computers, Intelligence, Surveillance, and Reconnaissance (C4ISR) concept provides the supporting architecture for UN- or NATO-led peacekeeping or peace support missions. Kolisnek examines the complexity of command and control in situations where authority and responsibility may be shared and also delegated. When deployed, command of forces may be temporarily delegated to a NATO or UN operational commander for the period of the deployment, but full command always rests and never leaves the national commanding officer of the country providing the forces. Kolisnek looks at the importance of communications in disseminating information and intelligence to mission commanders and decision-makers. Computers have greatly sped up the communications process, but the rapid technological development of computers has resulted in all levels of staff being inundated with overwhelming amounts of transmissions not readily absorbable or useable. Kolisnek goes on to discuss intelligence and the automatic assumption that it always involves covert collection and highly classified information. The use of OSINT means intelligence can be made available to more staffs and commanders without restrictions to conceal the sources or methods of collection used. Surveillance and reconnaissance, the use of sensors and platforms over large and limited geographic areas respectively, not only require a high degree of coordination, but also a wide spectrum of technologies. Kolisnek points out that many nations have begun to pool their resources since individual nations cannot afford to acquire the broad range of capabilities themselves. Fully understanding C4ISR, being aware of the limitations of each mission's architecture, and realizing the impact on the ability to make accountable decisions, all contribute to the capacity of commanders to achieve what Kolisnek terms "excellence in military operations."

The second part of the volume examines the "Evolution of intelligence in multinational peacekeeping missions," where both UN and non-UN mission capabilities are considered. In Chapter 6, Walter Dorn considers the consequences of the UN's historical reluctance to be involved in intelligence gathering, and he makes recommendations for improving UN intelligence capabilities. In the past, the UN avoided intelligence because it only wanted to be involved with open and overt sources. Nonetheless, in today's conflict environment, the UN is as likely to be a target as it is to be a peacekeeper; hence, force protection has become paramount. Experience has shown the need for, and benefits of, intelligence for peacekeeping missions. Because open-source material is simply no longer enough, Dorn argues that there needs to be a process in UN headquarters to get essential information (some of it secretive) into the hands of key decision-makers. UN members must discern what the UN needs to know so as to be able to carry out missions successfully and prevent attacks on UN personnel. Dorn explains that the UN not only needs to be willing to accept secrecy and create a balanced and adequate mix of open and secret sources, but once the UN has decided as a body what it needs, it then must pursue agreements with its information providers to set up standards, protocols, and guaranteed levels of accessibility and availability of the intelligence.

Chapter 7 examines the evolution of Network Centric Warfare (NCW) and its implication for PKI. Author Paul Mitchell asks why seamless interoperability of intelligence is not happening between member states of peacekeeping forces, despite the fact that technology makes interoperability increasingly possible. He suggests that the growing disparity in technology between partners (thus erecting tiers of capabilities) can partially be explained by some nations' militaries and intelligence communities' lack of appropriations to keep pace technologically with the more wealthy partners. The move from a multipolar world, where the numerous partners communicate and negotiate so as to reach compromises acceptable to each party's national interests, to a unipolar environment, has serious consequences. In this unipolar world of American domination, allies see little need to contribute, for the one superpower is under no obligation to listen to allies or to compromise on questionable national agendas. According to Mitchell, this raises some basic, yet fundamental, questions. Should efficiency be sacrificed as the US continues to resist sharing intelligence, or should the superpower abandon its fear of being vulnerable to its partners? Problems in peacekeeping immediately crop up when two different intelligence networks are maintained—a classified level for the US and an unclassified level for the rest of the coalition. Mitchell suggests that the US needs to seriously consider sacrificing its position of absolute control and pursuing unaltered national interests so that partners have a reason to invest in missions.

Drawing on field research in Bosnia, Kosovo, and Afghanistan, Christopher Ankersen's chapter, the eighth in the volume, analyzes the potential and actual role that civil–military cooperation (CIMIC) activities play in building the intelligence picture during peace operations. Owing to an ambiguous understanding of CIMIC amongst decision-makers and commanders, CIMIC can be seen as "all things to all people." Many formulations see CIMIC as an element of Information Operations, acting as a conduit for outgoing messages (psychological operations) and as a pipeline for gathering information about and from the local population (intelligence). Ankersen explains that such a utilitarian view of CIMIC is also prevalent in the perceptions held by many civil society organizations (CSOs), whether they are local or international in scope. In some cases, this has led to reluctance to cooperate with the military for fear of being "used." Consequently, "CIMIC *qua* espionage" features largely in the ethical debates surrounding the field. Though there is much to recommend such points of view, Ankersen contends that there are many cases which suggest that any intelligence function CIMIC provides is passive, accidental, and actually insignificant.

The third and final section of the volume examines "New elements of intelligence analysis" including small arms surveys and NGOs, war crimes, ethics, training, and early warning. Chapter 9, by Eric Berman, draws on the findings of the independent research project on the impact of small arms on Africa, which was conducted by the Small Arms Survey Organization of Geneva. The organization, of which Berman is a member, has been analyzing the distribution, circulation, and control of arms by having researchers visit African countries and interview people with knowledge about their impact. To construct a reliable picture of small arms usage and flows using HUMINT requires researchers to visit the subject countries and develop meaningful grassroots contacts. Because local populations have been more willing to talk with civilian interviewers than with uniformed personnel, the Small Arms Survey Organization, according to Berman, is a valuable intelligence source for peacekeeping nations. The analysis of the information gathered reveals what types of weapons are circulating and who (both state and non-state actors) pose the threats to civilians and peacekeepers. Analysis also considers the socio-economic impact of the weapons: the kinds of wounds that are occurring; the number of deaths; and the black-market prices of weapons that are encouraging people not to turn them in. Such research shows the wealth of HUMINT and the value of independent projects for peacekeeping missions.

Chapter 10, by Douglas Bond and Patrick Meier, maintains that peace-keeping nations not only have to recognize the importance and necessity of intelligence for their missions, but that they also have to consider what their nations' objectives are and what must be done in the realm of intelligence to achieve these goals. To meet these objectives, a system of locally owned and community-wide protocols governing intelligence collection, analysis, and sharing should be developed. Since analysts need to look at events happening before crises erupt, Bond suggests a variety of economic, social, and political indicators whose measurement and monitoring have proved useful to PKI. To this end, technology is not the most important element of intelligence gathering. For those on the ground, the creation of relationships with the local populace, interpreters, and NGOs is invaluable. Software can be designed to help standardize and aid the intelligence community in understanding and interpreting local information, but the focus needs to be less on technology and more on understanding the local context, on identifying conflict indicators, and knowing where a region is in the conflict cycle. Bond argues that PKI is more successful when ad hoc practices are replaced by careful consideration and clear objectives.

Christopher Penny's chapter focuses on the relationship between PKI and the prevention and punishment of international crimes. He concludes that the relationship between PKI and the prevention and punishment of international crimes must be limited, particularly with respect to post-conflict criminal prosecution. Mission effectiveness in robust peacekeeping operations requires the collection, analysis, and dissemination of information relating to the commission, or the planned commission, of international crimes by parties to the conflict. The failure of a peacekeeping force to collect intelligence on, and act to prevent, international crimes is a gross abdication of its responsibility, which will not only undermine the force's legitimacy, but also threatens its ability to consolidate peace and deter future crimes. While advocating the use of intelligence by peacekeepers to actively prevent the commission of international crimes, this chapter illustrates the dangers of relying on peacekeepers as primary investigators for the purpose of subsequent international criminal prosecution. Penny supports limitations on the use of PKI in criminal law fora; he argues that direct peacekeeper involvement in criminal investigations may have a detrimental impact on mission effectiveness and also undermine the success of any resulting criminal prosecution.

Chapter 12, by Angela Gendron, examines the ethics of using intelligence in PSOs. Gendron's analysis addresses the ethical implications of the use of, or failure to use, intelligence in peacekeeping and peace support missions. Consideration is given to the motives and objectives behind national and international decisions to embark on PKOs and PSOs, and to issues relating to transparency and accountability. The UN historically has been ambivalent about the use of intelligence in support of peacekeeping missions because of an intuitive moral judgment that deception is not an appropriate instrument in pursuance of peace. Whereas the traditional UN emphasis on impartiality and neutrality was considered essential for the effectiveness of peacekeeping and truce observation missions, the changing character of peace support and peace enforcement operations call into question the relevance—and indeed the appropriateness—of this passive approach. Peace support and peace enforcement missions may well require an intelligence capability for force protection and to prevent loss of civilian lives, not to say for mission credibility and effectiveness. Yet, as Gendron emphasizes, ideals matter as well as consequences. The acceptance of intelligence as an ethical tool of contemporary PSOs will be dependent upon rules being articulated and practices agreed which can command wider assent than at present. Gendron argues that the same moral tests used to justify international interventions and the use of force can also be applied to an ethical framework for intelligence in support of peace.

Chapter 13 by Robert Heibel, Tamal Bhattacharya, and Kristan Wheaton, identifies the importance of education and training for peace-keeping missions. Part of preparing for a peace support mission is tapping into intelligence already gathered and applying lessons learned from previous operations. According to Heibel, Bhattacharya, and Wheaton, by studying other nations' training, doctrines, and experiences, peacekeeping forces about to embark on a new mission can extract lessons and best practices; peacekeeping nations can also identify what has worked well for previous operations and what has not. Language skills, culture appreciation, lessons learned, doctrine comparison—all of these are vital to the training of peacekeeping forces and for a successful mission in a hostile territory. The authors argue that training must be tailored to meet the nature of the specific operation, and training must be comprehensive. Ad hoc approaches to peacekeeping can no longer be sustained in the new international order. The authors contend that true success in bringing peace, security, and humanitarian aid to the world depends on clear national objectives, carefully considered plans to achieve these objectives, and thorough training to carry out these plans.

The final chapter in the volume by Robert Grossman-Vermass, evaluates the application of effects-based concepts in the planning and execution of a multinational experiment. Though not exclusively an idea that is applied to PSOs, the relevance of effects-based operations (EBO) is clear. Today's complex situations require increased cooperation between NGOs and the military, and are a valuable way to ensure that all aspects of security and development are incorporated into the planning and implementation of PSOs. Grossman-Vermass, argues that EBO are necessary to enhance a nation's (or coalition's) strategic capabilities at the political, economic, technological, and information networking levels in order to achieve politically satisfactory outcomes for a nation or coalition. Success will depend upon the ability to forecast the end-state or *effects* desired and deploying in advance the appropriate resources to achieve such effects. EBO are a way of leveraging the resources available to achieve maximum impact; they allow a nation or coalition to achieve its strategic objectives at minimal costs. EBO are advantageous because they go beyond the initial military campaign to include economic factors and human development and participation. A successful PSO must include a detailed analysis of the desired effects and prepare a response that includes short-term military goals as well as long-term development and reconstruction goals. This planning process also requires acknowledgment and, consequently, a contingency plan for any unwanted or negative effects the campaign may encourage. All PSOs must include an analysis of unintended consequences complete with resources to handle unfavorable situations, as well as the mandate to act in such situations including, under extreme circumstances, the possibility of early withdrawal.

Notes

1 The term peacekeeping and peace support operations (PSOs) are used inter-changeably throughout this volume. It is recognized that the proper and current term is PSO, and peacekeeping is used only where it is construed as part of the historical context in which it was applied.

2 For example, the Canadian Joint Task List (CJTL) was established to describe and relate the various capabilities required for a range of operations. The CJTL is based on the Joint Mission Essential Task List (JMTEL) developed by the US and the Joint Essential Task List (JETL) created by the United Kingdom. In addition, to assist senior officers and officials in ranking the myriad options, the Canadian Forces can utilize a decision support tool known as Fundamental Investigation of Defence Options (FIDO) or a risk/gap analysis model known as the Scenario Operational Capability Risk Assessment Model (SOCRAM).

Bibliography

Arrol, L. (1996) "The Intelligence Fusion Family," *Military Intelligence*, 22 (3), July–September.

Berlin Information Center for Transatlantic Security (1994) *NATO, Peacekeeping, and the UN*, Berlin Information Center for Transatlantic Security, Germany. Available at: http://www.bits.de/frames/databases.htm (accessed March 11, 2005).

Boyd, A. (1998) "Joint Intelligence Support of Peace Operations," *Military Intelligence*, 24 (4), October–December.

BVD (2002) *General Intelligence and Security Service, Annual Report 2001*, The Hague: General Intelligence and Security Service, July.

DND (Canada) (2002) *Peace Support Operations Joint Doctrine Manual*, Department of National Defence, November 6.

International Peace Academy (1984) *Peacekeeper's Handbook*, New York: Pergamon Press, p. 39.

Nomikos, J. (2000) *Intelligence Requirements for Peacekeeping Operations*, Working Paper, Athens: Research Institute on European and American Studies

Richelson, J. and Ball, D. (1985) *The Ties that Bind: Intelligence Cooperation Between the UK–USA Countries*, London: Allen & Unwin.

Rudner, M. (2001) "Canada's Communications Security Establishment From Cold War to Globalization," *Intelligence and National Security*, 16 (1) Spring: 97–128.

—— (2002) "Contemporary Threats, Future Tasks: Canadian Intelligence and the Global Security Challenge," in Norman Hillmer and Maureen Molot (eds.),

Canada Among Nations 2002: A Fading Power? Toronto: Oxford University Press.

UN (2000) *Brahmini Report: Report of the Panel on UN Peace Operations,* A/55/305, S/2000 801, New York: UN, August. 21.

UN General Assembly (2000) *Resource Requirements for the Implementation of the Report of the Panel on UN Peace Operations: Report of the Secretary-General,* A/55/305-S/2000 801. Available at: http://www.un.org/peace/reports/peace_operations/ (accessed March 11, 2005).

Part I

PEACEKEEPING AND ITS INTELLIGENCE REQUIREMENTS

2

BEYOND THE NEXT HILL

The future of military intelligence in peace support operations

Robert Martyn

Wondering what is over the next hill, or beyond the next tactical bound, has always been a pressing concern for military and security practitioners. While no forecast is guaranteed, one may expect that certain features of the current security environment, notably the so-called global war on terrorism, will remain extant for the foreseeable future. Other factors, such as increasing globalization and environmental degradation, provide such clearly appreciable trends that one is able to estimate with a high degree of confidence several probable future flashpoints—many of which will require the deployment of a multinational interventionary force. This chapter will therefore provide a snapshot of a likely security environment, consider United Nations (UN) and coalition operations, and look at intelligence trends, in order to conclude how these factors intersect and affect future peace support intelligence.

Future security environment

While the near-term likelihood of global or nuclear war is minimal, the 2020 international environment will very likely feature numerous armed conflicts of various types (Taylor, 1992). Traditionally, war has taken place for reasons of religion, the pursuit of wealth or, simply, territorial expansion: god, gold, or glory. Peacekeepers have entered disputes based on all of these reasons, and will continue to do so into the future.

The September 11 attacks clearly altered the security landscape. Yet even before this dramatic series of events, it was obvious that the world was not the stable place cited by those demanding a peace dividend. This was eloquently expressed by former CIA Director James Woolsey, "We have slain a large dragon, but are now finding ourselves living in a jungle with a bewildering number of poisonous snakes. And in many ways, the

17

dragon was easier to keep track of" (Woolsey, in Ciccarelli, 1996: xi). Those snakes are readily seen in the internal conflict, humanitarian crises, and failed or failing states forecast in the US 1997 *Quadrennial Defense Review* (US Department of Defense, 1997). This circumstance will worsen as further governments lose their ability to maintain public order and provide for the needs of their people. Such disarray will generate conditions for civil unrest, massive refugee flows, and aggressive counter-actions, possibly including mass killings, by neighboring states.

Ethnic and religious fighting will persist as states established by imperial or colonial powers, but lacking a unifying sense of nationhood among their inhabitants, are challenged by other group identities. Consider the violence that swept Europe between the fourteenth and twentieth centuries, as non-viable states were annexed by or partitioned amongst stronger and more viable neighbors. This led to a reduction from 500-odd states to 25 viable, modern states by 1900 (Ayoob, 1995). Now picture a similar occurrence happening, but in reverse, based on increasing ethno-nationalism—5000 possible states (Hannum, 1990). There are already:

> 32 failed states within 20 complex emergencies declared by the UN, five of these in Africa. There are 66 countries with millions of refugees, 59 countries with plagues and epidemics, 41 countries using child soldiers, 33 countries with massive starvation, and active genocides now ongoing in 18 places, three of these in Indonesia.
>
> (Steele, 2004)[1]

Such increased threats to human dignity will be expanded by the perilous combination of diminishing natural resources, rising populations, and declining opportunities for prosperity. This is readily apparent in places such as India, which over the next decade faces a 30 per cent population increase, with a 50–75 per cent per capita water drop in availability. Of its 1.2 billion population, over 5 million will be considered to live in dire poverty (US Director of Central Intelligence, 2000). As globalization continues to draw income and skilled labor away from the "have-not" areas of the planet, there will be a concomitant increase in the pool of bored, unfulfilled, angry young males habitually drawn to violence as a solution to their woes (Peters, 2002).

Ethnic and religious strife, as well as ecological failures, will spark a growing impetus for intervening in the name of protecting human rights. This was the stated justification for such diverse missions as in the Balkans or Ivory Coast. This rationale will be further promoted in the guilty aftermath of humanitarian failures, such as Rwanda and Sudan. Contrasting with the trend in humanitarian intervention, however, will be the declining belief in a common set of human values. We will witness increasingly asserted value-based and cultural variations, such as "Asian Values" or

"Islamic Values" (Falk, 2004). Such differing perceptions between largely Western-driven peace operations and those non-Western countries in which intervention occurs will make the task of intelligence analysis that much more difficult. We shall return to the issues of culture and nuance shortly.

Future peacekeepers will also confront problematic tactics upon intervening. While not necessarily innovative, one lesson learned from recent terrorist successes is that antagonists can target political resolve via asymmetric means, rather than directly challenging peacekeepers militarily (US Office of Naval Intelligence and US Coast Guard Intelligence Coordination Center, 1999). Resultant civilian casualties will hasten demands for intervention. Once forces are deployed, this targeting, both of civilian and military sectors of society will require increased attention to intelligence issues as well as a heightened requirement to maintain a level of motivation amongst the nations contributing troops.

Future belligerents will further exploit established international bodies to legitimize their campaigns, such as occurred with Serbia accusing Belgium, Canada, France, Germany, Italy, the Netherlands, Portugal, and the UK of war crimes during the Kosovo conflict. Belgrade claimed, before the International Court of Justice, that the intervention was genocidal in its aim of killing the Serbian ethnic group (BBC News Online, December 15, 2004). While the Court dismissed these allegations, it does presage legitimacy issues for peacekeeping, with interventions becoming more challenging.

The future security environment is therefore more likely to be the "stepchild of Somalia and Chechnya" (Holzer, 1996: 4). Political decision-makers and deployed forces must adapt to ambiguity, with military personnel becoming accustomed to the chaos of operating in the absence of the comfort of a predictable, readily templated enemy force (Horn and Reshke, 2003). Such complexity will increase exponentially with antagonists' expected preference for confronting peacekeepers asymmetrically in difficult terrain. Conflict featuring networked, dispersed individuals using terrorist tactics, surrounded by non-combatants within an urban setting, will not seem uncommon.

Multinational coalitions

While General Dwight Eisenhower lamented, "history testifies to the ineptitude of coalitions," they are inevitable for peace support operations (PSOs) (Eisenhower 1948: 4). Though these earlier undertakings were almost exclusively the purview of the UN, this legacy began to unwind almost immediately following the culmination of Cold War. With multiple, inadequate missions in the Balkans, Cambodia, and Somalia commencing virtually simultaneously, 1992 marked the UN's decline. The spread of violent (often genocidal), low-tech civil wars with unconventional combatants, made the UN's forte of simply standing between two resting armies largely irrelevant. In a newspaper editorial, Douglas Bland states that the UN's traditional "peacekeeping model is passé. It's like the parrot in the Monty Python skit—dead" (Dimanno, 2004: A5). This changed security environment therefore makes lessons for the future more difficult to discern.

It is not merely traditional peacekeeping missions that have outlived their usefulness, but perhaps the UN itself. The past decade saw the institution stumble from one crisis to another: impotently watching the Balkans and Rwanda implode; routinely disregarded by the major powers; widespread belief in its corruption; allegations of sexual child abuse in the Congo and sex trafficking in the Balkans (Frum, 2005). Regarding its actual operational efficacy, the security environment does not support the UN in its current format; simply put, the UN is "a forum for the big players to settle their differences, eyeball to eyeball. You can't do that with Osama bin Laden" (Kerevan, 2005). UN bureaucrats' black-and-white attitude toward Chapter VI and VII missions denied any development of a more effective approach to the new environment. UN experts and peace-studies institutes could not react to the approaching doctrinal void (Mackinlay, 1994: 152). What was needed was military expertise, preferably familiar with counter-insurgency-type operations.

Despite its inability to keep pace with the world's changes, inertia will likely ensure the UN continues as an international player, albeit increasingly marginalized by its apparent role as merely a forum for America-bashing. This is not to imply that peacekeeping is dead though; it remains a booming business. During the UN's first forty years, there were thirteen deployments—a number surpassed in the four years following 1988 (Mackinlay, 1993; Serafino, 2004). The future, however, will see fewer deployments under a UN flag.

Future coalitions

Traditionally peacekeeping troops came from countries considered lesser powers, operating well outside their area of direct military and political interest (Smith, 1994). This is the natural outcome of two UN predilections: drawing peacekeepers from nations neutral toward the conflict, which often rules out neighboring countries; and this neutrality often eliminates some of the more powerful nations, given their need to maintain a Cold War balance. Despite the fall of the Soviet Union, lesser nations will continue to bear an undue burden of future peacekeeping operations. Freed of Cold War limitations on their actions, major nations are now addressing terrorism with a single-mindedness that will preclude extensive peacekeeping participation. Where they do become involved, it will be in the more violent conflicts, with the involvement marketed as fighting terror.

Increasingly complex, violent Chapter VII missions, or even the so-called "Chapter 6½," cannot be commanded or controlled without a proper military command structure (Mackinlay, 1993). The UN will remain incapable of producing such a command structure as long as it continues to make decisions by lowest common denominator, wherein everyone gets a turn, regardless of ability. The more demanding missions will therefore fall to a lead-nation coalition of the willing, regardless of UN sanction.

As the mission's intensity increases, there is a commensurate requirement for competent troops. The UN Operation in Somalia (UNOSOM I) was established as an Observer Mission on April 24, 1992. Being largely ineffective, it was strengthened with combat troops in July, though this also proved inadequate (Hillen, 2000). US military troops, under the auspices of the Unified Task Force (UNITAF), reinforced the mission, coming ashore on December 9, 1992. When the crisis of widespread starvation seemed to have subsided the mission was returned to UN control when UNOSOM II, as a Chapter VII mission, took over from UNITAF in May 1993. This suggests a division of labor between complex and traditional missions. As coalitions of powerful nations address the more difficult operations, traditional peacekeeping missions will not disappear. Without the interest of the major powers, however, customary peacekeeping missions will remain under-funded and likely supported by less than optimal troops.

But even traditional operations have witnessed the apparent erosion of the UN's principle of minimum force, such that there is now a greater acceptance of the use of military strength in mission accomplishment (Regehr, 1993). This reality has even jarred the UN into routinely authorizing Chapter VII mandates whether the mission is otherwise considered to be "peacekeeping" or "peace enforcement," in acknowledgment that even benign environments can become hostile (United Nations, 2004).

This militarization of peacekeeping has affected more than just the interventionary troops. The increased threat to the international relief structure is accepted by practically all but the most naïve idealists. With aid agencies accepting that belligerents use humanitarian relief as a weapon, armed security is necessary to protect both the aid workers and their supplies. A major exception appears to be the Red Cross, which in Iraq, preferred to close its offices rather than accept US military escorts (Schnieper, 2003).[2] In Canada, the military acknowledges this change through the requirement for greater inter-agency coordination, especially Foreign Affairs and the Canadian International Development Agency. The "3-D" approach—Defence, Diplomacy, Development—is thus the model for building stability in war-torn countries (Department of National Defence (Canada, 2004).

This more integrated approach, while previously present to some degree, will be more evident in all future operations. Coordinating these different groups within a theater of operations will be increasingly problematic, not least in the realm of providing intelligence support. Multinational coalitions, regardless of the mission's intensity, still "founder on the shoals of technical incompatibility, language difficulties, cultural asymmetries, and ignorance of key historical and geopolitical issues" (Scales, 1998–99: 10). Each of these issues is inextricably enmeshed with the intelligence function, particularly at the tactical level, where during deployments the various theories of intelligence collide head-on with the realities of operations. This reality is even more pronounced within UN operations, where intelligence has always led a colored existence—usually deemed unnecessary, and until very recently, never acknowledged.

Intelligence

Intelligence has but one purpose, unchanged from the days when it became "the second oldest profession"—namely, to reduce uncertainty in the mind of decision-makers. Perfect situational awareness remains unattainable despite technology's dramatic advances. Uncertainty, whether caused by information that is missing, unreliable, ambiguous, or too complex to be utilized, will not vanish (Klein, 1999).[3] The intelligence system must therefore strive to fill whatever knowledge gaps exist, and estimate the most likely, and most dangerous, situations facing a commander. For peacekeepers in particular, filling this intelligence gap has always been problematic.

Useful peace support intelligence products can include a range of materials not generally considered important for conventional war-fighting. For example, genealogical trees provide insight into the networks surrounding important people, where often the family structure is critical to that network, while focus groups, polls, and cultural materials offer up useful information not generally sought out.

Peacekeeping intelligence thus far

While the 1994 report of the International Institute of Strategic Studies observed that "intelligence is no longer a UN taboo," that verdict was premature, to say the least (IISS, 1994: 268). The Netherlands' Marine Corps Major-General Frank van Kappen once commented on PKI that:

> during my tenure as the Military Advisor to the Secretary-General
> of the United Nations, I have struggled with this topic more than

once and I have not always come out of the battle unharmed, to say the least. The subject matter is not only complex, but also controversial.

(van Kappen, 2003: 3)

The controversy is fueled by disreputable stereotypes surrounding intelligence as spying, and the UN-held view that peacekeeping's benevolent presence, welcomed by all sides in a conflict, supposedly eradicates any requirement for intelligence. That neither view is based in reality is irrelevant; the perception will continue into the future.

Attempting to utilize intelligence within multinational PSOs has created ludicrous situations, such as when Indian Lieutenant-General Satish Nambiar, commanding the United Nations Protection Force (UNPROFOR) in the former Yugoslavia was denied North Atlantic Treaty Organization (NATO) intelligence being provided to his staff (Smith, 1994). The intelligence-sharing situation was not particularly improved when the Force Command was transferred to NATO's Lieutenant-General Bernard Janvier from France, because his senior intelligence officer was Colonel Jan-Inge Svensson, from non-NATO Sweden (Svensson, 2002).

The intelligence way ahead

Despite the acknowledged changes in the security environment, intelligence priorities and resources have shifted only marginally from their Cold War focus, leaving peacekeepers poorly supported (US Department of Defense, 2001). A Johns Hopkins study of humanitarian mission fatalities noted that 17 per cent died within the first month of service and 31 per cent within three months. Of those operations studied, median length of service at death for UN peacekeepers was the shortest, at 5.5 months (Sheik et al., 2000). This unsettling statistic indicates a serious intelligence problem, in that even in peace support missions where intelligence is not shunned, such as NATO-led missions in the Balkans or Afghanistan, it still takes newly arrived contingents approximately four months to gain competency in the new surroundings (Vass, 2004). Force protection and operational efficiency will demand that intelligence operations receive greater emphasis.

The starting point for any intelligence problem is direction, wherein a commander understands the issues and knows what answers are required to formulate a plan of action. Yet PKI operations are seldom actually directed toward a specific end. They are mostly generic (Reinhelt, 2004). Information is accordingly collected in a haphazard and negligible manner. Peacekeeping missions require forceful, intelligence-savvy commanders, in order to make the system work effectively. Increasingly pervasive Chapter VII missions argue against tolerating inadequate leadership in light of the increased risk of casualties. Yet, if the UN continues to accept less competent leaders, in seeking greater organizational equity, such direction will remain an Achilles' heel.

Collecting adequate information to support decision-makers thus becomes a key issue. Despite peacekeepers operating in unfamiliar territory, some missions may have a head start on intelligence collection where the area of interest is a former colony, whose previously colonizing power backs the mission by providing relevant information. In many cases, however, the troops will either be without effective intelligence support, or be forced to trust whatever the more powerful nations choose to share. The absence of a credible intelligence capability led to Major-General Lewis MacKenzie's exasperation at relying upon the BBC World Service to ascertain what was happening 200 meters away from his own headquarters (*Gazette*, 1994). Such situations will become increasingly common given the convergence of media-savvy belligerents with a seemingly omnipresent media. PKI must therefore turn this to its advantage by embracing open-source intelligence (OSINT), while actively practicing counter-intelligence and operational security measures.

OSINT provides solutions to many ethical issues of secrecy and impartiality. Though information from open sources has always been used, it remains undervalued within the intelligence community—an attitude derived from people mistakenly equating secrecy with information's ultimate value to analysts and policy makers (Lowenthal, 2000). OSINT provides a Rosetta stone for other intelligence materials by providing a much-needed context for fruitful analysis and potentially cueing more covert or technical collection methods. Its overt nature therefore supports UN impartiality and allows for greater intelligence sharing.

This latter point is increasingly significant given the expanded number of peacekeeping dramatis personae—Robert Steele's seven "intelligence tribes": national, military, business, academic, law enforcement, NGO–media, and religious–citizenry (Steele, 2003). With OSINT providing an overwhelming amount of basic information required for PSOs, the other key information source acquired directly by the personnel on the ground is considered under the rubric of human intelligence, or HUMINT.

Because HUMINT is the collection of information by humans, it is often equated with "spying." In actuality, it is what the UN's Military Advisor calls "the Mark 1 Eyeball"—troops on the ground, observing and conversing with the local population (Cammaert, 2002). While most competent infantry patrols can produce excellent reporting during peacekeeping missions, there is a recurring communication problem in that peacekeepers often speak a language different from the local community. The difficulties inherent in locating and hiring suitable interpreters can often hinder information collection for several months (Sherman, 2004). But this certainly does not justify canceling patrolling as a source of critical information. The mere ability to gain entry to various communities and, like a police officer "walking the beat," be aware of any changes, adds immeasurably to the intelligence picture—more so if the patrol can determine why something has changed (Canadian Forces, 2001). Specialist HUMINT, which is conducted by soldiers specifically trained to elicit particular information in direct response to the commander's list of intelligence requirements, further enhances this general skill.

Because the principal advantage of HUMINT is that it can help one understand an adversary's intentions and capabilities, HUMINT will be progressively more important in future operations. It is worth again citing the UN Military Advisor: "contingents with a HUMINT collection orientation and their own organic intelligence structure and capabilities are several times more effective in controlling their Area of Responsibility than other contingents with only an equivalent combat capability" (Cammaert, 2003: 21). The downside is the fundamental challenge in selecting and training HUMINT operators. As well, peace support coalitions are demanding greater intelligence responsiveness, while relying on HUMINT, which is traditionally the slowest form of intelligence (Hunter, 1994).

Notwithstanding the growth forecast in OSINT and HUMINT, technical information collection has been featured in many peacekeeping missions, and its use will likely increase. The most prolific methods involve collecting imagery intelligence (IMINT) and signals intelligence (SIGINT). During the UN's first Congo mission, for example, the Swedish Battalion was particularly adept at radio intercept using Swahili interpreters (Eriksson, 1997). This operation also saw aerial photography provided by two Swedish S29C reconnaissance aircraft, cameras affixed to several of the six Indian Canberra bombers, and hand-held cameras used by transport aircraft crews (Van Nederveen, 2001). While photo interpreters were restricted by limited processing capability and their small numbers, their presence and capability definitely bolstered the intelligence contest.

Imagery collection, pictures worth a thousand words, routinely provides irrefutable evidence of treaty violations or border incursions. Given potential antagonism within distrustful societies still on the edge of hostilities, the future will see greater use of more surreptitious image collection methods. These range from vehicle-mounted optics to unmanned aerial vehicles (UAVs). While the latter have demonstrated inconsistent utility in PSOs, their growing popularity assures their continued use in the future (US Army, 2003). There will also be increased exploitation of sensors within these platforms, especially those that exploit the non-visible spectrum such as infrared, thermal, or millimeter wave.

For SIGINT, the proliferation of radios makes targeting communications systems more profitable for the intelligence staff. Electronic Warfare equipment collecting warring factions' radio traffic need not be particularly complex or expensive since many belligerents use unencrypted, commercial radios. In Rwanda, such a capability could have provided specific warning of pending atrocities, allowing the politically constrained force at least a chance of mustering some effective response, such as jamming the genocide-inducing radio stations, or at least providing direction finding to allow intervention (Dallaire, 2003). Surreptitious communications interception, increasingly providing peacekeepers with real-time warning of hostile intentions, will figure in most future operations (Williams, 1993).

Regardless of how the information is collected, it still falls to the intelligence analyst to make sense of it all. Analysis, or the intellectual task of understanding complex and often incomplete or contradictory information, is the key to the intelligence process. Developing competent analysts was difficult against a reasonably straightforward adversary, such as the Cold War's opposing alliances. Forecasting has become an increasingly difficult task in today's unstable environment. Common indicators and warnings, with which the modern intelligence system is comfortable, are inadequate when the cause is ethnic hatred and the weapon system of choice is a machete. The problem is further complicated in that the protagonists are seldom familiar Western-style soldiers: professionals are predictable; amateurs are dangerous. Some intelligence officers appear unable to make this transition to the more complex environment; those that can will remain in high demand.

Western militaries cannot presently support ongoing intelligence requirements (US Department of Defense, 2004). This analytic deficit is exacerbated by two factors: quality intelligence personnel often take years to develop, and the current terrorism focus had sparked a hiring frenzy for qualified analysts (Pfleger Shrader, 2004). Many non-standard analytic skills are transferable between counter-terror and peace support. Within Kosovo, for example, a local coffee shop gets blown up. Did the owner fail to pay protection money? Was the coffee *that* bad? Had the owner sold tobacco to someone of the opposing ethnic group? (Välimäki, 2002). In this example, the rationale turned out to be the latter supposition. While this sort of event appears on very few analytic templates, there have been tremendous advances in expanding the range of intelligence analysis within peacekeeping operations, counter-terrorism, and in this example, criminal extortion. Analysts, however, will most likely follow the money, which is not found in PKI.

If not received in time, even the most accurately analyzed intelligence is useless. While an unprecedented amount of information is available through technological advances in collection, dissemination systems have not kept pace (US House of Representatives, 1993). Dissemination within multinational alliances and ad hoc coalitions adds further hurdles to efficient information promulgation. Whereas in war fighting, security is often best attained through speed of operation, peacekeeping traditionally aims to freeze hostilities in order to allow attempts at diplomacy (Quist, 2002).

Peacekeepers therefore require a rapid method of sharing information that will provide the decision-maker with alternatives other than violence. While always problematic within peacekeeping missions, the increased number of military and civilian participants will only further cloud this issue.

Conclusion

When traditional justifications for peacekeeping operations are coupled with the growing quantity of conflicts and causes of instability, it is obvious that the number of such interventions will not decrease any time soon. As the scale of violence increases from traditionally envisaged benign peace-keeping to operations requiring more adversarial intervention, so too will the intelligence requirements and methods change. As PSOs become increasingly constrained by funding issues, the fiscal reality that intelligence makes operations less expensive will be acknowledged. Even the Canadian government concedes that an intelligence capability provides a potent force multiplier to a budget conscious military (Canada, Parliament, 2002).

All missions will progressively exploit the utility of OSINT and HUMINT information. Operations more closely resembling combat will perforce rely more heavily upon combat skills of tactical reconnaissance and the greater standoff safety inherent in technical collections methods. The major powers, previously operating within the constraints of Cold War politics, are increasingly occupied by fighting such insurgencies and terrorist campaigns. This may institutionalize a growing division of labor wherein the more developed countries will provide materiel and technical support to traditional peacekeeping missions, including that of intelligence, while it falls to the lesser-developed nations to provide a greater share of labor in the form of troops. Another possible outcome from this situation may be the recognition that PKI requires the more nuanced linguistic and cultural skills that are unavailable in Washington or London. Thus membership in the Organization of African Unity or the Arab League may provide greater credentials for future PKI staff.

Though the UN has been adamant that intelligence is "dirty," refusing to acknowledge its presence within the organization, it should be equally obvious that it must embrace intelligence or the organization's inevitable shortcomings will see it cast aside. Returning to Robert Steele, regarding the future of PKI within the UN:

> It may be that the United Nations simply cannot be helped, in part because the most powerful member nations do not want it to have an independent intelligence capability, and the level of ignorance about the craft of intelligence *sans* espionage is so low among UN and humanitarian officials as to represent a generational issue that

will require completely new blood, over the course of 20 years, before progress can be entertained.

(Steele, 2003: 223 n15)

Perhaps a ray of hope that PKI may move forward lies in UN Under-Secretary-General Marrack Goulding's acknowledgment that "few memories of my UN days disturb me more than the recollection of how little I knew when we plunged into new conflicts" (Goulding, 2002: 339). If more effective intelligence support to peacekeeping interventions is not forthcoming, the future security environment indicates that many regions will soon resemble Hobbes' vision of a life—"solitary, poor, nasty, brutish and short."

Notes

1 See also Litton–TASC (1998: 19).
2 That the ICRC accepted Russian Interior Ministry escorts within Chechnya, while refusing the same security arrangement in Iraq, is likely more attributable to anti-Americanism than any rational difference between the conflict areas.
3 Klein cites four sources of uncertainty: missing information, wherein information is unavailable, whether it has not been received or it has been received but cannot be located when needed; unreliable information, where the credibility of the source is low, or is perceived to be low even if the information happens to be highly accurate; ambiguous or conflicting information, in which there are multiple rational ways to interpret the information; and complex information, where it is difficult to integrate the various facets of the information.

Bibliography

Ayoob, M. (1995) "The New–Old Disorder in the Third World," in T. Weiss (ed.), *The United Nations and Civil Wars*, London: Lynne Rienner.

Cammaert, P., Maj.-Gen. (2002) Personal communication, November 15–16.

—— (2003) "Intelligence for Peacekeeping Operations: Lessons for the Future," in B. de Jong, W. Platje, and R. Steele (eds.), *Peacekeeping Intelligence: Emerging Concepts for the Future*, Oakton, VA: OSS International Press.

Canada, Parliament (2002) "Facing Our Responsibilities: The State of the Canadian Forces; Ch. 2: The Limits of Current Policy, Para D: Intelligence," *Report of the Standing Committee on National Defence and Veterans Affairs*, Ottawa: Public Works and Government Services.

Canadian Forces (2001) "HUMINT During Peace Support Operations," *Dispatches: Lessons Learned for Soldiers*, Kingston, Ont.: Centre for Army Lessons Learned, June: 8.

Ciccarelli, J. (1996) *Transnational Crime: A New Security Threat?* Canberra: Australian Defence Studies Centre.

Dallaire, R., Lt.-Gen. (ret'd.) (2003) Personal communication, August 29.

Department of National Defence (Canada) (2004) *2003–2004 Annual Report—Making Choices*. Available at: http://www.cds.forces.gc.ca/pubs/anrpt2004 (accessed December 10, 2004).

Dimanno, R. (2004) "Old Peace Model is Dead," *Toronto Star*, June 9.

Eisenhower, D. (1948) *Crusade in Europe*, New York: Doubleday.

Eriksson, P. (1997) "Intelligence in Peacekeeping Operations," *International Journal of Intelligence and CounterIntelligence*, 10: 1–18.

Falk, R. (2004) "Think Again: Human Rights," *Foreign Policy*, March/April: 18–26.

Frum, D. (2005) "This Disaster Exposes the Myth of the UN's Moral Authority," *Telegraph*, June 9. Available at: http://www.telegraph.co.uk/opinion (accessed January 10, 2005).

Gazette, The (1994) "MacKenzie: Disappointed by Lack of 'Inter-National Self-Interest'," February 12.

Goulding, M. (2002) *Peacemonger*, London: John Murray.

Hannum, H. (1990) *Autonomy, Sovereignty, and Self-Determination*, Philadelphia: University of Pennsylvania Press.

Hillen, J. (2000) *Blue Helmets: The Strategy of UN Military Operations*, Washington, DC: Brassey's, 2nd edn.

Holzer, R. (1996) "Krulak Warns of Over-Reliance on Technology," *Defence News*, October: 7–13.

Horn, B., Lt.-Col., and Reshke, R. (2003) "Defying Definition: The Future Battlespace," in B. Horn and P. Gizewski (eds.), *Towards the Brave New World: Canada's Army in the 21st Century*, Kingston, Ont.: Directorate of Land Strategic Concepts.

Hunter, J., Maj. (1994) "The Doctrinal Functions of Intelligence: Are They Applicable to Peacekeeping and Peace Enforcement Operations?" unpublished research paper, US Army Command and General Staff College, School of Advanced Military Studies.

IISS (1994) *1994 Annual Report*, London: International Institute of Strategic Studies.

Kerevan, G. (2005) "Has Impotent UN Finally Outlived Its Usefulness?" *Scotsman*, 5 January. Available at: http://news.scotsman.com (accessed January 5, 2005).

Klein, G. (1999) *Source of Power: How People Make Decisions*, Cambridge, MA: MIT Press.

Litton–TASC (1998) *Problem Identification and Definition Forecast 2020*, unclassified, Chantilly, VA: Litton–TASC.

Lowenthal, M. (2000) *Intelligence: From Secrets to Policy*, Washington, DC: CQ Press.

Mackinlay, J. (1993) "Defining a Role Beyond Peacekeeping," in W. Lewis (ed.), *Military Implications of United Nations Peacekeeping Operations: McNair Paper No. 17*, Washington, DC: National Defense University.

—— (1994) "Improving Multifunctional Forces," *Survival*, 36: 149–173.

Peters, R. (2002) *Beyond Terror: Strategy in a Changing World*. Mechanicsburg, PA: Stackpole Books.

Pfleger Shrader, K. (2004) "Analysts Are in Great Demand: Intelligence Agencies Scramble for Talent," *Washington Post*, December 30.

Quist, A. (2002) *Security Classification of Information*, Vol. 1: *Introduction, History, and Adverse Impacts*, Oak Ridge, TN: Oak Ridge Classification Associates.

Regehr, E. (1993) "The Future of Peacekeeping," in A. Morrison (ed.), *The Changing Face of Peacekeeping*, Toronto: Canadian Institute of Strategic Studies.

Reinhelt, L., Maj. (2004) Personal communication, June 10.

Scales, R., Maj.-Gen. (ret'd.) (1998–99) "Trust, Not Technology, Sustains Coalitions," *Parameters*, 28: 4–10.

Schnieper, M. (2003) "A Before and an After in Iraq: The Red Cross is 'Taking A Step Back' in Iraq," *Tages-Anzeiger*, November 8. Available at: http://www.icrc.org/Web/Eng/siteeng0.nsf/html/5T6HX7 (accessed November 8, 2003).

Serafino, Nina M. (2004) *Report for Congress (RL32321)—Policing in Peacekeeping and Related Stability Operations: Problems and Proposed Solutions*, Washington, DC: Congressional Research Service, March 30, p. 5.

Sheik, M., Gutierrez, M., Bolton, P., Spiegel, P., Thieren, M., and Burnham, G. (2000) "Deaths Among Humanitarian Workers," *British Medical Journal*, 321: 166–168.

Sherman, C., Capt. (2004) Personal communication (July 17, 2004).

Smith, H. (1994) "Intelligence and UN Peacekeeping," *Survival*, 36: 174–192.

Steele, R. (2003) "Information Peacekeeping and the Future of Intelligence: The United Nations, Smart Mobs, and the Seven Tribes," in B. de Jong, W. Platje, and R. Steele (eds.), *Peacekeeping Intelligence: Emerging Concepts for the Future*, Oakton, VA: OSS International Press.

—— (2004) Remarks to the Secretary of State's Open Forum, "The New Craft of Open Source Intelligence: How The U.S. Department of State Should Lead," US Department of State, March 24. Available at: http::/www.state.gov/s/p/of/proc/30870.htm (accessed October 20, 2004).

Svensson, J., Col. (2002) Personal communication, November 15–16.

Taylor, C. (1992) *A World 2020: A New Order Of Nations*, Carlisle, PA: US Army War College.

UN (2004) "A More Secure World: Our Shared Responsibility," *Report of the Secretary-General's High-Level Panel on Threats, Challenges, and Change*. New York: UN Headquarters.

US Army (2003) "Operation OUTREACH," *CALL Newsletter*, No. 03–27, Center for Army Lessons Learned.

US Department of Defense (1997) *Report of the Quadrennial Defense Review*.

—— (2001) "Executive Summary," *DoD USS Cole Commission Report*, January 2.

—— (2004) *Defense Science Board 2004 Summer Study on Transition to and from Hostilities*. Washington, DC: Office of the Under Secretary of Defense for Acquisition, Technology, and Logistics, December.

US Director of Central Intelligence (2000) *Global Trends 2015: A Dialogue About the Future with Non-government Experts*, Washington, DC: National Intelligence Council.

US House of Representatives (1993) *Intelligence Successes and Failures in Operations Desert Shield/Storm*, House of Representatives, Committee on Armed Services.

US Office of Naval Intelligence and US Coast Guard Intelligence Coordination Center (1999) *Threats And Challenges to Maritime Security 2020*, Suitland, MD: National Maritime Intelligence Center, March 1.

Välimäki, P. (2002) Personal communication, November 15–16.

—— (2003) "Bridging the Gap: Intelligence and Peace Support Operations," in B. de Jong, W. Platje, and R. Steele (eds.), *Peacekeeping Intelligence: Emerging Concepts for the Future*, Oakton, VA: OSS International Press.

Van Kappen, F., Maj.-Gen. (ret'd.) (2003) "Strategic Intelligence and the United Nations," in B. de Jong, W. Platje, and R. Steele (eds.), *Peacekeeping Intelligence: Emerging Concepts for the Future*, Oakton, VA: OSS International Press.

Van Nederveen, G., Capt. (2001) "USAF Airlift into the Heart of Darkness, The Congo 1960–1978: Implications for Modern Air Mobility Planners," unpublished research paper, USAF Air University College of Aerospace Doctrine, Research, and Education.

Vass, J. Maj. (2004) Personal communication, May 18.

Williams, C., Com. (1993) *Intelligence Support to U.N. Peacekeeping Operations*, Washington, DC: Industrial College of the Armed Forces, National Defense University.

3

A READING OF TEA LEAVES

Toward a framework for modern peacekeeping intelligence

Michael A. Hennessy[1]

The renowned Danish Physicist Niels Bohr said once that: "Prediction is extremely difficult, especially about the future." I will not quibble with him. Frameworks require foundations. Abstract ideas are one possible source of such foundations. But far more solid are ideas grounded in practical experience. Knowledge from experience is more certain. This chapter takes an inductive-historical approach to developing a "framework" for intelligence support to future "peacekeeping" operations. The historical-inductive approach offers for contemplation the vagaries of intelligence support to peacekeeping intelligence (PKI) operations by developing a solid sense of "ground truths." Recent practice is an important basis for any analysis. But each case could be the subject of a major and lengthy study—in essence, then, this account provides only a reading of certain surface details, and the picture is necessarily incomplete; however, like the practice of reading tea leaves the object is to speak to the future. Given that caveat, there remains a complexity to the lived realities of recent intelligence support to peace operations that needs to be apprehended, and not avoided, in framing discussion of future requirements. Recognizing the imperfectability of doctrine, rather than decrying imperfections, is a fundamental step. For instance, in all the cases examined here the intelligence organization was task-tailored for specific deployments.

For the purpose of this chapter the term peacekeeping is employed in its widest possible sense. It must be construed to include peace support operations, stability and humanitarian relief operations—because the limits of United Nations Emergency Force (UNEF) I style "traditional" peacekeeping are clearly too rigid. Rather than traditional peacekeeping operations, these recent operations range from humanitarian relief deployments, to small- and large-scale contingency operations to bring or secure peace. Rather than survey all the record of intelligence support to PKOs a

32

survey of four missions conducted in the recent past, conducted in four different regions, illustrates issues and problems that should inform future PKI operations. The missions addressed are:

1   Operation Assurance—a UN mandated Humanitarian Intervention in Zaire-African Great Lakes Region: November–December 31, 1996.
2   Operation CONSTABLE—Haiti: July 29–November 30, 1997.
3   SFOR—Bosnia: January 1997–
4   INTERFET—UN-sanctioned mission to East Timor: September 1999–January 2000.

Operation Assurance: November 1996–December 31, 1996

Operation Assurance has been called the largest humanitarian intervention operation that never happened—and is known affectionately by many in the Canadian military as the "bungle in the jungle." Only a brief thumbnail sketch is warranted here. The operation's origins lie in the 1994 genocide and civil war in Rwanda. The Tutsi tribal groups responsible for the genocide had been vanquished. A large number of them were driven into refugee camps along Zaire's eastern border (the Great Lakes region) and prevented from returning home first by Rwandan forces but then also by their owned armed factions, particularly the Interahamwe, which used the refugee camps as staging areas for raids into Rwanda. Fighting along the border sparked by a resurgent Interahamwe prompted growing calls for a repatriation of the innocent who were being held among them in the camps. In discussions within the UN Security Council, the US, and France made it clear they would not take a leading role in such a mission. Canadian diplomats and politicians took the opportunity to advance the proposition that Canada should lead the mission. That commitment facilitated finalizing UN S/C Resolution 1080 (November 15, 1996) authorizing a UN humanitarian intervention force to enable the repatriation. Canada dispatched its advanced reconnaissance party under the nominal force commander Lieutenant-General Maurice Baril the following day. It promised to be an auspicious mission, because Canada had not taken the lead in a new UN operation since the Suez Crisis of 1956.

However, the real tests never came. Reacting to the UN vote, the Hutu/Rwandan military redoubled their attacks on the refugee camps. These attacks resulted in the "liberation" of approximately 400,000 refugees (estimates vary) back into Rwanda within the course of the week. This movement soon clearly obviated the need for a large UN mission. Nevertheless, several hundred thousand refugees were reported by a number of non-governmental organizations (NGOs) and a UN agency to be seen heading deeper into Zaire. While Baril was attempting to establish his headquarters and, indeed, to get Rwandan authority to place UN troops in their country, press coverage of the "refugee crisis" fueled calls for air relief operations. Baril negotiated with the local Zairian warlord, Laurent Kabila, and the Zairian government to allow uncontested air passage over the region—both parties had threatened to engage UN aircraft. The Canadian's had little or no idea who Kabila was or that he had led a thirty-year struggle against the Mobuto government in Kinshasa. Kabila took this opportunity to go on the offensive, and within several months was on the outskirts of Kinshasa, and Mobuto's regime collapsed.

For the UN mission air access proved of limited worth. While many NGOs touted figures of hundreds of thousands lost in the forests of Zaire, these numbers could not be verified by teams on the ground. Baril took the initiative to insist that air photographs would constitute the only intelligence on which relief efforts should be based. This step was critical for resolving a debate within the ad hoc international coordinating group to whom Baril reported. While Canada did not have suitable air reconnaissance assets both the US, and Britain provided overflights (and it appears France provided photos taken by aircraft allegedly flown by Médicine sans Frontières). By early December these flights demonstrated that the mass refugee crisis had passed. Only groups of several thousands could be spotted in Zaire, and these were judged too small, or too militant, to warrant further UN intervention. With that the mission was wound up.

Without overdrawing the lessons, the mission from conception to execution yields some valuable lessons. Canadian politicians, diplomats, and senior military staffs all overestimated Canada's ability to lead such a mission. Canadian planning was inadequate for the task—as demonstrated by the failures not to anticipate Hutu actions to evacuate the camps on the eve of UN intervention, or by the intelligence failure regarding Kabila that resulted in intervening in a long-standing civil war; perhaps even tipping the balance.

Second, Intelligence Preparation of the Battlefield (IPB) ran concurrent to the deployment of forces. Whereas both the US and Britain (both of whom refused to lead the mission) had previously dispatched strategic reconnaissance teams into the region in the early stages of the impending crisis, Canada did not—though it might be asked if Canada had sent a team that recommended against the mission would such a conclusion have been accepted by the Prime Minister's Office.

Third, the absence of nationally controlled strategic and operational reconnaissance aircraft or high-resolution satellite imagery complicated the Canadian mission and delayed timely decisions. Canada could have availed itself of the technical capacities of its RADARSAT but did not. The grace of others solved the dilemma. Most particularly, a Canadian planning staff forward deployed to Germany was able to avail itself of US imagery and communications, but that access became available only once the mission was underway.

Operation CONSTABLE—UN support mission to Haiti, July 29, 1997–November 30, 1997

Following the US intervention in Haiti in 1994, the UN authorized serially three separate peacekeeping forces to help reduce the American footprint and stabilize the political and security situation in Haiti. Canada led the last two of these missions, the UN Support Mission in Haiti (UNSMIH) and the UN Transition Mission in Haiti (UNTMIH). Regarding the latter, its primary task was to complete within four months the training of a local police force capable of taking over the general security mission being fulfilled by foreign forces while also ensuring a stabilized security situation. The security effort aimed particularly at thwarting political factional violence, and the formation or expansion of organized gangs such as the Tontons Macoutes.

UN forces filled in the security void left by departing US forces. Canada provided the largest contingent and developed a well fleshed out intelligence program that employed its conventional military forces, air assets, psychological warfare, and other elements into a comprehensive intelligence effort. Helicopters provided surveillance and maneuver. A reconnaissance platoon provided detailed observation and patrols. Indeed, a complete intelligence net was constructed during the operation. Aggressive patrolling provided local "street" intelligence. Police-type intelligence was gathered on neighborhoods, local gangs, power brokers, and political aspirants through an intelligence net that included espionage operations by paid informants from the general population and local government officials. The fact that French speakers predominated in the Canadian contingent enabled the troops to be intelligence ears. The Canadian operation typified the art of the possible. Basic Canadian intelligence doctrine proved sufficient and the operational lassitude provided in the Force Commander's tasking allowed an essentially full-blown intelligence operation. Neither Ottawa, nor New York interfered. Throughout the mission the security situation appeared to notably improve and the local police trainees finished their indoctrination. From an operational point of view, Canadian actions, predicated on a solid intelligence picture and organization, were highly successful.

But the Canadian effort cannot be viewed in isolation. Indeed, it followed in the wake of some rather heavy-handed security measures imposed by the US forces during Operation Restore Democracy (1994), and then built upon the constant patrol and intelligence network established by the previous UN mission. That force had also been led by a Canadian officer with a robust mandate. The IPB that informed the follow-on commander therefore was well grounded in experience. Very intimate knowledge of key personalities and local issues was well developed within the Canadian intelligence community rather than deduced from the ether. Moreover, it must be stressed that that knowledge was available to the incoming

35

commander because of his national ties. That it was available and could be fully utilized illustrates perhaps two unique elements of the mission: the handover between mission forces proved seamless because of the continuity between national forces involved.

Nevertheless, if UNTMIH can be judged a tactical or operational intelligence success it must still be pointed out that shortly after the departure of the contingent's heavier military forces, political and security instability returned to the island—it remains the case to this day.

SFOR—Bosnia, January 1997

The long agony of the civil strife and international intervention in the former Yugoslavia need not be recounted in any detail here. The Dayton Accords brought an end to much of the formal fighting and North Atlantic Treat Organization (NATO) forces created the Implementation Force (IFOR). IFOR's force of 55,000 troops began operations in December 1995 to develop a safe and secure civilian environment. In January 1997, a Stabilization Force (SFOR) was formed from a scaled-down IFOR and began the second phase of the stabilization campaign, nation building. Organized into three separate Multinational Divisional Areas SFOR reflected the dispositions of the three major troop-contributing nations, namely, France, the US, and Great Britain.

SFOR is a NATO mission and the major troop contributors are all NATO "allies." But even that formal alliance relationship did not allow the "allies" to transcend narrow national interests. This is particularly true of intelligence sharing. Initial efforts at the time of SFOR's creation to create a Combined Joint Allied Military Intelligence Battalion to coordinate activities across the sectors fell apart. A compromise remains in place wherein national intelligence cells (NICS) tend to be located in close proximity to those of their allies.

The continuing reluctance of various members to share and plan intelligence is seen in the three sectors. Intelligence within each sector can be said to have been developed according to the visions of the various commanders and has served their various interests. Within each sector, intelligence, psyops, civil–military cooperation (CIMIC), and espionage are all conducted differently—all with some degree of real success, as the ability of SFOR to roll up pockets of Islamic terrorists resident in Bosnia illustrated. However the lack of cooperation and coordination to secure the capture of various war criminals illustrates something to the contrary, in particular that the national interests or proclivities of various contingents can play a rather negative role.

Moreover, while the security environment is greatly improved, the HUMINT collection effort remains hampered by a shortage of language skills and a reluctance to exploit CIMIC as an intelligence source—CIMIC is a staff function of the organization of Joint Forces Command and its allied partners (J9s). An integrative element has been the Multinational Specialized Unit (an Italian-led police formation). It may well play a crucial intelligence role but how their information is provided to the military authorities or what is filtered from the CJ2 SFOR remains an open question.

SFOR intelligence cannot be called a failure; however, it has been operationally focused and remains of unknown significance in shaping the success of nation building. It clearly aided the creation of a more stable security situation and what else is needed is perhaps best carried out by political intelligence beyond the ken of military operational forces. The interface between the two is perhaps a gray area yet to be explored and can prove a major limiting factor. Tactical military intelligence can accomplish so much if geopolitical interests do not share a vision of "success." Obviously where there is no unity of purpose there cannot be unity of effort.

INTERFET—East Timor: September 1999–January 2000

A period of marked internal strife followed a UN-monitored referendum on independence from Indonesia in the former Portuguese colony of East Timor in September 1999. UN monitors found themselves rapidly evacuated and NGOs and other international observers were confined to their compounds where they found themselves under threat of violence or death from pro-Indonesian "militias" that rampaged in the wake of the election. A forced exodus of refugees also ensued. In response, and with Australian leadership and US prodding, the UN sanctioned the creation of an 11,000-strong intervention force to restore stability and prevent further operations by pro-Indonesian "militias." The multinational force included Canadian, Irish, Fijian, New Zealand, and several southeast Asian contingents. However, Australia provided the force commander and most of the initial troops for the brigade-sized land force were drawn from the Australian 3rd Brigade, the ADF's Rapid Deployment Force.

Much as Haiti had been a Canadian area of interest, Timor had been an Australian area of interest for some time. The Rapid Deployment Force's annual training the year before had gamed such a deployment to Timor. The exercise facilitated development of an extensive IPB that was quickly brought into play when the real crisis blossomed. As well, because of its long-standing interest in the region, the Australian forces also had a large number of troops able to speak the local languages (especially Tetum). Thankful for the security it brought, the UN force found much willing cooperation from all of resident NGOs, which provided much timely and intimate information in the initial days after the landing and thereafter.

UN headquarters allowed the Australian force commander a free hand to plan and conduct operations as he saw fit. Operations included deployment of a brigade-level intelligence organization augmented with several staff positions. Drawing on experiences with counter-insurgency operations, the Australian intelligence organization was also charged with conducting psychological operations and coordination with CIMIC activities. Strategic imagery allowed gaming the deployment to East Timor's capital Dili on a 3D map, and aerial photography ranged from strategic third-party assets to fixed-wing and helicopter-borne collection. Local informants took some time to cultivate, but Field Intelligence teams were active throughout the area. Signals intelligence (SIGINT) and electronic warfare (EW) also found vital roles. Psyops included the creation of East Timor's only newspaper, which was printed in four languages. In short, Australian forces were able to employ a substantial, but conventional, military intelligence organization and employ their pre-existing doctrine to good effect. Within six weeks a great degree of stability was achieved and plans for turning over the mission to a successor UN force were in hand.

Conclusions

So what can be induced from these various cases? First, a normative template would be difficult to fashion because each mission is so unique. Each mandate is unique and those explored here entailed a wide range of missions. These included humanitarian assistance; conflict reduction through active force; separation of combatants; supervision of disarmament; "nation building"; facilitation of local politics and elections; shoring up a new or transitional government, and general "stability" operations. Each mission also had unique command relationships that affected the role, tasking, and structure of intelligence resources. These ranged from oversight by committee, such as Operation Assurance, to coordination amongst a trinity of great powers, to near complete autonomy from New York, or large alliance structures, as typified by missions in Haiti and East Timor. It is unlikely a coincidence that the full panoply of traditional intelligence methods and resources were so clearly employed by force commanders in these two missions. That is to say, in Haiti and Timor the intelligence doctrine and basic organization and operational structures of the lead nation's military intelligence assets proved solid bases from which to proceed. Such bottom line "realities" allow one to venture that perhaps the ability, agility, and willingness to task tailor is essential, but that solid basic doctrine and organization is also essential. Further, the full range of assets can only be employed if you have them—and mission leadership clearly implies you should.

Second, some old truths about intelligence can be seen in all these missions. Language skills, cultural empathy, and a willingness to use and cultivate HUMINT proved essential. Canada found itself sending troops into two missions where innate French language skills proved useful for intelligence gathering. Australia's willingness to train a sizeable group within its forces on local languages, at least those found in areas of long-term strategic interest and instability, clearly paid dividends. Larger forces with global interests might well find it difficult to predict areas of operations, but this only makes their problem greater in scale, not in kind. As well, given free rein to employ forces according to intelligence doctrine, force commanders allowed employment of the full range of traditional intelligence assets, from HUMIT to SIGINT. It should be noted this was most possible when the force commander controlled forces that possessed these assets. That is to say, when all the cards held were played—perhaps a cautionary tale because cooperation between contingents from different nations cannot be taken for granted. Problems of unity of effort—domestic or international—can undermine greatly the intelligence effort.

Little has been revealed about offensive intelligence operations, or the ability of commanders in these missions to exploit intelligence for attacks, i.e. to disarm or spoil efforts by those opposed to peace, but it appears that in the case of SFOR and INTERFET these were clearly undertaken.

Finally, the political element within all the missions examined here warrants emphasis. Whereas Op. Assurance had only a humanitarian objective, the political agendas of the forces that would have to cooperate or facilitate success of the mission placed politics over "humanity." In the other missions the intervening forces that brought stability remained somewhat constrained to security roles—and intelligence played its clearest role in stopping surprises and violence. The role of the PKI forces in doing more than bringing security, that is, in helping create long-term political stability as a means of preventing further violence once the intervention force has departed, is perhaps the path most unexplored, because it is obscure and difficult to achieve by traditional military intelligence assets. The absence of war does not mean a viable peace. Achieving stasis may remain the most acceptable goal for intervention forces. The pursuit of larger objectives, for instance a more durable peace, can well prove too costly or destabilizing.

Note

1   The author thanks Dr. Sean Maloney, L.-Col. John Blaxland, Dr. Walter Dorn, and all the anonymous officers who contributed information for this chapter. Many comments here are based on interviews with participants, but material was also derived from Zymaris (1998).

Bibliography

Blaxland, J. (2000) "On Operations in East Timor: The Experiences of the Intelligence Officer, 3rd Brigade," *Australian Army Journal*: 1–13.

—— (2002) *Information-era Manoeuvre: The Australian-led Mission to East Timor*, Land Warfare Studies Centre Working Paper No. 118, Canberra: Australian Defence Force.

Cirafici, J.L. (1999) "SFOR in Bosnia in 1997: A Watershed Year," *Parameters*, Spring: 80–91.

Corrigan, C. (2002) "Bosnia Revisited: A Recent National Commander's Perspective," *Canadian Military Journal*, Autumn: 29–36.

Department of National Defence (Canada) (1997)"Backgrounder: United Nations Support Mission in Haiti," BG-97.007, January 30.

—— (2002) "Operation CONSTABLE: July 29, 1997–November 30, 1997," briefing note, ADM (Public Affairs), December 23.

Dorn, W., and Elneus, L. (1998) "Notes on UN Intelligence Sources in Haiti," June 17, n.p.. Copy provided by Walter Dorn to M.A. Hennessey.

Economist (1997) "Peacekeepers Out," October 30.

Economist (1999) "Friend or Foe in East Timor," September 23.

Economist (2001), "The UN in East Timor: Any Lessons For Others?" *Economist*, October 11.

Gagnon, J.J.R., B-Gen. (ret'd.) (n.d.) Comments.

Grunau, S. (2003) "The Limits of Human Security: Canada in East Timor," *Journal of Military and Strategic Studies*, Spring/Summer.

Guzman, Janina de (n.d.) "Department of State's Comments on Peacekeeping Lessons for Kosovo: PAST PEACEKEEPING EXPERIENCE SHAPING KOSOVO PLANS." Copy in author's possession.

Hennessy, M.A. (2001) "Operation 'Assurance': Planning a Multi-national Force for Rwanda/Zaire," *Canadian Military Journal*, Spring: 11–20.

Massey, S. (2000) "Operation Assurance: The Greatest Intervention that Never Happened," *Journal of Humanitarian Assistance*. Available at: http://www.jha.ac/ articles/a036.htm (accessed June 3, 2000).

McPherson, D.E., Maj. (1996) "Intelligence and Peacekeeping in Haiti," *Military Intelligence Professional Bulletin*, April–June.

UN Department of Public Information (1996) "Haiti-UNMIH," August 31.

—— (1997) "Haiti-UNSMIH," c.July.

Zymaris, C. (1998) "Shoulders of Giants—A Paper on the Inevitability of Open Source Dominance," p. 6. Available at: www.cyber.com.au/users/conz/ shoulders.html.

4

SIGINT AND PEACEKEEPING
The untapped intelligence resource

Matthew M. Aid

The need for reliable intelligence in peacekeeping

I would like to begin by making a simple, but I think critically important, observation about the importance of intelligence in peacekeeping operations (PKOs), which in large part explains the relative importance of signals intelligence (SIGINT) in contemporary peacekeeping. There is an age-old adage among intelligence professionals, which is, "Don't give me guesses—I want facts." Over the years I have met a number of senior US military officers who have told me that they have never been angrier with their intelligence officers than when the first words out of their mouths at the morning intelligence briefing are, "We estimate that..." One senior American field commander, who served with distinction in Bosnia and Kosovo during the 1990s, put it most colorfully when he said that "If I wanted estimates, I would have brought along my Ouija board instead of my intelligence staff" (confidential interview)

At its most basic and fundamental level, international PKOs are essentially low-intensity military exercises with a large and extremely important diplomatic component thrown in for good measure. From the peacekeeper's perspective, the *only* way these extremely delicate and inherently complicated operations can be carried through to a successful conclusion is with reliable, timely, fact-based intelligence information. Military commanders, regardless of which country they come from or the type of military operation being conducted, want hard facts from their intelligence staffs, not best guesses. It is true, as intelligence historian David Kahn has recently written, that "Intelligence cannot discover everything or foresee all. Such expectations exceed human capacity" (Kahn, 2004: A27). But it is also a sad fact that if intelligence officers cannot produce timely and accurate current intelligence during PKOs, then there is a natural tendency on the part of military commanders around the world to pay little attention to what their G-2 has to say. And history shows that the failure to provide peacekeeping commanders with this type of intelligence information, I am sad to say, usually has resulted in botched operations and/or the needless loss of life among the peacekeepers themselves.

Anyone who has spent any appreciable amount of time in the foreign intelligence business knows full well that the partisans of HUMINT (human intelligence), SIGINT, IMINT (imagery intelligence) and OSINT (open-source intelligence) argue *ad infinitum* about the relative value, cost-effectiveness, and importance of the intelligence produced by their own personal favorite intelligence discipline. Bluntly put, this seemingly never-ending argument is specious, a waste of time, and misses the point. The fundamental truth is that each discipline is vitally important in PKOs, each in its own particular or peculiar way. When one talks to the peacekeepers themselves, most of whom are not intelligence professionals, their only thought on the subject is that they will take the best intelligence information available from wherever they can get it, regardless of the source. The only consistent requirements that they have are that the intelligence information be reliable and timely, and that it be presented in a form that they can use.

No man is an island

With this in mind, SIGINT should *not* be viewed as a stand-alone source. Unlike the many partisans of the utility of air power in the US military, who believe with religious fervor that the massive and unrelenting application of strategic bombardment can win wars all by itself, one must admit that the same is not true of SIGINT. The seventeenth-century English poet John Donne wrote that "No man is an island, Entire of itself. Each is a piece of the Continent, A part of the main" (Donne, 1624). The same is true for all of the intelligence disciplines when viewed individually, including SIGINT. SIGINT cannot win the intelligence war all by itself. It is only truly valuable when its product is merged with the materials being produced by other intelligence sources, such as IMINT, HUMINT, and even OSINT. This is where SIGINT comes into play.

SIGINT: the under-appreciated resource

Signals Intelligence, or SIGINT, refers more specifically to Communications Intelligence (COMINT), which is concerned with the interception and processing of adversarial radio communications traffic in all its varied and wondrous forms. What truly separates SIGINT from the other major intelligence disciplines is not that it is necessarily better or has a higher utility value than other intelligence sources. Rather, what puts SIGINT in a special niche all by itself is that, historically, it has been the most difficult intelligence information for peacekeeping commanders to get their hands on, and even more difficult to use because of the extreme secrecy attached to SIGINT product by the nations who produce it. One North Atlantic Treaty Organization (NATO) field commander I spoke to who served in Bosnia during the late 1990s recalled being made to feel as if he had to "pledge his first male-born child" as security in order to gain access to even the lowest-level SIGINT (confidential interview).

Why is SIGINT treated as if it were a religious relic by those who collect it? In and of itself, the SIGINT collection process is not particularly sensitive, since virtually every current nation state of any import, and many non-governmental organizations (NGOs) besides, engage in it. SIGINT's intrinsic value is that, in the proper environment, and especially in the context of military operations, it will almost always be one of the most productive sources of hard intelligence. According to a CIA historian, "SIGINT is not only a high-gain but also a low-risk business. Electronic signals can be grabbed off where no agent can go, and the target doesn't even know" (Fischer, 1998: 143). Moreover, according to a declassified CIA report, intelligence consumers tend to prefer SIGINT because "... the intelligence return on effort invested is considerably greater than is the case with human assets operating in a hostile environment" (CIA, 1969: 2). Moreover, SIGINT: "... contributes reliable administrative and organizational information which serves as the basic framework for all other analyses, and furnishes a check on the reliability of information from other sources" (CIA, 1949: 3). For example, SIGINT serves as a reliable verification tool for OSINT information, which can be just as unreliable as HUMINT reporting, as demonstrated by the recent embarrassing intelligence disaster over Weapons of Mass Destruction (WMD) in Iraq. A leaked Australian intelligence assessment conducted during the late 1970s found that "By far the most valuable secret intelligence source was SIGINT, without which it would have been very difficult to evaluate effectively the often wild and alarmist reporting in some sections of the press" (Toohey and Wilkinson, 1987: 134).

This author would argue that a SIGINT collection and processing organization should be, in the best of all possible worlds, an essential component of any intelligence collection package dedicated to PKOs, both now and in the future. Frankly speaking, it is too important an intelligence source not to have. A former CIA officer with significant experience in PKOs, Helene L. Boatner, argues that "Tactical signals intelligence (SIGINT) is essential to PKOs, and can also make a significant contribution to humanitarian operations, sanctions enforcement, arms control regimes, and many other activities in which international organizations engage" (Boatner, 2000: 9).

When should SIGINT be employed in PKOs

The next question becomes which types of PKOs are best suited for SIGINT. The answer is that there is a clear and direct correlation between the relative value of SIGINT and the level of military activity in the geographic region where the PKO is taking place. The general rule of thumb should be that the higher the level of violence endemic to the region, the more you need SIGINT, because of its well-recognized ability to quickly and accurately chart military activities and movements. If peace-keepers are stepping into a war zone with the intent of separating warring parties, as in the recent PKOs in West Africa, or if one of the PKO's principal missions is to monitor the movements and activities of opposing armed forces in the region in order to keep them apart, such as in Bosnia and Kosovo, then success relies upon the peacekeeping commander having access to a robust SIGINT collection capability (Bash, 1995)

An excellent example how SIGINT has produced important intelligence in the context of previous PKOs took place in Bosnia. In February 1996, a US Army listening post in Bosnia intercepted a transmission which showed that Bosnian Serb forces were prepared to resist American efforts to inspect a Serb weapons storage site near Han Pijesak, the location of the headquarters of the Bosnian Serb General Staff. In March 1996, a US Army listening post in Bosnia intercepted a Bosnian Serb military message that indicated that the Serbs were hiding artillery pieces in barns in north-eastern Bosnia from US infantry patrols searching for the weapons (Atkinson, 1996a: A14, 1996b: A1). Another example comes from 1997–98, when the British SIGINT organization, the Government Communications Headquarters (GCHQ), deployed small teams of radio intercept specialists belonging to the British Army's 14 Signal Regiment to Sierra Leone to provide West African peacekeepers with intelligence support on politico-military developments in the war-ravaged country (ISC, 1999: 3). Timor is also an excellent example of how SIGINT can be used effectively in a peacekeeping environment. SIGINT intercepts collected by the Australian SIGINT service, the Defence Signals Directorate (DSD), in the fall of 1999 revealed that the Indonesian military was furiously trying to cover up atrocities committed by its troops in East Timor before the arrival on the island of United Nations (UN) peacekeeping troops and human rights investigators, including silencing militia leaders who could point the finger at the Indonesian military as having been behind some of the massacres previously committed on the island (Daley, 1999: 1).

Unfortunately, three years earlier, in 1994, no SIGINT collection resources were available to the UN Assistance Mission for Rwanda (UNAMIR) before the Rwandan government, then dominated by members of the Hutu tribe, embarked on a systematic campaign of genocide directed against the country's Tutsi tribe.

SIGINT has also proven itself to be an invaluable tool in monitoring whether opposing sides in a conflict pose a direct security threat to the peacekeepers on the ground. For instance, during the UN's PKOs in the Congo (MONUC) in the early 1960s, COMINT (Communications and

Intelligence) provided UN peacekeepers with advance warning that Katangese Premier Moïse Tshombé and his Interior Minister were using radio broadcasts to incite their supporters to attack UN peacekeepers in the region (Dorn and Bell, 1995). During the evacuation of British and American diplomats and their dependents from war-ravaged Beirut, Lebanon on the night June 18–19, 1976, the National Security Agency (NSA) and GCHQ closely monitored Lebanese and Syrian radio traffic for any indications that the diplomats were facing a threat to their safety. SIGINT intercepts noted artillery and mortar exchanges between Lebanese Christian, Palestinian, and Syrian forces in Beirut and outlying areas; a shift of Syrian MiG-21 fighter aircraft from Palmyra Air Base in central Syria to Al Qusayr Air Base in northeastern Syria, where they could be used in Lebanon; coupled with expanded Soviet naval surveillance of US Sixth Fleet forces in the eastern Mediterranean. Needless to say, the evacuation went smoothly and there were no casualties among the evacuees (CIA, 1976).

By the same token, there have been in recent years PKOs in parts of the world that arguably were sufficiently stable, both in political and military terms, and where the allocation of expensive SIGINT resources may not have been appropriate, much less necessary. I am thinking in particular of the UN peacekeeping and observation missions in the Sinai, Cyprus, Cambodia, and Namibia.

Geographical considerations

SIGINT's value and import in PKOs is also largely determined by the level of technological sophistication of the region where the operation in question takes place. In previous PKOs in more developed parts of the world, such as Bosnia and Kosovo in Europe, SIGINT has been amply demonstrated to have considerable ability to generate high-quality intelligence information for peacekeepers. SIGINT has also demonstrated in the past high utility in the Middle East, where there is a high density of communications and electronic emitters. This was aptly demonstrated during the 1976–82 Sinai Field Mission and during PKOs in Lebanon in the 1980s. But the relative value of SIGINT tends to decline commensurate with the drop in technological sophistication of the geographic area in which it is used.

Take, for example, what happened in Somalia during the early 1990s. By all accounts, SIGINT did not play an important role during Operations Restore Hope and Continue Hope, the US military intervention in the war-torn African nation of Somalia between December 1992 and March 1994, undertaken in conjunction with the UN. HUMINT in fact turned out to be a far more useful intelligence source here. But an officer who served in Somalia recalled that SIGINT "was probably the most reliable source of intelligence" (Casper, 2001: 136). The reasons why SIGINT did not perform well in Somalia are numerous. The principal reason was that the militias of the Somali warlords did not use radios to any appreciable degree, and the Somali economic infrastructure had deteriorated to such a degree that the nation's telephone exchanges had long since ceased to work. When the militia forces of Somali warlord Mohammed Farah Aideed did use walkie-talkie radios, they were of such low power that it was difficult for the NSA and the CIA to intercept these transmissions, much less locate them. Some COMINT was obtained, such as monitoring the radios used by Aideed's militiamen who were directing mortar and artillery fire at UN positions in the city of Mogadishu in the fall of 1993 (bin Laden, 2001: 4458–4459). These intercepts were used by US forces to arrest a number of Somalis who intelligence analysts were able to identify as Aideed's radio operators based on their recorded "voice prints" (INSCOM, 1993: 35). But when Aideed learned that the US was monitoring his communications, according to a postmortem document "Aideed effectively thwarted US SIGINT collection by merely turning off his radios," and relied on messengers instead (Cooling, 2001: 92)

To come on bent knee

Now comes the really hard question: how does a peacekeeping commander get SIGINT collection resources allocated for his operation. The problem always comes when the commander or his political masters have to come "hat in hand" to the various nations contributing intelligence resources for a PKO. At present, the process of selecting intelligence resources for specific peacekeeping missions is done in reverse of how it should be done. Senior military and intelligence planners in Washington and other world capitals determine what national collection resources to contribute to specific peacekeeping missions based upon case-by-case political considerations and detailed pre-formatted plans that are "cookie-cutter templates" rather than country-specific. The author would respectfully suggest that we turn this process around on its head and let the peacekeeping force commanders determine what intelligence collection assets they need based upon their first-hand assessment of what is required for them to perform their mission.

One frustrating problem repeatedly faced in previous PKOs is that many of the nations contributing troops to the operations have been highly reluctant, if not outright hostile, to directly placing their SIGINT collection resources under the direct command of the peacekeeping commander, preferring instead to keep these resources under their national control. This led to the ludicrous situation in Bosnia during the early to mid-1990s, where almost twenty countries operated their own independent SIGINT collection operations. Some of these national SIGINT collection operations were larger than others, but with each largely duplicating the efforts of the others in order to meet the specific intelligence needs of their own national force commanders in Bosnia (Wiebes, 2003).

The truth is that the current system of nations giving force commanders only that SIGINT information which their governments authorize is a waste of time and effort, and more importantly it does not work. For SIGINT to be truly effective in the context of future PKOs, the force commander must have operational control of all intelligence collection and analytic assets supporting the operation, including SIGINT. But up until now, only the four Scandinavian nations and the Benelux nations have demonstrated any willingness to contribute first-line SIGINT collection and processing resources to international peacekeeping efforts.

Organizing for the mission

The author is aware that what follows is not a novel suggestion, but I know a number of US field commanders with peacekeeping experience who would be overjoyed if we got away from the previous practice of being wedded to a strict paper formula (in the US military this is called a Troop Organization and Equipment, or TO, document) in determining what intelligence collection resources to commit to a PKO. Too often this has led to situations where we have sent SIGINT collection equipment designed for use against Soviet forces on a European battlefield to PKOs whose operational environment bears no resemblance to what the equipment was designed for. In one particularly painful example, in Haiti and Somalia the US Army sent intelligence units to these countries, including their full wartime load of electronic intelligence (ELINT) intercept and processing equipment, despite the fact that there were no working radars in either of these countries. One US Army ELINT intercept team in Haiti kept itself busy by pretending that the landing radar at Port-au-Prince International Airport was an enemy radar before they were finally sent home (confidential interview).

In other words, if peacekeepers are sent to a country with little in the way of radio equipment but lots of cellular telephones, then don't send radio intercept equipment. Send collection equipment that is designed exclusively for cell phone exploitation. Our Scandinavian brethren have done a far better job along these lines, I am afraid to say, than their larger and better-funded American counterparts. US Army intelligence units about to take part in the invasion of Iraq in March 2003 did not receive their allotment of theater-appropriate SIGINT collection equipment until literally days before they crossed the border, which of course meant that they had no time to learn how to use it before the invasion began (3ID AAR, 2003: 16)

Those countries that routinely commit forces to international PKOs perhaps should give some serious consideration to committing to each

PKO a multinational battalion-sized intelligence collection and processing unit structured along the lines of the old US Army's Communications, Electronic Warfare and Intelligence (CEWI) battalions, but minus the extravagant ELINT intercept and communications jamming equipment that the US units included, which does not appear necessary for a peace-keeping mission. The unit should be mobile, flexibly structured so that they are capable of being broken down into task-oriented sub-units, and comprise dedicated SIGINT (including cellular intercept), IMINT (UAVs, or unmanned aerial vehicles), MASINT, or measurement and signature intelligence (ground-based radars), and HUMINT collection and processing elements. The SIGINT equipment should be mobile, rugged and durable, and capable of monitoring a wide range of signals found in the operational environment. The motivating concept behind this unit should be "Simple is best."

Some nations with considerable experience in PKOs have organized highly mobile, tactical SIGINT collection units that specialize in intelligence collection support in a peacekeeping environment. For example, since the early 1990s the British Army's 14 Signal Regiment, based since December 1995 at RAF Brawdy in Wales, has spent an inordinate amount of time providing British forces with tactical SIGINT support during PKOs. For instance, sizeable elements of the 14 Signal Regiment, together with linguists and analysts belonging to the British Army's 9th Signals Regiment in Cyprus and the RAF 399th Signals Unit from RAF Digby in England, were stationed in Bosnia throughout the mid-1990s. Together, these units maintained a fifty-man SIGINT collection detachment at Banja Luka providing COMINT and ELINT data to British Army peacekeeping commanders in Bosnia. The main British listening post was located at Gornji Vakuf, a town situated west of Sarajevo, which was also the head-quarters of the British Army military contingent in Bosnia (McPeek, 1996: 23; British Army Intelligence Corps, 1996: 43, 1997: 83, 85; Urban, 1996: 216).

During the PKOs in Bosnia and Kosovo in the mid- to late 1990s, the Scandinavian SIGINT organizations from Denmark, Norway, and Sweden openly cooperated and pooled their SIGINT collection and processing resources. In 1995, the Norwegian Intelligence Service (Forsvarets Etterretningsteneste, or FO/E) sent a small mobile SIGINT unit to Bosnia to support Norwegian peacekeeping forces there. The SIGINT unit was deployed to the town of Doboj, and a National Intelligence Cell (NIC) was set up at the same time in the nearby town of Modrica to service the intelligence needs of the Norwegian field commander in Bosnia. In 1997, the Norwegians, Swedes, and Danes merged their respective SIGINT collection and processing units into a single integrated SIGINT collection and analytic organization based at Doboj. The Norwegian Intelligence Service was also active in Kosovo. In 1999, the FO/E deployed a Norwegian NIC to a location just outside the Macedonian capital of Skopje, and a mobile SIGINT unit (Task Force MIKE) was deployed to a mountain-top position near the town of Ravno in order to provide tactical SIGINT support to Norwegian aircraft participating in the Kosovo bombing campaign. After Kosovo was occupied, the FO/E established a new SIGINT site, designated Task Force KILO, inside Kosovo at Camp Sotor, northeast of Pristina, and deployed two mobile SIGINT units to Macedonia to provide KFOR and NORDBAT with tactical SIGINT. In January 2000, a joint Norwegian–Swedish–Danish intelligence cell, called the Scandinavian National Intelligence Cell (SCANIC), was activated outside Pristina, which in March 2001 was joined by Finland. In November 2002, TF KILO pulled out of Kosovo with its mission accomplished (Pedersen, 2002; Shukman, 2000: 79).

In the mid-1990s, the Finnish national SIGINT organization, Viestikoelaitos (VKL or VKoeL), which translates either as "Communications Research Institute," "Signals Test Facility," or "Intelligence Research Institute," expanded its activities to include tactical SIGINT collection and electronic warfare (EW) in support of Finnish troops deployed in the Balkans on peacekeeping duties (confidential interview). Initially, the Finnish Battalion (Suomen Pataljoona) operating in Kosovo in the late 1990s depended on British intelligence assets for their tactical SIGINT and EW support, which was provided by 640 Troop (EW) from the British Army's 14 Signal Regiment (Välimäki, 2002). As of 2002, there was a small Finnish SIGINT intercept station supporting the Finnish Battalion in Kosovo at Camp Ville near the village of Lopljan.

The Dutch military intelligence service has also configured tactical SIGINT collection units to support Dutch international PKOs. Since January 1, 1998, Dutch tactical SIGINT has been the responsibility of a new joint services COMINT organization called the Operational Signals Intelligence Center (Operationeel Verbindings-inlichtingen Centrum, or OIVC) based at Eibergen in northeastern Holland. From 2000 to 2003, Dutch military SIGINT personnel were deployed to the nation of Djibouti to provide SIGINT support to the 4300 Canadian and Dutch troops performing peacekeeping duties in Eritrea as part of the UN Mission in Ethiopia and Eritrea (UNMEE) peacekeeping force.

The Belgian Army also formed in the 1990s its own small tactical SIGINT collection force for use in PKOs. The Belgian Army maintains an intelligence unit called 17 Escadron de Reconnaissance (17 Verkenning-seskadron), or 17 Recce, at the Kwartier Meerdaalbos in Heverlee near the Belgian city of Louvain. Heverlee is also the headquarters of the Belgian Army's premier international rapid deployment force, the Airmobile Brigade (formerly the Para-Commando Brigade). The Belgians sometimes refer to 17 Recce as the Escadron or Eskadron "Intelligence & Information Warfare." In addition to a HUMINT detachment, 17 Recce also consists of two Information Warfare platoons (*pelotons* "Information Warfare"), which collect and process tactical SIGINT.

The new SIGINT collection environment

The technological revolution is also changing the face of communications on the world's battlefields. The NSA has found in the last decade that some foreign military forces, particularly in Europe, have begun using new advanced telecommunications technologies, such as spread spectrum links, laser point-to-point communications, fast frequency-hopping technology, tactical satellite communications, increased usage of millimeter-wave communications systems, data compression techniques, burst transmitters, imbedded decoy signals, increased signal directionality, better signals encryption at all levels, and greater use of low-probability-of-intercept communications systems, such as walkie-talkies and even cellular telephones. All of these relatively new technologies are making NSA's SIGINT collection mission in support of US military operations overseas more difficult than it was ten years ago (US Army, 1993: 1–7; DoD, 1995: 2; Hewish and Janssen, 1997: 28).

Linguistic issues

Regardless of where SIGINT is used around the world, the only way it can be effective is if the peacekeeping SIGINT unit brings with it a supply of linguists who are capable of speaking the local languages. This is perhaps the single largest hurdle facing the effective use of SIGINT in the less-developed countries of the world. Though communications security (COMSEC) procedures by warring parties in West Africa were poor, Western intelligence personnel participating in PKOs in Liberia and Sierra Leone did not speak the dialects local to these countries, making effective SIGINT collection near impossible. For example, it proved next to impossible to find linguists capable of translating the intercepted walkie-talkie transmissions of rebels in Liberia, who spoke the local Mende or Kwa dialects rather than English. The same problem occurred during PKOs in Sierra Leone, where, though intercepting the traffic of the warring parties proved to be a relatively simple matter, no one trustworthy could be found who could translate the tapes of intercepted radio traffic in the local Mende, Temne, or Krio dialects. Further, local interpreters proved to be politically too biased to be objective translators (confidential interview). During the UN PKOs in Somalia during the early 1990s, native speakers of the numerous Somali dialects were in such short supply that it severely hampered effective SIGINT operations. When translators with a fluency in the Somali dialects became available, they revealed one of the inherent weaknesses of SIGINT, namely—do you believe what the targets you are monitoring are saying? A US Army officer who served in Somalia wrote that "SIGINT was probably the most reliable source of intelligence, though what you heard may not have represented the truth. The Somali militiamen always seemed to outdo one another with their exaggerations. It didn't matter if they were submitting a report to a superior or having a casual conversation with a crony—it was as if embellishment was embedded in the culture" (Casper, 2001: 136). In Kosovo during the late 1990s, the Finnish SIGINT service, the VKL, experienced difficulty finding linguists with sufficient clearance who understood Albanian. They managed to find a Finnish woman married to an Albanian, but she proved to be so unreliable because of her intense pro-Albanian sympathies that she was sent back to Finland after only a couple of months (confidential interview).

Getting intelligence to the consumer

It is an oft-spoken truism in the intelligence profession that all the best intelligence in the world is worthless if it does not get to intelligence consumers in a timely fashion and in a form that they can understand and use. As one author has stated: "Information is power. But it is useless when not shared" (Karoly, 2001). Historically, this has proven to be the biggest obstacle to using SIGINT effectively in the peacekeeping environment, with the world's largest intelligence agencies, invariably those who have collected the SIGINT, proving resistant to complete, across-the-board sharing of their sensitive product in previous PKOs. In Bosnia and Kosovo, for example, the US intelligence community deliberately excluded American commanders on the ground in Bosnia from high-level SIGINT that was freely available to American commanders at US European Command (EUCOM) headquarters in Stuttgart, Germany. These commanders had to subsist on a diet of low-level COMINT and ELINT that hardly qualified as the best material available to the US intelligence community. Attempts to "sanitize" the data so as to protect "sources and methods" have only delayed the delivery of this time-sensitive product and reduced it to a format that left commanders wondering where it came from or how reliable it was (confidential interview). This situation led a senior US Army intelligence officer who served in Bosnia during the mid-1990s to state that the NATO-releasable SIGINT reporting he received "… consistently was a day late and a dollar short." He noted that the sanitized SIGINT he received usually consisted only of marginally useful information that was as much as three-to-four days old. Moreover, SIGINT on Bosnia was available in abundant quantities to US intelligence officers working within the US military command structure in Europe, but severe restrictions on the dissemination of SIGINT to US intelligence officers working within the NATO command structure in Bosnia, as well as even further restrictions on how this intelligence could be passed on to non-American intelligence officers, even on a sanitized basis, only served to reduce dramatically the value and import of information derived from this source (Gramer, 1996: 13).

Sharing the wealth with your friends

There have been too many examples in recent years of SIGINT organizations, including but not limited to the NSA, failing to adequately share information with friends and allies around the world. In August 1998, UN intelligence officers in Iraq complained that the raw SIGINT data they were sending to the US about Iraqi efforts to hide their weapons of mass destruction was not being processed and sent back to Iraq (Wilkinson, 1999). During the 1999 war in Kosovo, the NSA experienced serious problems sharing intelligence information with its NATO allies, in large part because many of these partners were not parties to any of the bilateral and multinational SIGINT sharing agreements that the US had helped broker in the late 1940s. Bill Nolte, then head of the NSA's Legislative Affairs office, stated that "compartmentalization of intelligence doesn't really work anymore in modern coalition operations and complained about the current problems of getting the NSA to modernize both its practices and mentality" (IN, 2000: 3).

The US does not hold a monopoly on this issue. The intelligence establishments of a number of other countries have been equally chary about fully and completely sharing their SIGINT and other sensitive-source intelligence with other countries engaged in peacekeeping duties. For example, in Western Europe, where there is extensive cross-border cooperation among clandestine intelligence agencies and security services in the field of counter-terrorism, evidence indicates that multinational SIGINT joint ventures are practically non-existent. A study by a European scholar found that, in Europe, "WEU [Western European Union] intelligence cooperation has focused primarily on imagery intelligence (IMINT), however, with a notable lack of emphasis on signals intelligence (SIGINT), human intelligence (HUMINT), and tactical intelligence cooperation" (Villadsen, 2000). This finding was confirmed by a recent European Union report, which stated:

> It has to be said that at the present time there is no real technical [intelligence] cooperation as each country takes the view that the electromagnetic situation in a given zone is a matter for its sovereignty. This means that any European potential will be confined to national equipment and approaches existing side by side.
>
> (WEU, 2002)

This is not to say that collaborative arrangements are not within the realm of possibility when it comes to SIGINT during international PKOs. In

1995, following the end of the war in Bosnia, the NSA brokered a tripartite airborne tactical SIGINT exchange program between the US, German, and French Air Forces. As part of the agreement, the Germans flew daily SIGINT collection missions over the Adriatic in support of PKOs in Bosnia, while the French Air Force was tasked with collecting SIGINT with its airborne reconnaissance platforms over the Mediterranean Sea. The American, German, and French air forces agreed to share all intelligence collected through the headquarters of NSA/CSS Europe in Stuttgart, Germany (Sitze, 2001). This collaborative agreement probably dates back well before 1995. At the height of Operation Deny Flight in October 1993, a source saw an airborne reconnaissance mission schedule which showed a French C-160G *Gabriel* SIGINT aircraft on duty station over the Adriatic from 0530 to 1130 GMT; a British *Nimrod* R-Mk.1 SIGINT plane on duty from 0830 to 1345 GMT; a US Navy EP-3E *Aries* reconnaissance aircraft on duty from 1345 and 1830 GMT; the French *Sarigue* DC-8 reconnaissance plane from 1730 to 2130 GMT; and a US Air Force RC-135 *Rivet Joint* SIGINT aircraft on station over the Adriatic from 1830 to 2230 GMT. Clearly, the significance of the 1995 collaborative agreement was that it brought the Germans into the fold in order to supplement the ongoing Bosnian reconnaissance operations (Streetly, 2000: 387). German military SIGINT units deployed in Bosnia with the French-led Multinational Division (MND) provided their intercepts to the French divisional commander and his intelligence staff for analysis and reporting purposes (Villadsen, 2000).

Multinational SIGINT collaboration improved and intensified during the war in Kosovo in 1999–2000. The end of the war there did not end the important role played by SIGINT however. As of the summer of 2001, there were eight multinational SIGINT intercept sites deployed along the Kosovo–Macedonian border monitoring Yugoslav communications traffic, with another five sites due to be activated the following year (NATO, 2001). These SIGINT sites were truly coalition operations. According to a British publication: "The working environment in Kosovo is uniquely multi-national, working in a Finnish cell, alongside a Swede, reporting to a German, an American and a British sailor via a Frenchman, a Norwegian and another American. We sometimes even talked to G2 too. With detachments deployed 50 meters from, or 50 meters into Macedonia (depending on which map series you were using) the [237 Signals] squadron was at the cutting edge of EW for KFOR, sometimes providing half the available intelligence" (British Army Intelligence Corps, 2002: 36).

The impact of 9/11

Sadly, the situation has worsened since the terrorist attacks in New York City on September 11, 2001. Today, the reigning school of thought within the US intelligence community is to become less reliant on liaison with foreign intelligence services, which will be a hindrance to further SIGINT sharing and cooperation between the US and other nations (confidential interview). Driving this shift in policy is the widely held perception in Washington that America's allies are not doing enough in the SIGINT field to make continued American hand-holding and subsidization a worthwhile proposition. This school of thought was succinctly summarized in a secret 1999 memo from the NSA's then-Deputy Director for Operations, Richard L. Taylor, to the Director of the NSA:

> Issues for our foreign relationships are, in some ways, very much analogous to the military relationships we see in our coalition warfare. The U.S. maintains the lead, both in technology and operational readiness; we bring our partners along. This is also the rubric for our SIGINT relationships with our Second and Third Party partners. While they may exhibit excellence in particular areas, they depend on us for leadership in operational method-ology and advanced technologies. It was apparent in Desert Storm that it is becoming more difficult for the military to operate in coalition because we are moving more rapidly than [our] partners in technology and doctrinal change. Partners are having a difficult time keeping up. This trend is accelerating. Care must be taken to deal with impacts of acceleration away from key partners.... *We must have a sound business strategy, based both on mission require-ments and geopolitical realities, which directs the conditions and extent of sharing, joint operations, and continued access.*
>
> (NSA, 1999: 4–5, emphasis added)

The unfortunate consequence of this widely held belief is that US intelli-gence officers now generally hold that the potential intelligence contributions of even its closest NATO allies in PKOs are minimal. For instance, an unclassified US Army "Lessons Learned" study based on the experiences of US forces in Bosnia and Kosovo during the 1990s found that "When you look at what NATO countries can contribute, you realize that there is only a limited Imagery, Human, and Signals Intelligence capa-bility." The report went on to note that most of the SIGINT resources America's NATO allies could contribute were ground-based and had extremely limited ranges of between 50 and 80 kilometers from the inter-cept site (CALL, 1999).

Learning the lessons of history

We must free ourselves from the practice whereby conscientious military officers and NCOs come back from PKOs and write "Lessons Learned" reports, identifying problems and suggesting solutions, but do nothing about these reports other than file them away. Some officers I know have stopped writing these documents because nobody higher up in the chain of command reads them or does anything about them.

Bibliography

Atkinson, R. (1994) Rick Atkinson, *Washington Post,* January 30: A27.

——(1996a) "GIs Signal Bosnians: Yes, We're Listening," *Washington Post,* March 18: A14.

—— (1996b) "Warriors Without a War," *Washington Post,* April 14: A1.

Baker, C. (1993) "Manhunt for Aideed," *Armed Forces Journal International,* December: 18.

Bash, L. (1995) "Air Power and Peacekeeping," *Air Power Journal,* Spring. Available at: http://www.airpower.maxwell.af.mil/airchronicles/apj/bash.html.

Belgium (2002) Unit details. Available at: http://www.mil.be/armycomp/org/index.asp?LAN=E&PLACE=22; (accessed 2002). The Belgian military has since closed this page.

Bin Laden (2001) Trial transcript, April 23, in 98 Cr. 1028, *United States of America v. Usama bin Laden et al.,* US District Court for the Southern District of New York, New York City.

Boatner, H. (2000) "Sharing and Using Intelligence in International Organizations: Some Guidelines," *National Security and the Future,* 1 (2), Summer.

Bowman, T., and Shane, S. (1995) "Battling High-Tech Warriors," *Baltimore Sun,* December 15: 22A.

British Army Intelligence Corps (1996) The Rose and the Laurel: Journal of the Intelligence Corps, 1996 edition.

—— (1997) *The Rose and the Laurel: Journal of the Intelligence Corps,* 1997 edition.

—— (2002) *The Rose and the Laurel: Journal of the Intelligence Corps,* 2002 edition.CALL (1999) *CALL Bulletin,* Center for Army Lessons Learned, November–December.

Casper, L (2001) *Falcon Brigade: Combat and Command in Somalia and Haiti,* Boulder, CO: Lynne Rienner Publishers.

CIA (1949) Memorandum, Hillenkoetter to Executive Secretary, NSC, *Atomic Energy Program of the USSR,* April 20, enclosure to Memorandum, Allen to Secretary of the Army et al., *Atomic Energy Program of the USSR,* April 28, RG-319, 1949–1950 TS Hot File 091.412, Box 165, File: 091 Soviet Union, NA, CP.

—— (1969) Memorandum, CIA Special Assistant for Vietnamese Affairs to Kissinger, *Intensified Collection Program Targeted Against the Logistics Network Used by North Vietnam to Support Communist Activity in South Vietnam,* July 18, RG-263, CIA Reference Collection, Document No. CIA-RDP80T01719R000300080002–2, National Archives, College Park.

—— (1976) Central Intelligence Agency, SC No. 07362/76, *Intelligence Memorandum: Lebanon Evacuation Situation Report No. 2,* June 18, RG-263, CIA Reference Collection, Document No. CIA-RDP83M00171R001800080031–7, NA, CP.

Cooling, N. (2001) "Operation RESTORE HOPE in Somalia: A Tactical Action Turned Strategic Defeat," *Marine Corps Gazette*, September: 92.

Daley, P. (1999) "Indons 'Purge' Militia," *The Age*, October 11: 1.

DoD (1995) *FY96 Electronic Warfare Plan*, US Department of Defense, April, FOIA.

Donne, J. (1624)"Meditation XVII" from *Devotions Upon Emergent Occasions*. Available at: http://www.bedfordstmartins.com/introduction_literature/essays/donne.htm.

Dorn, W., and Bell, D. (1995) "Intelligence and Peacekeeping: The UN Operation in the Congo 1960–64," *International Peacekeeping*, 2 (1), Spring. Available at: http://www.mc.ca/academic/gradrech/politics-9e.html.

Fischer, B. (1998) "One of the Biggest Ears in the World: East German SIGINT Operations," *International Journal of Intelligence and Counterintelligence*, Summer: 143.

Gramer, G. (1996) "Operation Joint Endeavor: Combined-Joint Intelligence in Peace Enforcement Operations," *Military Intelligence Professional Bulletin*, October–December.

Hewish, M., and Janssen, Lok J. (1997) "The Intelligent War: Signals Intelligence Demands Adaptable Systems," *Jane's International Defence Review*, December: 28.

IN (2000) "How Cooperation in Balkans Works," *Intelligence Newsletter* (385), June 29.

INSCOM (1993) *Annual Historical Report, U.S. Army Intelligence and Security Command, Fiscal Year 1993*, U.S. Army Intelligence and Security Command, FOIA.

ISC (1999) *Sierra Leone*, CM 4309, Intelligence and Security Committee, April. Available at: http://www.archive.official-documents.co.uk/document/cm43/4309/slrpt.pdf

Kahn, D. (2004) "How Good Intelligence Falls on Deaf Ears," *New York Times*, March 27.

Karoly, B. (2001) *21st Century Comint Possibilities in the Mirror of 3rd Generation Mobile Systems*: Available at: http://www.zmka.hu/tanszekek/ehc/konferencia/april2001/balogh.html

Loeb, V. (2000) "After-Action Report," *Washington Post Magazine*, February 27: 9.

McPeek, R. (1996) "Electronic Warfare British Style," *Military Intelligence*, January–March.

NATO (2001) *Nato Fact Sheet: Facts and Figures – the Former Yugoslav Republic of Macedonia*, August 10. Available at: http://www.nato.int/docu/facts/2001/ff-macedonia.htm.

NSA (1999) *Thoughts on Strategic Issues for the Institution*, Memorandum, Taylor to DIRNSA, April 9: 4–5.

OIVC (2004) Dutch language website. Available at: http://www.898vbdbat.nl/historie.htm.

Pedersen, O. (2002) Presentation of Colonel Odd Egil Pedersen, Royal Norwegian Army (Norwegian Intelligence Service), at the 2002 NISA conference, The Hague, The Netherlands, November 15.

Shukman, H. (ed.) (2000) *Agents for Change: Intelligence Services in the 21st Century*, London: St. Ermin's Press.

Sitze, G. (2000) Biography, Lt. Colonel Garry E. Sitze, USAF, undated. Available at: http://jitc-emh.army.mil/iop_conf/bios/sitze.htm. This site has since been disconnected.

Smith, J. (1993) "Tracking Aideed Hampered by Intelligence Failures," *Washington Post*, October 8: A19.

Streetly, M. (ed.) (2000) *Jane's Electronic Mission Aircraft* (London: Jane's Information Group Limited).

3ID AAR (2003) *Third Infantry Division (Mechanized) After Action Report: Operation IRAQI FREEDOM*. Available at: http://198.65.138.161/military/library/report/2003/3id-aar-jul03.pdf

Toohey, B., and Wilkinson, M. (1987) *The Book of Leaks*, Sydney: Angus & Robertson Publishers.

Urban, M. (1996) *UK Eyes Alpha* , New York: Faber & Faber.

US Army (1993) *The United States Army Modernization Plan*, January, Vol. II, Annex I Intelligence/Electronic Warfare, US Army FOIA.

Välimäki, P. (2002) Presentation by Major Pasi Välimäki, Senior Staff Officer, Finnish Defense Staff, C3 Division, at 2002 NISA Conference, The Hague, The Netherlands, November 15.

Villadsen, O. (2000) "Prospects for a European Common Intelligence Policy," *Studies in Intelligence*, Summer. Available at: http://www.cia.gov/csi/studies/summer00/art07.html.

WEU (2002) Assembly of WEU, Document A/1775, *The New Challenges Facing European Intelligence—Reply to the Annual Report of the Council*, June 4, 2002. Available at: http://www.assemblee-ueo.org/en/documents/sessions_ordinaires/rpt/2002/1775.html.

Wiebes, C. (2003) *Intelligence and the War in Bosnia: 1992–1995*, Munster: Lit Verlag.

Wilkinson, M. (1999) "Revealed: Our Spies in Iraq," *Sydney Morning Herald*, January 28. Available at: http://www.smh.com.au/news/9901/28/pageone/pageone1.html.

5

C4ISR

The unified theory of support to military operations

George Kolisnek

C4ISR is an acronym used in modern military doctrine to describe a single supporting military architecture that encompasses Command, Control, Communications, Computers, Intelligence, Surveillance, and Reconnaissance. The purpose of this chapter is to provide a brief and simple introduction to the C4ISR concept and some of its challenges.

Command and control

Command and control are commonly used terms within the hierarchical architecture supporting military operations. While seemingly clear and simple to understand, these terms actually are quite complex ideas representing a broad range of responsibilities and authorities. Command, for example, ranges from Full Command, normally the authority and responsibility of the most senior national military officer within a nation's armed forces, to Commanding Officer, the responsibility and authority vested in the most senior military officer within a particular unit varying in size from a handful to several hundred personnel. There are varying levels of command in between these two extremes, which are delegated to either operational or administrative commanders. For example, when forces are deployed on North Atlantic Treaty Organization (NATO) or United Nations (UN) Operations, command may be temporarily delegated to a NATO or UN operational commander for the period of the deployment. Command in this context involves the assignment of authority and responsibility for the conduct of operations to the NATO/UN Commander. However, Full Command, the authority and responsibility for the training of personnel, their logistic support and, ultimately, the legality of their conduct, while deployed, always rests and never leaves the Chief of Defence of the nation providing the forces to NATO/UN. Thus, for example, while aircraft and troops assigned to UN/NATO or other coalition-type operations are carrying out operations in foreign countries, the Chief of Defence never relinquishes his authority and responsibilities for the actions of his deployed forces. This is a very important point that is central to creation of the C4ISR acronym, since each Chief of Defence in any troop-contributing nation within a coalition is able to effectively exercise Full Command only when he has the proper communications, computers, intelligence, surveillance, and reconnaissance in place.

Control is a term used to describe a level of authority and responsibility below that of operational command, which is that normally assigned for a specific operational or tactical level task. While successful accomplishment of the task rests with the officer having control of the forces assigned, accomplishment of the mission rests with the officer in command. Therefore while the first two letters stand for Command and Control, it is really Command that requires the broadest degree of support from the remaining letters, namely Communications, Computers, Intelligence, Surveillance, and Reconnaissance in order to accomplish the mission assigned. Senior officers in command must have the level of knowledge required to make good and timely decisions. To achieve the degree of knowledge required of them, they need to have situational awareness, which comes in part from tactical and operational levels of intelligence, as well as surveillance and reconnaissance reporting. They must also have strategic level intelligence, which provides them with basic background information, such as relevant historical events, and estimative information, such as indications and warning of future developments and events. The rest of this discussion will be devoted to just how the remaining letters of the C4ISR acronym serve this function.

Communications and computers

Communications stands for all the methods of communicating available to any force commander. In modern military operations this usually encompasses a broad range of technologies and methodologies. The technologies range from simple radio to satellite relay, and the methods range from voice through audiovisual to data links between computers. While this broad range in capabilities will usually exist, their primary purpose is to pass information and allow for exchanges of information between all parties involved either in command of a particular mission or providing decision-making support in the form of intelligence, surveillance, and reconnaissance reporting. This primary purpose sometimes gets lost in the fascination with, and reliance on, the highest available technological solution to a communication problem. That said high-speed reliable satellite communications around the globe are a significant addition to the ability to supply the right information to the right place at the right time.

Mission success in modern military operations that span broad geographic areas and a wide variety in the types of tasks assigned to forces is heavily dependent on reliable and redundant communications. The types of information being communicated have also become critical success factors for commanders who have access to imagery and audio-visual tools that bring a high degree of situational awareness to them and their staff. Situational awareness will be covered later, but it is the essential plank upon which decision-making rests.

Computers were initially employed by the military to handle tasks that required a degree of number crunching, for example in the calculations associated with ballistics and artillery. However, at some more recent point in time it was discovered that computers could also help with the communications of messages and the passing of information. As a consequence, computers greatly sped up the passing of communications and information, so much so that there are vast amounts of information and messages being passed throughout a military operation today. While this result is very useful, the overwhelming amounts being transmitted around a force need to be organized into a content that is readily absorbable and usable by all levels of staff. It is this aspect of the use of computers that is hardest in concept and their employment. Technological development of computers has outpaced the development of a mature concept for their employment, especially as the users of these new technologies are not always equipped to fully and properly exploit the technology these developments bring. Military users have been faced with rapidly adapting their methods and techniques for the increased sharing of information to take advantage of each new development. As a consequence there is little time left to spend on the more in-depth thinking required to develop more detailed concepts of content and meaning of the information and knowledge before the next new technological capability arrives. The internet is a parallel example where vast amounts of information and true knowledge reside, yet how, when, and where it is created, as well as validation of content, is an impossible task. In the Internet environment this may not be an issue, as every user knows that there is a dark side and consumers must beware, but for military operations that require oversight and accountability these are real core issues.

Intelligence

Within the concept of C4ISR the word intelligence represents information that has been put through a process that determines whether it is of value and use to the decision-makers involved in command and control. This process either confirms there is value in the information itself or uses the information along with further analysis and other information to produce information that is of value. It includes evaluation of the source, assessment of the validity of the information and, finally, analysis to produce intelligence for commanders who have requirements for intelligence in support of situational awareness and future operational and strategic-level planning. It should be noted that the above use of the word intelligence focuses around information of value; it is not defined by either the method of collection or the classification of the information itself. It is a commonly held view that use of the word intelligence always and automatically involves covert collection and highly classified information. This perception often leads to misunderstandings. Many outside the intelligence community believe that intelligence analysts are always engaged in exploiting highly classified activities and documents. While many covert sources and methods are available and could be used within the C4ISR concept, any information gathered by these means results in highly classified intelligence reporting that is often restricted in its use through limited distribution and fear of revealing the sources and methods used. Therefore the use of open sources has some degree of added value in that any intelligence gleaned through its analysis will likely be more capable of being widely distributed and available to more staffs and commanders. The aim is to produce intelligence that is of value to those exercising command and control, no matter what the sources and methods used.

The processing of information to gain intelligence goes through many steps. Firstly, there is the collection process, which is normally handled by individual specialists who are knowledgeable about their particular method of collection. This includes the complete range of so called "ints" such as human intelligence, normally referred to as HUMINT, etc. In the case of open sources this would include library scientists. Within the C4ISR concept the complete range of source reporting, from open source to the most covert, must be made available to intelligence analysts, who are for that reason called "all-source" analysts. These "all-source" analysts will then produce intelligence that meets the needs of a wide variety of consumers within the C4ISR architecture. Intelligence in support of situational awareness perhaps meets the needs of the largest number of consumers, but there are also other requirements. There is intelligence required in direct support of tactical-level operations such as targeting. There is operational-level intelligence required in support of force protection that includes such topics as the capabilities and intentions of any organization posing a threat to the success of the mission in the immediate future. There is strategic-level intelligence required in support of force generators, planners, and force protection that includes topics such as medical and environmental intelligence, and any organization posing a threat to successful completion of the mission and its capabilities and intentions over the longer term, sometimes out to several years. These requirements for intelligence support in the past were broken down neatly into tactical, operational, and strategic levels, with specialist organizations at each level.

Rapid advances in technology in communications and computers have significantly altered that paradigm. In the types of military operations being conducted today, something less than all-out war and with an increased eye on legal and human rights issues, all operations have tactical-, operational- and strategic-level implications. In this environment it is essential that all levels of command and control have the same degree of situational awareness and assessment of threats and risks to force protection in order to ensure the proper employment of forces as well as maintaining a chain of accountability. Therefore, within the C4ISR concept, the intelligence architecture and its products must be capable of supporting all levels in the chain of command. This places a heavy reliance on the communications and computers portion of the C4ISR concept, but it also places a heavy reliance on the fast turnaround of intelligence collection and analysis and an emphasis on the coherence of intelligence products at all levels of command. Thus the C4ISR concept places new, more rigorous demands on the supporting intelligence architecture as well as all-source analysis production.

Surveillance and reconnaissance

Surveillance within the C4ISR concept is a term used to describe the use of sensors and platforms to cover large geographical areas for a sustained and relatively long period of time. Surveillance can involve the use of a single sensor, such as imagery satellites, or multiple sensors and platforms, such as aircraft and ships employing radar and passive acoustic sensors to watch a broad ocean area. Communications and computers have significantly increased surveillance capabilities to provide near real-time coverage across a wide spectrum of sensors including digital imagery, infrared, and night vision devices. The planning for deployment of surveillance resources and their use along with pre-planned courses of action, once something of interest has been located, requires a high degree of coordination. Modern military operations also normally require situational awareness across a broad geographical area due to an increase in the range of weapons systems as well as better understanding of how events in areas other than the area of responsibility impact on force protection. Therefore there is an increased need for input to the employment of surveillance assets and their collected information at all levels of command within any particular mission. C4ISR is designed to provide the vehicle for this coordinated approach.

Reconnaissance is normally used to describe the use of sensors and platforms either within limited geographic areas or against particular targets of interest. Reconnaissance assets can also assist in providing support to particular courses of action. That said, reconnaissance assets can employ the same types of sensors and platforms as surveillance resources, but usually in a specific and more focused manner. Surveillance and reconnaissance support to modern military deployments during peacekeeping operations are an essential element to the success of any mission. Not all nations have the means to acquire the broad range of capabilities required and many have begun pooling their resources in order to share the burden brought about through new technologies and increased costs.

Modern digitized sensors and versatile platforms such as unmanned aerial vehicles (UAVs) have blurred some of the difference between surveillance and reconnaissance sensors in particular. The ability to refine, and in some cases measure, the information collected exists at both levels. This is particularly important because it enables commanders to transition quickly from broad area surveillance to executing courses of action against particular targets without further deployment of other resources. Accordingly, the C4ISR concept provides the supporting architecture needed for these types of rapid transitions from broad area search to selection of the appropriate course of action. These types of transitions are usually rapid in nature due to the changing targets, and all parts of the C4ISR architecture must be able to respond accordingly. The environment of most modern military operations in other than war situations poses particular challenges at such times. Avoidance of what has come to be called collateral damage to innocent civilians, along with situational awareness of illegal activities outside the rules of engagement of deployed forces, places demands on surveillance and reconnaissance assets over and above their normal coverage. Commanders at all levels of the mission must now make decisions within relatively short time frames. They cannot do this without the highly specialized support that C4ISR integration of resources brings to the problem.

Concluding remarks

While C4ISR has the appearance of a long acronym covering a complex concept of military operations, it is in fact a relatively short term for a simple vision, namely excellence in military operations. It is in the detailed architecture of C4ISR that complexities arise that can bring challenges and risks to its role in support of commanders and planners. In today's operating environment any military operation at any level has the capability of being catapulted into international news coverage and consequently quickly rising to a strategic policy level. Therefore C4ISR must be fully understood by commanders and planners so that they are aware of the strengths and limitations of each particular mission's architecture and how it affects their ability to make decisions for which they are accountable. It is not something that should be left to the specialists that contribute individual capabilities to C4ISR to put together. Each mission has unique requirements in each of the specialized fields of C4ISR, and these need to be identified prior to the deployment of forces and agreed upon by all levels of command involved in the mission.

Given the issues briefly identified and discussed above, as well as the wide range of geographical regions where forces are deployed on peace-keeping and related operations, from jungles to deserts, and the wide scope of operations, from humanitarian aid to peace enforcement, C4ISR is a concept whose time is now.

Part II

EVOLUTION OF INTELLIGENCE IN MULTINATIONAL PEACEKEEPING MISSIONS

6

INTELLIGENCE AT UNITED NATIONS HEADQUARTERS?

The Information and Research Unit and the intervention in Eastern Zaire (1996)

Walter Dorn

Introduction

To some people, the term "United Nations intelligence" is an oxymoron. Not that the UN is "unintelligent," but to them the organization and its peacekeepers in the field should not dabble in the murky practice of "intelligence gathering" or deal in the trade of secret information; it should only use information from direct observation and open (overt) sources. There is a growing recognition, however, that the world organization needs much information, some of it secret, when dealing with raging conflicts and human barbarity. Especially when UN staff in the field are themselves at risk, it is vital to know in advance about the possibilities and intensions of attackers. The bombing of the UN compound in Iraq on August 19, 2003 reinforced the need for threat analysis and early warning. Fortunately, the terms "intelligence" and "intelligence gathering," once banned from the lexicon of the UN, are becoming acceptable, if not fashionable, in the organization. They are now often, if not formally, used in the UN peacekeeping operations (PKOs) and field offices, in the sense of processed or analyzed information relating to security (both open and secret), something clearly separate from the cloak and dagger activities (" covert action") practiced by some national intelligence agencies. The UN has even advertised positions for "intelligence analysts" to work with the International Criminal Tribunal for the Former Yugoslavia.[1]

UN intelligence gathering has also grown rapidly as a scholarly field in recent years, though almost all of it relates to peacekeeping intelligence (PKI). Since the publication of the first case study of intelligence in a UN PKO by Dorn and Bell (1995), there have been detailed examinations of PKI in Bosnia, Haiti, Lebanon, and other conflict areas. Despite the proliferation of papers, there remains a lacuna in PKI: the literature still does not deal with the vital issue of intelligence at UN headquarters.

Indeed, the term "headquarters intelligence" is viewed by field personnel as yet another oxymoron for yet another reason. UN headquarters is often seen as a black hole into which information from the field regularly disappears, with little or no information or feedback returned. It is also seen as a place where very little *analysis* is done to convert information into intelligence, certainly nothing comparable to the work of national intelligence agencies. A long-standing sense of these deficiencies has led several recent Secretaries-General to attempt to do something about the situation. This chapter will outline these efforts and describe in detail the most advanced intelligence body yet created by the UN at headquarters: the Information and Research (I&R) Unit that was part of the Situation Center (SitCen) of the Department of Peacekeeping Operations (DPKO) from 1993 to 1999. The story begins earlier, however, with the establishment of the Office for Research and the Collection of Information.

An early effort: the ORCI

At the end of his second term as UN Secretary-General in 1991, Pérez de Cuéllar remained frustrated by a great lack of information that had inhibited him from being more proactive and from practicing early warning and preventive diplomacy. He had tried unsuccessfully to solve this problem by creating, in 1987, the Office for Research and the Collection of Information (ORCI). In the cost-cutting environment of the day, the ORCI's establishment was justified as an effort to streamline the Secretariat and cut repetition in functions relating to political assessments and analysis (Jonah, 1990). But its mandate was far more ambitious. It was to assess global trends, prepare "profiles" of various countries, regions, and conflicts, and give early warning of emerging "situations" as well as monitor refugee flows and other emergencies.

There was an immediate backlash from a group of conservative US politicians, including Senators Bob Dole and William Roth. They co-sponsored a bill in 1987 to withhold US funding for the ORCI. In a letter to the UN Secretary-General they charged that the new office could "provide a cover" for Soviet espionage in the US and that it would "gather information on the internal political situation of member states—a definite United Nations intrusion" into domestic affairs (*New York Times*, 1987: 4). They did not allege that the office might challenge US intelligence agencies, though this was almost certainly on their minds. The US State Department managed to convince the Senators that the office was useful however, and it replaced the Political Information News Service (PINS) that, as part of the Department of Political and Security Council Affairs (DPSCA), had been managed by a Soviet national. The officials also argued that the new

68

UN office would save money since it was amalgamating several other UN sections. At its establishment and during its tenure, the ORCI was placed under the control of a long-standing international civil servant James Jonah of Sierra Leone. The organizational diagram of the ORCI is given in Figure 6.1.

Even though the US Senators backed down over their Bill, the office continued to face resistance. The ORCI was branded undesirable by other governments, who also feared UN intrusion into sovereign affairs. In addition, the ORCI suffered from a number of problems: with an initial staff of twenty members (less than half of which were in the professional category), at a time of a recruitment and funding freeze, and with little automation, it was understaffed, under-equipped, and unable to hire new staff from outside the UN system. Jonah made light of all this by saying it was "better to be overworked than to be overstaffed" (Jonah, 1990: 7). The office was equipped with only primitive teletype machines to receive news from the wire services. The UN only caught up with the computer/information age a half decade later. The lack of technical and human resources, combined with an incessant demand for speech writing by the Secretary-General and senior UN officials, meant that the ORCI could not devote the time and effort needed for deeper analysis of pressing international issues. Though it had an "Early Warning Service" it did not issue significant early warnings.[2]

When Boutros Boutros-Ghali arrived as Secretary-General in 1992, he created the DPKO to manage the burgeoning practice of UN peacekeeping that was quickly becoming a centerpiece of the organization's response to the many post Cold War conflicts.[3] The ORCI was disbanded and a new organization within DPKO was established.

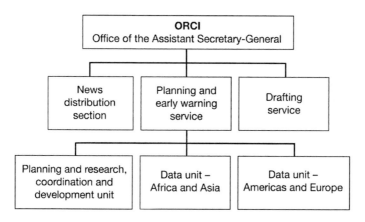

Figure 6.1: Organizational diagram of the Office for Research and the Collection of Information (1987–92)

The situation center and the I&R Unit

To manage the new set of multidimensional field operations, the UN had to find middle ground between the concept of an "Operations Center" (which was not possible, given the meager resources and the paucity of political will among the member states) and a "Situation Room" (which was found to be inadequate in scope). Hence a "Situation Center" was created within the DPKO in 1993.[4] This was to be more than the "cable room" that had existed in the Office for Special Political Affairs, but not the nerve center for command and control commonly found in national defense establishments. The "Sitcen," the 1996 organizational structure of which is shown in Figure 6.2, included a 24/7 Duty Room where knowledgeable officers could promptly refer field officers to appropriate headquarters officials.

This was done in part to respond to the criticisms of peacekeepers like Major-General Lewis Mackenzie, who accused headquarters staff of being unreachable, even as life-threatening crises were unfolding in places like Sarajevo where Mackenzie was the sector commander. The Duty Room, which had three or four officers on duty 24 hours a day, divided the world into three or four regions, as is commonly done in military headquarters. Each duty officer was responsible for communications, including the daily

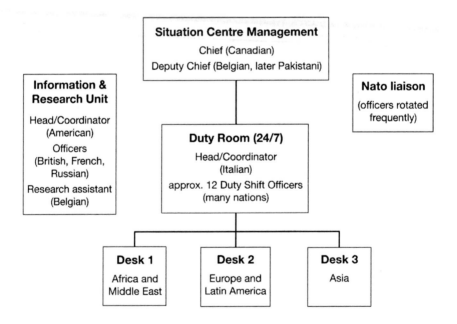

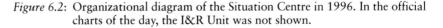

Figure 6.2: Organizational diagram of the Situation Centre in 1996. In the official charts of the day, the I&R Unit was not shown.

70

situation reports (SitReps), for between four and seven peacekeeping missions. The initial SitCen goal of uninterrupted communications with all UN missions around the globe was achieved for all PKOs. At the height of PKO deployments in the mid-1990s, it was possible to boast that the sun never set on UN peacekeepers. And this when, in many places, tensions were running high. Headquarters was particularly busy.

Information from UN peacekeepers in the field was clearly not sufficient, however, if the UN wanted to engage in early warning and preventive diplomacy, as Boutros-Ghali had advocated in 1992 in his landmark report *Agenda for Peace*. To uncover the deeper forces underlying conflicts, the DPKO needed a way to tap into the vast information networks of national governments, with their numerous embassies and sophisticated intelligence agencies. But the major powers didn't want to send information to the Secretariat without having someone linked to them ("their man") inside the UN to "handle" and more carefully disseminate sensitive information. The result was the creation within the SitCen in September 1993 of the Information and Research (I&R) Unit, composed of officers on secondment from the governments of four of the five permanent members of the Security Council: France, the UK, Russia, and the US.[5] China declined to send an officer; apparently, it was unwilling to share information, a prerequisite for membership. Besides, it was not contributing substantially to peacekeeping and others felt it could not be counted on to provide useful or unbiased information (which could also be said of the others as well!). The four I&R Unit staff were *gratis* officers, whose salaries were paid by their home governments but who still were subject to UN direction and, in theory, to UN discipline (another oxymoron to some, especially concerning officers on secondment). These individuals maintained substantial links to the intelligence services of their home countries, most having come from these agencies. The Unit was headed by a US Air Force intelligence officer for the first few years. A Canadian headed the SitCen but the officers in the I&R Unit did not consider themselves responsible to the SitCen chief or subject to his authority. It was under his initials, however, that many of the reports were sent to the UN's senior officials.

In the first few years of the DPKO and its SitCen, the US sought to build up the UN's peacekeeping capacity, identifying intelligence as a key deficiency. It provided substantial assistance for the development of the I&R Unit, though many in the UN Secretariat were uneasy about relying on US intelligence agencies. The USA Defense Information Systems Agency (DISA) performed an "audit" in 1994, recommending that a new US system, the Joint Deployable Intelligence Support System, or JDISS, be provided to the Unit. This system had been deployed by the US to Somalia in 1992–93 (Operation Restore Hope and UNOSOM II) and to the former Yugoslavia in 1993 (Operation Provide Promise). It was offered free of charge but the UN insisted on purchasing it. Thus, a JDISS terminal was installed in one corner of the room occupied by the I&R Unit on the 32nd floor of the UN's Secretariat Building. This terminal was to facilitate information transfer on a "need to know basis" to the UN, i.e., when the US thought the UN needed to know. To the officers in the Unit, JDISS was a limited tool, useful only for certain types of information. Normally the Unit would submit a Request For Information (RFI) to the US Mission across the street. Within the US Mission, an officer from the Defense Intelligence Agency/J2 (Joint Staff, Intelligence Directorate) would coordinate the response to the request. The Bureau of Intelligence and Research (INR) in the State Department was an important resource but it was the newly created "UN Support Desk" in the National Military Joint Intelligence Center (NMJIC) that was tasked to gain "properly sanitized" responses from the US intelligence community. Most responses could be sent in standard formats using JDISS, though more sensitive information was hand-delivered.

There were fears that the US could manipulate UN decision-making by providing selective and biased information, but officers in the I&R Unit claimed that this was not so. Certainly, the intelligence officers from the other three countries kept a close eye on the information provided by their colleagues, and to a certain extent this provided "checks and balances." The papers and reports issued by the Unit were, as a rule, a joint project, requiring a consensus of all the officers covering a situation. Their "consolidated report" was intended to remove "national orientations." The reports were then delivered to a number (typically between three and seven) of high-ranking officials in the Secretary-General's office, in the Department of Political Affairs (DPA) as well as the DPKO. However, the regular feed of political and military information from them was deemed important. The US supplied substantial intelligence on conflicts in Angola, the Balkans, Burundi, Cambodia, and Haiti. As we shall see, in the case of Zaire (now called the Democratic Republic of the Congo), it was problematic.

The other countries also provided valuable and timely information. In particular, France sent its officer information on "trouble spots" in Africa: Eastern Zaire, where a refugee crisis had erupted after the 1994 Rwandan genocide; Sudan, where there was an ongoing war between the "Muslim" government in the North and "Christian" rebel groups in the south; Burundi, which had Hutu/Tutsi ethnic divisions similar to Rwanda; Hanish Islands, which were claimed by both Yemen and Eritrea; and Angola, where rebel leader Joseph Savimbi was fighting to gain power after losing the 1993 election. The British officer had the lead for the Balkans, though he also contributed to the Zaire case and other "hot spots" as they arose. The Russian officer worked mostly on the Commonwealth of Independence States (CIS) region, especially in areas like Georgia where the UN had deployed PKOs. In addition, the North Atlantic Treaty Organization (NATO) posted to the SitCen a liaison officer who gave twice monthly briefings to SitCen and I&R Unit staff.

What kind of intelligence did the I&R Unit provide to the UN? Was the information accurate and its analysis unbiased? Did it improve the effectiveness of peacekeeping? To answer these important questions, it is helpful to make a case study. The crisis in Eastern Zaire in 1996 provides plenty of useful examples, insights, and lessons. Fortunately, the I&R Unit reports on Zaire (1994–98) were made available to the author. A summary and analysis of these "information products" during the crisis period of 1996–97 is provided here for the first time.

Eastern Zaire was the center of world attention after the 1994 Rwandan genocide (Adelman and Suhrke, 1999). Over a million Hutu refugees, including many former *genocidaires*, fled Rwanda for camps in the Goma, Bukavu, and Uvira regions of neighboring Zaire. From these refugee camps, the defeated Rwandan government forces (the Force Armée Rwandese, now called ex-FAR) staged attacks into Rwanda. They were in turn subject to attacks from Tutsi-led Rwandan government forces and local Tutsi (Banyamulenge) forces allied to them as well as other rebel groups in Eastern Zaire. The situation was dubbed a potential genocide and there was a constant clamor for the UN to do something to avoid "another Rwanda." The UN authorized a Canadian-led peacekeeping and humanitarian mission in November 1996. But soon after the UN announcement, the Hutu camps were attacked outright, an event perhaps catalyzed by the news of the impending peacekeeping mission that might provide protection to the camps. The UN-authorized mission was aborted a few weeks later. Events in Eastern Zaire had overtaken the mission and then cascaded further, with the rebel groups sweeping across Zaire to the capital Kinshasa. The authoritarian Zairian President, Mobutu Sese Seko, who had installed himself in the mid-1960s with CIA backing, fled the country, leaving the rebel group leader, Laurent Kabila, to govern an impoverished, war-torn, and deeply divided land. But Kabila's Rwandan patrons soon turned against him and the country was again divided by civil war in 1998. The newly named Democratic Republic of the Congo, far from being "democratic," became a vast battlefield for over a half a dozen African nations who took opposing sides. Other nations of the world also had an interest in the region, not only for partisan or humanitarian reasons, but because of the lucrative mining contracts in the mineral-rich region.

The American, British and French officers in the I&R Unit all provided substantial information on the situation in Eastern Zaire, but the French officer took the lead in preparing the I&R Unit reports. As the crisis grew to pandemic proportions in late 1996, and as a new mission was being launched, objective information was crucial for the UN. I&R Unit officers

73

occasionally briefed the commander of the Multinational Force (MNF), a mission authorized by the UN to provide humanitarian assistance to the refugees and to facilitate their repatriation to Rwanda. The Secretary-General maintained an open-door policy for I&R staff though only he and his chief-lieutenants were allowed to brief the Security Council. This present chapter focuses on the reporting of the I&R Unit during the period of greatest crisis in late 1996. It is based on reports (I&R Unit, 1996–97) and interviews (Dorn, 1996, 2004).

Zaire case study

During the years 1996–97, I&R Unit "memoranda" on the situation in Eastern Zaire (Kivu province) were issued about once a month. Most of them were classified as "UN Confidential," though some were also "Eyes Only" reports for designated UN officials. During critical times, like November–December 1996, when the MNF was being assembled, reports were more frequent. Most reports had standard section headings: introduction, event, significance and conclusion (on one page) followed by a detailed analysis. Maps, disclaimers, and confidentiality provisions were often included.[6]

One early event was President Mobutu's agreement on June 6, 1996 that UN observers could be stationed in Kivu to monitor the Security Council-mandated ban on arms exports to Hutu refugees, who included extremists from the defeated Force Armée Rwandese (ex-FAR). The I&R Unit warned of the risks to UN officials posted there on such a sensitive mission. Those selling, delivering, or using the illegal arms would not want to be caught or have any sinister plots exposed. The report of June 20, 1996 provided both insightful analysis and a prediction (accurate as it turns out):

> Despite President Mobutu's insistence on declaring the FAZ [Force Armée du Zaire] as being neutral vis-à-vis the ethnic groups in Kivu, the obvious pro-Hutu attitude of the Zairian military authorities in this area and their non-intervention policy would suggest that the bottom line would be the removal from Masisi [in North Kivu] of all the Banyarwaranda/Tutsis in order to resettle the Hutus from the refugee camps. Should such a solution, covert or otherwise, be initiated the Rwandese authorities would react: they would definitely not tolerate such a potential threat in the form of a "Hutuland" close to their borders.
>
> (I&R Unit, June 20, 1996)

The reports give much information that was sensitive at the time and would have laid the UN open to criticism of "interference in internal matters," however relevant the information was to conflict management and resolution. But the details about many nefarious activities in Eastern Zaire would have been hard if not impossible for UN staff on the ground to learn by themselves. Such information necessitated intelligence-gathering methods in which the UN itself could not engage. As is natural in the intelligence world, I&R reports don't specify the sources or methods of information gathering. They usually begin with an intentionally vague statement that a variety of informed sources were used. It was understood that information usually came from the intelligence networks of one or more of the Great Powers represented in the Unit.[7]

Among the many topics covered in the reports, four areas stand out for their potential importance to the mission. These are described in detail below:

1 arms shipments;
2 military (belligerent) activities;
3 refugee numbers and status;
4 predictions and warnings.

In citing and quoting the Unit's reports below, only the date is given. The title of most was merely "memorandum" or "information on Kivu (Zaire)."

Arms shipments

The UN had a responsibility to stop the violations of the arms embargo it had imposed on the former Rwandan government forces in Eastern Zaire. Thus, it needed to identify those transferring weapons into the region and expose them. In theory such persons would then be arrested by the government of Zaire, which claimed to be strictly abiding by the embargo, but the I&R Unit implicated the government itself at the highest levels. Knowledge of illegal arms shipments was also important for the UN because weapons infusions caused a great danger to UN aid workers and also served as early warning indicators of escalating violence. It was a very combustible situation in a region with a long history of animosity and attacks, the existence of several marauding tribes and militiamen (Zairian, Hutu and Tutsi), and the recent arrival of the desperate former Rwandan government army (the Hutu ex-FAR).

The I&R Unit revealed that illegal shipments were made to the Hutus by persons with close ties to the Mobutu regime, despite its claims of compliance with the embargo. The reports even point to Mobutu's own adventure-seeking sons piloting 727s filled with weapons. At the local level, a wealthy Zairian woman in Kivu, named in one report, channeled funds and arms to the Hutu rebel groups. She was the "front person," as the nominal director-general of a tobacco company, whose hangars were used to transfer weapons, ammunition, and other amenities. She supported the extremist Hutu radio station, *Radio Democratie*, located on company premises, and chartered planes to medivac certain senior Zairian officers wounded during a transfer operation. She was protected from authorities in the Zairian government by the Prime Minister himself. She was also described as a mistress of a radical Burundian Hutu commander (also named).

The two main routes for arms flows are described: in one route, planes leave Belgium, load weapons and ammunition in Bulgaria, Egypt and even Sudan before landing in Kinshasa (Zaire); in the other, cargoes depart South Africa, from a secret facility run by former South African Special Forces affiliated with Executive Outcomes (a company that closed down in 1999 after South Africa regulated private military corporations and its growing but disreputable mercenary export market). The reports also claimed that large cargo plane[s] from Uzbekistan were found to be unloading arms and new military uniforms at the airport outside Kinshasa. The weapons were stored at Kinshasa airport before being shipped to Bukavu (Eastern Zaire), as well as to Angola and Cabinda to help rebel leader Joseph Savimbi. The Army Chief of Staff facilitated the storage of the cargoes at the Kinshasa airport. In Eastern Zaire, the main caches were located in two *Parcs national* in Kivu and one training camp was located in Kigonga, near Mugunga. The weapons were paid for by the ex-FAR from funds they took out of Rwanda at the time of their withdrawal. According to the report, politicians and militaries at the highest level in Kinshasa were involved in the FDD (Burundian armed rebel group) arms trafficking. One of the Unit's reports reveals an interesting incident: two Officers of the Zairian Corps of Engineers were caught delivering arms to Hutu rebels in Uvira. The local military system in Goma, it was written, was paid US$15,000 to cover up the case. (This suggests some close, if not inside, sources for information in the report.)

Military activities

The reports give order of battle information, including new military assets like the arms mentioned above for each of the warring factions. The Hutu military in exile was estimated at about 30,000 ex-FAR and Interahamwe members, among the estimated 850,000 Hutu refugees. In Kivu three military training camps were supported covertly by the Zairian government.

In opposition, an estimated 3000 Banyamulenge (Zairian Tutsis) were, according to the report, armed, equipped, and trained in Rwanda. They benefited from the incorporation of mercenaries from South Africa, Angola (UNITA), Serbia, France and Belgium. (For the UN, this was all too reminiscent of its problem with the "soldiers of fortune" in the 1960s when it had a mandate to identify, capture, and repatriate mercenaries from the Congo.) Executive Outcomes, not generally known to have operated in the Congo, recruited 154 highly skilled personnel to manage military air assets which included MiG-21 fighters and Mi-25 attack helicopters (I&R Unit, 1996).

The I&R Unit reports describe night raids by the Zairian rebel forces. In the town of Lemera, the rebels killed twenty Zairian soldiers and seized "200 small arms, 2 × 81 mm mortars, 3 radio communication sets and a lot of ammunition" (October 24, 1996). In an act of deception, the government of Rwanda stationed its forces "under the disguise of Banyamulenge" in Zaire to protect hydroelectric plants that provide power to both Rwanda and Burundi (December 19, 1996). In November 1996, the Rwandan forces took control of Goma, an international seizure that was made quite apparent when the Rwandan flag was raised over the main administrative buildings (February 6, 1997).

Despite Rwandan government denials of involvement, its army provided two battalions in direct support of the rebels and also anti-aircraft artillery to secure airports in Bukavu and Goma. In one instance, Rwandan attack helicopters left more than 100 [Zairian] soldiers dead. Further, Rwandan Special Forces troops spearheaded an attack on at least one of the refugee camps.

Rwanda was not the only country supporting the Zairian rebel forces, who were now amalgamated under the leadership of Mobutu-opponent Laurent Kabila. His forces had received long-standing support and training from Libya (Annex I, January 1, 1997). And Uganda also sent troops to Zaire to support the rebels (at first denied by Uganda, but later admitted).

A more controversial allegation is that the United States "strongly supported and established the rebellion" (December 19, 1996). The I&R Unit boldly asserts that the Tutsi rebellion was backed by "American teams" (February 6, 1997). Despite official US support for the Canadian-led humanitarian mission in November–December 1996, the Unit alleges that the US sought to undermine the operation: "On the American request to deter the deployment of a UN-authorized Multi-National Force led by a Canadian General, the FRP [Rwandan army] along with ADFL [rebel group] elements lured the ex-FAR and Interahamwe in a combat operation north of the Muganga camp (Zaire)." If this allegation were true, it has a striking parallel with duplicity in the Congo mission in the 1960s. While UN forces were protecting the Congolese leader Patrice Lumumba, as part of a UN operation explicitly backed (and partly paid for) by the US, CIA operatives in the Congo were trying to assassinate him (Church Committee, 1975).

As a result of the attack on the camps, more than 800,000 refugees began the trek home. The emerging MNF was withdrawn "despite a remaining 400,000 scattered in Kivu" (February 6, 1997). This highlights one of the most contentious intelligence issues of the Zaire crisis:

the number of refugees allegedly "abandoned" by the international community.

Refugee numbers and status (an intelligence gap)

How many refugees remained in Zaire after the coordinated attacks on their camps in mid-November 1996? The estimates vary from as little as 20,000 to over 400,000. The US claimed the lower figure, while aid groups and the I&R Unit alleged the number was 10 to 20 times higher (PeaceLink for Africa Campaign, 1997). The "numbers game" had important political ramifications. The UN and the MNF needed to know if a sizeable refugee group remained and needed assistance in Eastern Zaire. The US position after the attack on the camps was clear: it wanted the mission aborted. It stated categorically that aerial and satellite reconnaissance backed its claim that almost all the refugees had returned to Rwanda. But Lieutenant-General Maurice Baril, the MNF Commander, was suspicious of US reports, in which "the numbers were sliding downwards" (Baril, 2004). Members of the I&R Unit had briefed him on what they believed was disinformation.[8] Both the French and British officers in the Unit were tracking the numbers, the former using French intelligence sources and the latter gaining information from UN agencies on the ground (e.g., UNHCR, UNICEF, WFP). They concluded that the US numbers were far too low. Baril's multinational force (mostly Canadian) engaged in a desperate attempt at reconnaissance and he himself flew over the territory for a first-hand impression. But the counting was difficult because the frightened refugees, many fearful of aircraft, were dispersed over large areas under thick jungle cover. The issue has never been resolved. Many thousands may have perished in the jungles of Zaire.

Predictions and warnings

I&R officers took on the difficult and potentially embarrassing challenge of predicting the future, something rarely done in the UN. In some instances their warnings were prescient. For instance, months before Rwandan government forces and Zairian rebel allies attacked the Hutu camps in November 1996, the Unit made the following dire but rather general warning (June 20, 1996): "Rwanda would be happy to put together a contingency plan to eradicate the ex-FAR troops and Interahamwe militias with the covert acceptance of Uganda" (I&R Unit, June 20, 1996).

A more precise warning came in August but was couched in cautious language, perhaps to hedge against an incorrect prediction: "No one can rule out a quick operation launched by Kigali [Rwanda] with the support of Kampala [Uganda] to terminate the ex-FAR and Interahamwe threat" (August 26, 1996).

In October, by contrast, a large scale Rwandan operation was ruled out "during the absence of General Paul Kagame [Rwanda's leader] who is currently visiting Israel and Italy." The main attack on the camps occurred in mid-November. As for the larger picture, the Unit postulated that the Rwandan training of Banyamulenge was indicative of a larger design aimed at seizing part of Kivu and potentially destroying the ex-FAR. It did not foresee the ambition and ease with which the rebel forces would sweep across Zaire and seize Kinshasa, nor that the ex-FAR would be easily defeated in attacks and would be dispersed so widely afterward. But the British officer in the Unit did develop scenario flow charts (November 12, 1996). In one of these scenarios the government of Zaire collapses and the country is de facto partitioned. Another scenario is that the rebels become the government of Zaire. Alternative scenarios were for a stable situation and the success of political efforts. Such model development showed that the Unit was aware of potential outcomes, but it was not predicting them.

Some warnings proved premature. The November 4, 1996 report warns the Unit of a coup plot against Mobutu "very soon," naming "three main plotters" who were top Zairian generals. The update of December 19 noted that one of these was dismissed while another was promoted. Again it warned that "a military coup should be expected soon." For the UN, risk assessments are an important part of any mission start-up. Thus I&R Unit warned that "aid workers could easily be caught up in the unrest or even targeted because of their relative wealth; four-wheel drive vehicles are prized and are often the first to be hijacked during a period of unrest" (August 26, 1996). In North Kivu, the Unit identified several other threats: landmines, "the ill disciplined behaviour of the FAZ [Force Armée Zairoises] soldiers, the rampant crime, and the lack of adequate means of evacuation" (August 26, 1996). The Unit also warned that the UN could unwittingly assist the fighting factions. For instance: "World Food Programme's supplies are being used to feed the military and militias, and to build up stocks in their ration depots" (August 26, 1996). Further "UN agency transportation assets are also used to smuggle arms and ammunition," in violation of the UN's own arms embargo (June 20, 1996)!

On December 19, 1996, the Unit described the offensive launched by government troops in Eastern Zaire and their subsequent retreat. It incorrectly predicted that the recent rebel successes, gained through surprise, would not continue in the intense fighting of the future. Later reports correctly describe FAZ in a total disarray, with soldiers deserting, joining the enemy, or engaging in rampages of "looting, raping and killing" (February 6, 1997). The rebel march progressed across the vast country and only ended after the forces loyal to Laurent Kabila had seized Kinshasa and control of the government. In an effort to protect his regime, Mobutu had called other African governments for support, leading to Africa's "continental war."

Conclusion

The reports of the I&R Unit were valued by UN officials like Kofi Annan, who was Under-Secretary-General for peacekeeping at the time. Even if the UN could not deal directly with nefarious activities in conflict zones, it had to know about them in order not to unintentionally get caught up in them. The game in Zaire was for high stakes and powerful forces were at play, including long-standing ethnic hatreds, displaced armies, and the economic interests of Western mineral resource companies.

To execute its mandate to assist refugees, the UN needed to know many things. The critical/priority information requirements (CIRs and PIRs) in the Zaire crisis included:

- refugee numbers, dispositions and locations;
- potential threats against UN personnel;
- external influences and the attitudes of major powers (expressed and unexpressed);
- weapons flows and military preparations;
- controlling forces;
- potential scenarios for the future.

It is clear from the I&R reports that the Unit provided much important and useful information on these categories, though this was still insufficient overall. Even if it was impossible to verify or corroborate all the intelligence, at least UN officials had an idea of what was likely to happen. UN officials could find opportunities to privately query governments, to seek further information on the ground, and in some cases to expose misinformation and disinformation. For example, Zairian assertions of non-involvement in illegal arms imports were later exposed by a UN Commission of Inquiry.

The revelations in the I&R reports include: clear evidence of the powerful influence of money, weapons, and illegal trafficking in the region; the complicity of governments in activities that they denied; and revelations of plots of a coup d'état in Zaire. The conflict analysis included estimates of the numbers and movements of troops (foreign and Zairian) and mercenaries, tracing arms shipments violating a Security Council embargo, exposing diversions of UN humanitarian aid and corruption at the senior levels of Zairian society, providing early warnings about potential violence against UN workers, and identifying military officers planning a coup against President Mobutu. The Unit also performed scenario-building and analysis of motivations of political and military leaders, practices which the UN has traditionally shunned.

Were the reports biased? A French bias can be alleged, but since the truth about many of the contentious statements is uncertain, this is difficult to prove. Several I&R reports advocated the same position as the French government. In one report (February 6, 1997), the Unit advocated that the mission in Zaire should have been continued. In another, there are allegations that the US strongly supported and aided the Zairian rebels, including their attacks on the refugee camps, and disseminated disinformation on the number of refugees remaining after the attacks. One I&R report questioned US analysis of the problems in the region. For instance, it criticized a "US security report," saying it "does not address the key factors; i.e., the military and paramilitary balance in the area, the short and mid-term struggle of the main current political leaders, the control of economic assets (minerals, diamonds) and hard currency generating profits (weapons smuggling)" (August 26, 1996). The issue of the control of economic assets was a sensitive one, since American firms were known to have cut deals with the rebels for access to the strategic minerals in the region.

Further, the French government was known to be partial to the francophone Hutus and maintained long-standing connections with the Hutu leadership. It is possible that this influenced the Unit's reports, which relied heavily on French intelligence. For instance, one report (February 6, 1997) admitted indirectly French complicity with ex-FAR in helping the Hutus to cross into Zaire in 1994 with most of their heavy equipment during the French-led "Opération Turqoise." The lesson for the UN in Zaire is similar to that learned by Canada the lead nation in the MNF—the need for an independent information-collection capability.

> The CF [Canadian Forces] lacked an independent strategic intelligence capability causing reliance on allies for virtually all in-theatre collection. This brought with it the danger of data manipulation or distortion for political reasons as was evident during the debate over refugee numbers.
>
> (DND (Canada), 1998: para. 23.5)

To be truly independent, the UN would have to directly gather information about the nefarious, criminal, and duplicitous world of warlords, rebels, and dictators. For an organization dedicated to transparency and openness, this would be a great challenge. It cannot run covert intelligence-gathering operations since this would open the UN to criticisms of partiality and stain its credibility. But at least the UN should have channels to receive such information and have the means to openly verify the information where possible. For the UN to cover its eyes, ears, and mouth saying "hear no evil, see no evil, speak no evil" would be to ignore the reality of the many evil atrocities committed in the war zones where it operates (Power, 2003; Dorn and Matloff, 2000). To reduce national bias, the UN would need to rely on a larger number of countries for information. This case study shows that there are many important facts the UN *should* know if it going to be effective in providing a peaceful alternative to war.

In Zaire 1996, the UN did not know enough. It was therefore possible for the US to lead the UN away from engagement in late November 1996, one of the principal reasons the mission was forced to abort (Baril, 2005). The I&R Unit gave UN officials and mission leaders a sense of what might be the US agenda but this came too late to stop the chain of events set off by the attack on the camps. The attacks brought about at least one positive development however: hundreds of thousands of refugees returned to their homeland.

The UN lost the I&R Unit inadvertently in February 1999 when all the gratis personnel working at the UN, mostly in its peacekeeping and humanitarian departments (some 500 people, including 219 military officers), had to leave because of a General Assembly resolution pushed by the developing world. Perceiving an unfair advantage to the developed world, these nations wanted positions to be opened up for their nationals. Since they could not afford to post their nationals to New York using meager national budgets they sought new UN positions, paid for by the UN, for which their nationals were eligible. But new funds, posts and units for information analysis were not forthcoming.

The SitCen currently has no I&R unit. The SitCen's present information gathering and reporting draws almost exclusively from UN field missions and open sources (the media in particular). It does not have the human resources even to acquire all the open source information needed for missions. Data analysis is conspicuously missing. The SitCen does no scenario-building and its links with government intelligence agencies (as well as UN agencies like the UN Development Program) ranges from weak and ad hoc to non-existent. The Brahimi Report (UN, 2000) recognized the need for intelligence and boldly proposed the creation of an "Information and Assessment Secretariat" but this proposal was resisted by many governments, despite pleas from the UN Secretariat.

In the field, there have been advances in intelligence gathering: Joint Mission Analysis Cells (JMACs) have become a standard feature in new PKOs. For instance, the present UN mission in the Congo (MONUC) provides surveillance training (however rudimentary) and deploys at airports and border flashpoints. A 2004 UN report found that much more was needed including lake patrol and air surveillance capabilities, including appropriate nocturnal, satellite, radar and photographic assets. But at headquarters the need is greatest. Further, any intelligence system needs to provide for robust data sharing between the field and headquarters in both directions.

In delving into the murky world of intelligence agencies, the UN must determine the proper balance between secrecy and openness. Given the recent emphasis on the safety of UN personnel, the balance is now swinging toward secrecy. In order to uncover secret, nefarious plots to attack UN personnel or other aid workers or to derail peace processes, the UN will need to delve more deeply into the world of terrorists and those who seek to sabotage the peace process. After the Baghdad bombing, with the loss of the chief of mission Sergio Vieira de Mello, the UN has become galvanized in its quest for prevention.[9] This involves the SitCen (whose chief is now also the focal point for security within the DPKO) and a quest to find new links to national intelligence agencies.

Should a future intelligence unit be modeled after the I&R Unit to include only nationals from the Permanent Five members of the Security Council? To do so would raise the rancor of much of the rest of the world. But without providing guarantees of confidentiality to the major powers the flow of intelligence from them would dry up. A balanced system must therefore be created based upon a strong confidentiality mechanism, expert analysis, and an effective but limited distribution mechanism. Should the UN enter into formal agreements with information/intelligence providers in various nations? Many believe this is desirable, particularly when UN missions are subject to threat. But to play in that game, the UN must become intelligence-savvy. Does it have the wherewithal to do so?

The unofficial motto of the I&R Unit was "Keeping an Eye on the World." The Unit proved that intelligence was extremely useful to understand the fast-moving currents of the Zaire crisis. It proved to be a useful early example of what can be done within the intelligence-sharing sphere. It is clear that the UN must have an even more vigilant eye if it is to be effective in its ambitious task of peacekeeping.

At the same time, the UN must determine the proper limits of its intelligence gathering and sharing, legally, politically, morally, and in terms of resources. As the UN gains more experience and an institutional evolution takes place—as in nature, in a non-linear fashion—we can hope that the UN is becoming not only more intelligence-savvy but also more intelligent.

Notes

1 The advertised "Intelligence Analyst" position was in the Investigations Section of the Office of the Prosecutor of the International Criminal Tribunal for the Former Yugoslavia. The job description was to conduct "in-depth research and analysis regarding criminal investigations of the conflict with information obtained from multiple sources related to the activities of persons under investigations" which required "specialized areas of analysis (military, police or federal/national intelligence analysis agencies)."

2 Some in the office have suggested that it played a role in warning the Secretary-General of ethnic strife in Burundi and helped with initiatives to end the Iran–Iraq War and to cope with conflicts in Sri Lanka and Fiji. Other officials in ORCI suggested that its role in these cited cases was not important and that the warning role had been played by others (author's interview with ORCI officials, 1990).

3   At the time of the ORCI's creation there were less than a half a dozen UN missions in the field, all small. By late 1993 there were over 70,000 peace-keepers under UN "operational control," in over a dozen missions, in some of the most difficult "hot spots" of the world (e.g., Bosnia, Somalia, Rwanda).

4   Initially called the "Situation Room" (SitRoom) in April 1993, the name "Situation Centre" (SitCen) was adopted in October 1993.

5   A US intelligence officer came to the I&R Unit in October 1993 and was joined two months later by a French military intelligence officer and a British logistics/intelligence officer. A Russian officer arrived in March 1995. Page numbers are not specified for quotations from I&R Unit memos.

6   An example of a disclaimer is found in the report "Zaire/Kivu," June 20, 1996: "The following text reflects a variety of informed sources, which in turn have [been] drawn from a number of individual reports. As such, the information necessarily includes elements which may be regarded by some as speculative or [that] cannot be independently substantiated." One confidentiality provision was that the reports were often "hand-numbered" and "hand-delivered" to the indicated recipients.

7   These agencies would, in turn, have relied on the traditional methods of intelligence gathering: human sources (HUMINT), signals (SIGINT), imagery (IMINT) and other technical means (measurement and signature intelligence or MASINT). They would use both open-source (OSINT) and cover methods of information gathering.

8   One I&R Unit officer, who requested anonymity, said it was obvious that the US was providing faulty satellite imagery. For instance, the sky over Kivu was perfectly clear while the pictures were alleged to have been taken recently during the rainy season, indicating that the pictures were actually from a much earlier period when refugees were much fewer. Besides, reconnaissance gathered with Mirage 4 planes showed a completely different situation.

9   At the time of the 1996 Zaire crisis, de Mello held the position of Regional Humanitarian Coordinator with the UN's Department of Humanitarian Affairs for that situation. In 2003, when he lost his life in the attack on UN headquarters in Iraq, he was the UN Envoy for Iraq and responsible for the UN mission there.

Bibliography

Adelman, Howard, and Suhrke, Astri (eds.) (1999) *The Path of a Genocide: The Rwanda Crisis from Uganda to Zaire*, Rutgers, NJ: Transaction Books.

Allen, Robert J. (1997) "Intelligence Support for Peace Operations" in Perry L. Pickert (ed.), *Intelligence for Multilateral Decision and Action*, Washington, DC: Joint Military Intelligence College.

Annan, K. (1993) "Memorandum from Mr. Annan to Mr. Baudot," New York: UN (internal memo), author's collection, June 22.

—— (1996) Transcript of press conference by Secretary-General Elect Kofi Annan (Ghana), Press Release GA/9212, December 18. Available at: http://iggi.unesco.or.kr/web/iggi_docs/01/952476023.pdf.

Baril, M. (2004) Private communication with the author, Toronto: Royal Canadian Military Institute, September 22.

—— (2005) Private communication with the author, New York: UN, February 17.

Boutros-Ghali, Boutros (1992) An Agenda for Peace: Preventive Diplomacy, Peace-making, and Peace-keeping: Report of the Secretary-General Pursuant to the

Statement adopted by the Summit Meeting Of the Security Council on 31 January 1992, New York : UN, UN Doc A/55/305 – S/2000/809.

Carlson, S. (2003) Email to the author, December 4.

Church Committee (1975) Report of the Senate Select Committee to Study Governmental Operations with Respect to Intelligence Activities, *Alleged Assassination Plots Involving Foreign Leaders*, 94th Congress, 1st Session, Senate Report 94–465, Washington: Government Printing Office.

Dallaire, Romeo (1995) "Our Man in Rwanda," Lecture to the Canadian Institute of International Affairs, Trinity College, University of Toronto, March 15.

De Jon, Ben, Plathe, Wies, and Steele, Robert David (2003) *Peacekeeping Intelligence: Emerging Concepts for the Future*, Oakton, VA: Open Source International Press.

DND (Canada) (1998) "Operation Assurance: Lessons Learned Staff Action Directive" (declassified parts), 3452–12–8 (J3 Lesson Learned), Department of National Defence, February 25.

Dorn, A. Walter (1996, 2004) Interviews on this situation were provided by the I&R Unit and SitCen officials during the Zaire crisis, November–December 1996, as well as in 2004.

—— (1998) "The Cloak and the Blue Beret: The Limits of Intelligence-gathering in Peacekeeping," Pearson Paper No. 4, Nova Scotia: Pearson Peacekeeping Centre.

Dorn, A. Walter, and Bell, David J.H. (1995) "Intelligence and Peacekeeping: The UN Operation in the Congo 1960–64," *International Peacekeeping*, 2 (1) Spring: 11–33. Available at: http://www.rmc.ca/academic/gradrech/dorn9_e.html

Dorn, A. Walter, and Matloff, J. (2000) "Preventing the Bloodbath: Could the UN have Predicted and Prevented Genocide in Rwanda?" *Journal of Conflict Studies*, XX (1) Spring: 9–52.

Interdependent, The (1987) "UN Veteran takes on New Role," *The Interdependent*, Washington: UN Association of the USA.

I&R Unit (1996) "I&R Information Memorandum, Subject: Scenario Flow Charts to Support I&R Analysis Work on Eastern Zaire," November 12, unpublished.

—— (1996–97) "Zaire/Kivu," reports dated June 20, 1996; August 26, 1996; October 24, 1996; November 4, 1996; December 19, 1996; January 1, 1997; February 6, 1997, unpublished.

Jonah, J.O.C. (1990) "Office for Research and the Collection of Information (ORCI)," in H. Chestnut (ed.), *International Conflict Resolution Using Systems Engineering: Proceedings of the IFAC Workshop in Budapest, Hungary, 5–8 June 1989*, Amsterdam: Elsevier.

New York Times (1987) "9 Senators Try to Block Funds for U.N. Office Asked by U.S.," *New York Times*, April 18.

PeaceLink for Africa Campaign (1997) "Goma/Bukavu: Eye-Witness Report November 1996–January 1997," February 19. Available at: http://web.peacelink.it/africa/za_297e.html.

Pérez de Cuéllar, Javier (1991) *Annual Report of the Secretary-General on the Work of the Organization*, General Assembly Official Records (GAOR), Supplement No. 1, UN Doc. A/46/1, September 1991, New York: UN.

Power, Samantha (2003) *A Problem from Hell: America and the Age of Genocide*, Toronto: Harper Collins.

Smith, Hugh (1994) "Intelligence and U.N. Peacekeeping," *Survival*, 36 (3) Autumn: 174–192.

UN (2000) *Brahimi Report: Report of the Panel on United Nations Peace Operations*, A/55/305, S/2000/809, New York: UN, August 21.

UN News Service (2004) "UN Experts Find Broad Rwandan Involvement in Eastern DR of Congo Conflict," New York: UN, July 21.Available at: http://www.reliefweb.int/rw/rwb.nsf/AllDocsByUNID/8119ccbcabd839dc85256 ed8006f2f0a.

7

INTERNATIONAL ANARCHY AND COALITION INTEROPERABILITY IN HIGH-TECH ENVIRONMENTS

Paul T. Mitchell[1]

The Revolution in Military Affairs is beginning to generate concrete operational concepts for the prosecution of war. Network-centric warfare (NCW) is central to the majority of these emerging operational doctrines. Despite overwhelming superiority in most indices of power, however, the US still relies on the support of allies and coalition partners to assist it in the enforcement of international order. Nevertheless, alliance operations will become increasingly difficult as the US military proceeds down the road of centralized information. Seamless interoperability, seemingly promised by NCW, will in fact remain chimerical between alliance and coalition partners because of how the international environment impacts on state behavior, especially with regards to national security. Should the US wish to maintain effective alliances rather than simply "flags at the table," it will be forced to choose between operational efficiency and strategic expediency.

Introduction

The United States is the undisputed military leader in the present international system. Few operations can be undertaken without its leadership, or at least its support. With this development comes a related issue: the rapid advance of American military technology and doctrine. While pre-eminent in power, the US has not yet reached such heights that it can operate long with impunity. Allies and coalition partners still figure prominently in US security policy. And yet, the rapid pace of technological and doctrinal developments challenges this need for cooperation. Effectively, the US, while capable of mounting large, rapid, and decisive operations to achieve certain limited ends, remains tied to its allies to assist it in maintaining international order. At the same time, however, the march of technology suggests that its allies and partners may soon be challenged in their ability to support this goal (Mitchell, 2003).

The US is not ignorant of these challenges. The role of allies is prominent in the current US national security strategy despite its discussion of pre-emption and unilateralism. Further, the US military has devoted a great deal of effort to studying the problem of coalition interoperability, particularly by its Joint Forces Command in Norfolk. Nevertheless, the nature of the current evolution of military technology and doctrine toward information-centric models presents troubling issues that may be impossible to resolve in any technological sense. In effect, the NCW paradigm, which informs all present military operational concepts, threatens the ability of allies and coalition partners to take part in American-led military operations.

This chapter suggests that the political constants, imposed by the nature of the international environment and the role played by warfare within that environment, will ultimately frustrate the desires of the US to keep its alliance partners fully engaged in its security policy. The ultimate result of this development may be increasing unilateralism in terms of American security policy, and a growing reliance on its partners to play subordinate roles, limited largely to peace support operations. This chapter will first examine the nature of NCW as its proponents, principally David Alberts and John Gartska, have described it (Alberts et al., 2001). Second, the chapter will consider the nature of international anarchy and its impact on the behavior of states in terms of what is commonly referred to as the security dilemma. Third, the chapter will look at the challenges of alliance formation and management and how the international environment shapes these issues. Last, the impact of politics on military operations will be studied through a discussion on the nature of limited warfare. Essentially, the chapter will suggest that the free flow of information desired by NCW cannot be achieved in the present international environment, and prognostications that NCW will represent a new paradigm for military operations will ultimately prove hollow for those who would seek to operate with the US, including its most trusted military allies.

NCW

The Revolution in Military Affairs has reached a sufficiently mature stage that the technological forecasts of visionaries like Admiral Bill Owens and Arthur Cebrowski are developing into doctrinal prescriptions. Theorists such as Alberts and Gartska have laid the underpinnings of these new concepts by describing how networks and information impact on military operations.

At the root of the theory, Alberts postulates the existence of three separate but related "Domains," the physical, the information, and the cognitive.

The *physical domain* is the one we are all familiar with as it is the location where humans reside and interact. Military operations take place in this domain, and it is where networks reside in a material sense. The *information domain* is where information is "created, manipulated and shared," essentially providing the conduit for the exchange of data between actors. As the study's authors suggest, it "is increasingly the information domain that must be protected and defended to enable a force to generate combat power in the face of offensive actions taken by the adversary" (Alberts et al., 2001: 2). Finally, the *cognitive domain* exists in the minds of the actors, and is where their perceptions, awareness, and understandings reside. Thus, the NCW model is the interaction between the physical domain where the events of "reality" are converted into information shared between participants in the information domain, and thence transformed into awareness and understanding in the cognitive domain (2001: 12–14).

While shared knowledge and understanding is not perfect between actors in these domains, the goal is to create a shared awareness amongst humans, programs, and technology. The level of commonality between actors' perceptions of the battlespace will impact directly on the types of operations that can be employed and the actions undertaken therein (Alberts et al., 2001: 24–26). In order to achieve the highest levels of shared awareness, each element in the physical domain must be connected to one another through a network capable of transmitting information from one part to every other. In the information domain, each element must have the ability to "share, access, and protect information to a degree that it can estimate and maintain an information advantage over an adversary" (2001: 24). Finally, in the cognitive domain, elements on the network must be capable of developing an awareness and sharing it amongst themselves (2001: 57–58).

The end result of this sharing of information and awareness is the creation of additional combat power through enhancing the utility of information provided to decision-makers. Information can be characterized by its richness (or the quality of the information), and its reach (or its ability to permeate every area on the network). Typically, in most scenarios, the higher the level of richness, the less reach it has. We see this in the case of classified information, which is generally closely held by those with a "need to know." However, those in the field with proper clearances may be unable to access this information because of their distance from those who control it. Lower-level information will spread much further along a network than the most highly classified material. This is depicted graphically in Figure 7.1.

Nevertheless, the realization of this vision in terms of current operations has to date been less than perfect, especially in coalition environments.

NCW was not a panacea for warfighting connectivity in the NATO [North Atlantic Treaty Organization] alliance setting, as realized upon examination of some unintended consequences in the Kosovo conflict. A major stumbling block was realized in the lack of US and European information interoperability, where communications were hamstrung by both equipment incompatibility and classification or releaseability mismatches.

(Stuart, 2000: 15)

While Stuart refers to releaseability concerns, the majority of analysts focusing on interoperability issues have characterized the problem as technical in nature and resolvable through upgrades and capital investment. Black (2000: 66) characterizes the issue as similar to the challenges faced by militaries in integrating their forces in a joint fashion. Others portray the issue as one of standards to be decided amongst allies in the same fashion that NATO developed its "STANAGS" (Coloumbe, 2001: 17–18). Some point out that coalition operations have always been problematic for military commanders and that technology has simply added one more degree of complexity with which they must be familiar (Geraghty, 1999: 15). However, some are beginning to recognize that the problem goes much deeper than all these concerns. Some have suggested that since the US has generally created the problem through its rapid development of technology, it must assist its partners if it truly wants them to continue to cooperate in security missions (Carr, 1999: 19; Pope, 2001: 19).

It is well recognized that NCW is changing how militaries operate in both battle and operations other than war, and that information sharing will only grow in importance as armed forces continue their never-ending quest for competitive advantage. It is also well recognized that the potential for failure in coalition operations exists should partners diverge too greatly in terms of their ability to interoperate. At the present time, however, there is still a great deal of hope that this problem can be solved through a variety of largely technical means. The search for an "interoperability black box" continues to attract the US and its partners. In the past several years, the US and its closest allies have established a number of

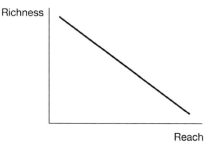

Figure 7.1 The traditional battlespace information richness and reach

venues to explore this issue. These concerns are being addressed by the ABCA (American, British, Canadian, and Australian) nations. Seven nations have established the Multinational Interoperability Council to explore common concerns. The US sponsors a yearly "Coalition Warrior Information Demonstration" where technical systems, designed to assist foreign partners to operate together and share information, are examined and tested in operational experiments. Finally, a number of "limited operational experiments" have been developed by the J9 organization of Joint Forces Command and its allied partners to test evolving concepts of information exchange in operational scenarios.

What those in either the technical or policy communities have not yet recognized is that the problem they are attempting to resolve actually may have no answer. The nature of the international environment creates policy barriers that hinder allies, even close allies, from sharing information amongst themselves in a transparent fashion. In effect, then, issues of allied and coalition interoperability are not about to fade anytime soon. The result may be that, in the face of continued rapid advancement of communication and computing technology in military operations, the US will gradually find itself able to operate with fewer and fewer partners until ultimately it may be forced to act unilaterally.

The international environment and state-to-state cooperation

To date, there has been no consideration of how the nature of the international environment, and the role states play there, will impact on the assumptions made by NCW theory on cooperation between forces of different nationalities. The principle reason for this may be because much of the literature has been written from a technical point of view. As well, the theory springs from observations of developments in the business world, especially on how major US companies, such as Walmart, have modified their business practices based on changes in the information

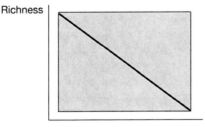

Figure 7.2 The new competitive space

technology sector. Finally, American authors writing about American developments and experiences overwhelmingly dominate the literature. Allied perspectives have been limited largely to major partners like the British, who still have some capacity for independent action and unilateral operations.[2]

Coalition operations are intensely political affairs in general, so perhaps it is not odd that they have been largely ignored in the mainstream literature on NCW.[3] The thrust of NCW is about increasing the efficiency of military operations. There may be an unstated assumption that the problems raised by coalition and alliance management may be overcome through the construction of networks and the development of an alliance-wide "common operating picture." There are serious reasons to doubt that such an unstated goal is realizable given the present nature of international relations, particularly as it relates to security affairs.

The nature of international anarchy is a well-debated affair amongst analysts of international relations. It is safe to say that most analysts congregate around four separate poles of opinion on how anarchy affects the behavior of states. Marxists, including most in the development literature, contend that anarchy is a social construct of the dominant classes in order to advance their particular interests. Constructivists share similar assumptions about the social origins of anarchy. However, they believe that it is a product of power relationships in the international system, rather than reflecting any narrow class agenda. Neo-liberal institutionalists accept the role that power plays in structuring relations between states; however, they assert that those power relations are mediated by the influence of international regimes. These regimes influence the outcomes of interactions between actors of unequal strength. Finally, Realists assert that power and its balancing between states is the primary determinate of outcomes in the international environment, including the construction of regimes and other institutions for maintaining order.

The product of Realist assumptions is the creation of a "security dilemma" wherein the state's quest for security and survival in the anarchic environment, the preparations to ensure its own welfare, lead to a decrease in security for all other members of that system. In turn, this leads to further insecurity for all states through the initiation of arms races. This is equally true in a system populated by actors all of benign intent, as it is in a system populated entirely by aggressors. As Collins (1997: 20) notes: "...it is the irresolvable uncertainty in the mind of the potential or actual target state about the meaning of the other's intentions and capabilities which create the dilemma" (see also Snyder, 1997: 17). While states may believe that few threats to their existence are present, they can never be certain if that condition will persist into the future for very long.

This paradoxical condition creates additional complications for states that attempt to alleviate their insecurity through cooperation. As Snyder (1997: 17) points out, "anarchy is the basic cause of alliances and their

Achilles' heel." Security fears create the need for alliances, and yet the same anarchic conditions lead to doubts as to the reliability of any agreement made at the international level. Lacking a "leviathan" to enforce the sanctity of contracts, parties to an international agreement can never be completely certain as to its inviolability. The moment of greatest danger for most alliances comes when it seems apparent that the *casus foederis* of the agreement is likely to be implemented. Most alliance agreements are purposefully vague on the conditions that would permit its members to request assistance from other partners. While there is a good deal of nostalgia for the Cold War and the certainty of its security environment, we must not forget that even close and effective alliances such as NATO were continually riven by disagreements that threatened to split the alliance apart.[4] While power is the motor that drives politics in the international arena, within alliances and coalitions the primary force is that of interest. Indeed, it is interest that distinguishes alliances from more limited coalitions.

According to Snyder (1997: 4), "alliances are formal associations of states for the use (or non-use) of military force, in specified circumstances, against states outside their own membership." Coalitions, rather, are based solely on common interests. Osgood agrees, stressing both the formality of agreement as the mark of a true alliance, and its obligation to use, or at least consider the use of, force. Furthermore, Osgood notes that, unlike collective security, which is simply an agreement to abstain from using force against a collective membership, alliances specify a threat around which the membership can coalesce. Alliances become a "contract" that "is simply an attempt to make more precise and binding a particular obligation or relationship between states, which is part of a continually changing network of interests" (Osgood, 1968: 18).

Both alliances and coalitions are a means of prosecuting conflict within an anarchical environment, rather than a means for preventing or lessening conflict within that environment. However, the distinguishing characteristic between alliances and coalitions are the constancy of those shared interests. While coalition partners may share a limited number of interests, they are not shared to the same depth or for the same length of time as those of true alliance partners. Indeed, coalition partners may be competitors in other issue areas, or may choose to oppose the interests of each other even on related issues. This confusing set of conditions was demonstrated easily in the recent conflict between traditional NATO partners and the United States in the lead-up to the Iraq war in 2003. While many nations like Germany, France, and Canada cooperated extensively with the US in its initial War On Terrorism, some members of that coalition actively opposed US policy in Iraq.

While shared interests and threat perceptions create dependent relationships between states in their search for security, this condition does not necessarily ensure perfect cooperation between partners, even in alliance situations. As both Chernoff and Keohane have pointed out, cooperation does not imply a perfect harmony of interests. Cooperation, rather, is the mutual adjustment of policy by two or more states (Chernoff, 1995: 17; Keohane, 1984: 54). As states can never be certain that their partners completely share their own interests, every state participates with the goal of minimizing its contribution while maximizing the obligations of its partners (Snyder, 1997: 17). This typically leads to a complex internal dynamic which, if left uncontrolled, can tear apart the alliance. Napoleon once remarked famously that he would rather fight coalitions than be a member of one. Because of the influence of anarchy and the resultant emphasis on security, the aggregate strength of alliances and coalitions can be difficult to determine. Legal, operational, and diplomatic elements all place limits on what is permissible, and thus on the very potency of an alliance. Divergent positions on legal issues, different operational doctrines, and clashes of interest all serve to slow decision-making in an alliance environment (Waxman, 1997: 40–42).

Osgood remarks that:

> In the American vision of international order, multilateral "regional" alliances have a special place because they presumably transcend and subordinate separate national interests, represent indigenous harmony and initiative, and permit the US to be one among several "partners," even if it is the senior partner.
>
> (1968: 2)

This probably explains why so many Americans were shocked and hurt by some of their allies' reactions to their policies on invading Iraq. But as Walt (1987: 26) points out, threat is the "lens" through which states perceive the environment around them. Given the global role that the US plays in the international system, it is often the hub through which threats are transmitted to its individual partners. Thus, the US may perceive threats in areas in which its allies have few engaged interests. Writing over forty years ago, Wolfers notes presciently:

> Any American military action or exercise of brinksmanship on behalf of an ally in immediate danger tends to strike other more remote allies not only as a diversion of American attention and strength to tasks of minor importance, but as a risky maneuver that may involve them all in conflicts incapable of being localized.
>
> (1952: 7)

In sum, while alliances and coalitions serve to reduce threats to a nation's security, they also reduce a state's freedom to maneuver, increase its dependency on other states in terms of obligation to come to its assistance, and introduce the possibility of catalytic conflicts. Paradoxically, alliances also lead to additional security complications for their members (Kegley and Raymond, 1990: 58–59). Thus, the requirements of collaboration and the requirements of security may often be at odds with each other, no doubt a situation acutely perceived by the Bush administration throughout last year.

This condition introduces a further paradox into alliance cohesion and management. The bargaining power of any state within an alliance is related to its overall dependency on its alliance partners. Given that states will share some but not all of their interests, and that cooperation is the mediation that occurs between these competing interests, bargaining within alliance usually assumes the form of placing the agreement deliberately at risk in order to coerce alliance partners into acquiescing. States that are able to effectively exploit asymmetrical relationships within an alliance will gain greater bargaining power (Kegley and Raymond, 1990: 55). As Snyder (1997: 170) puts it, "dependency refers to the degree of harm that partners could inflict on each other by terminating the relationship...." Those with a crucial supply of an important asset, be it military or diplomatic resources, will enjoy enhanced bargaining power with their partners. By threatening to deny access to those resources, they are able to manipulate their partners' fear of abandonment in the hopes of gaining concessions on interests that are in conflict (Walt, 1987: 43: Snyder, 1997: 171). Ravenal (1985: 23) points out that this leads to a "contradiction" between the demands of military effectiveness and political sovereignty. Likewise, Kissinger (1965: 246) notes there is an "inconsistency between the technical requirements of strategy and the political imperatives of the nation state" that cannot be resolved so long as sovereign states compose alliances.

International structure or polarity will also have an important impact on the supply of these critical resources. Structure is an important determinant of threat in the perception of states. Osgood anticipated the impact of the end of the Cold War, noting that in the absence of a Soviet threat to Western interests, "the psychological burden and political liability of maintaining American military preponderance in Europe seemingly for an indefinite period [will grow] heavier" (Osgood, 1968: 3). The polarity of the international environment will determine the rigidity of alliance obligations.

Multipolar environments are characterized by a high degree of fluidity in terms of alliances. From a purely theoretical standpoint, every power is able to form an alliance with every other power. Bipolar environments tend to be far more stable, however. Neither pole can ally with the other as each represents the only possible threat to their existence. If ideology is an important variable, the alliances each pole forms with its security partners will be similarly rigid as there are few options other than outright defection for them. As the Cold War waned, however, the declining threat from the Soviet Union permitted the NATO partners greater flexibility in arriving at positions independent from those of the United States (Kegley and Raymond, 1990: 266–267).

The present unipolar environment has had a distinct impact on how states approach security cooperation. Contemporary coalitions are characterized by the speed of their formation, the tendency to coalesce around issues of peace support and international stability, their lack of a strict hierarchy (and thus the absence of any disciplinary features), and relative lack of strong national interests guiding their creation (thus the cost of withdrawing from them is relatively small). This is to be expected when a unipole represents the sole guarantor of international order, and there is an absence of competing powers to impose a substantially different set of norms on international order, and there is general agreement that the norms represent all states' best interests. In the post Cold War period, we have tended to see far more flexible and temporary "coalitions of the willing," even when these have involved strict alliance partners such as in the Balkans, the Middle East, and Central Asia, when a variety of NATO partners assisted the US with peace support and anti-terrorism operations.

Limited war and interoperability

Gause is one of the few contributing to the literature on NCW who have recognized that interoperability is not just a question of technology but one concerning the nature of participation.

> For those allies that want to operate closely with the US in prominent positions, even in high threat environments, the level of interoperability will have to be high, possibly bordering on seamless. However, for other allies, the demands of interoperability will be lower
>
> (Gause, 2000: 7).

Still, Gause makes no mention of the role politics plays in shaping these decisions on the level of participation. How directly a state is willing to commit itself to any given conflict will have a direct impact on the level of interoperability between partners at all levels of warfare. Commitments to fight in a particular war, or decisions to align with a specific nation, are ones based on strategic rationales rather than on operational ones. Kegley and Raymond (1990: 53) note that it is possible to distinguish between alliances made during wartime and those made during peacetime. Wartime pacts are made to fight against a specific country, while peacetime pacts are usually less specific in nature.[5] Across the theoretical divide between war and peace lies an important boundary that delineates differences in terms of both commitment and compliance. Morgenthau makes a similar observation on the distinctions between pacts made by states during war and peace. He observes that, during war, alliances are frequently temporary and aimed at winning. They are general in nature and comprise the total interests of the signing parties. In peacetime, however, alliances are more commonly limited to a fraction of the total interests of a state (Morgenthau, 1970: 84). When engaged in a struggle for survival, states are usually not as choosy with whom they will align. As Churchill famously remarked on relations with Russia during the Second World War, "If Hitler invaded Hell, I would try to find some kind words to say about the Devil."

The level of commitments states are willing to make depend on the stakes involved in the conflict. States commit themselves to any given conflict along a spectrum of policy options stemming from open hostility, to neutrality, and through to outright assistance in combat. The role these limitations play in affecting operations is an important issue for determining the nature of cooperative relations between each participant. The literature on limited war has much to offer the debate over the emerging electronic environment.

Limitations in warfare are generally described in terms of geography (where operations can or cannot take place), objectives (how a state defines victory), means (what weapons a state is willing to employ in order to achieve its ends), and targeting (whether to engage in counter-force or counter-value strategies) (Garnett, 1975: 122–124; Osgood, 1968: 93). Clausewitz remarked that war naturally tends toward the maximum effort if left unchecked. However, states will not commit forces blindly to a conflict, but instead invest according to the sought-after aims and objectives. It is necessary to examine the political aim in order to determine the operational commitment and thus the limits under which a state will employ force (Clausewitz, 1976: 585–586). Even in his day, the subordination of the operational to the political must have rankled some military officers, as he alludes to in the following passage:

> ...when people talk, as they often do, about the harmful political influence on the management of war, they are not really saying what they mean. Their quarrel should be with the policy itself, not with its influence. If the policy is right—that is successful—any intentional effect it has on the conduct of the war can only be to the good. If it has the opposite effect, the policy is wrong.
>
> (Clausewitz, 1976: 607)

Cooperation in wartime is a matter conducted in much the same way between allies in peacetime, involving the coordination of policies between two or more partners. Again, Clausewitz notes:

> If two or more states combine against another, the result is still politically speaking a single war. But this political unity is a matter

of degree. The question is then whether each state is pursuing an independent interest and has its own independent means of doing so, or whether the interests and forces of most of the allies are subordinate to those of the leader. The more this is the case, the easier will it be to regard all our opponents as a single entity, hence all the easier to concentrate our principle enterprise into one great blow.

(1976: 596)

The problem, according to Clausewitz, is that state interests are never identical. Were allies mercenaries, then the issue of what they would be willing to do in order to achieve the war's objectives would be moot. However, Clausewitz observes that states enter warfare more in terms of a business deal, wherein the risk is weighed against the profit and an appropriate investment is made. "Only in recent times did the extreme danger emanating from Bonaparte ... force people to act (without additional consideration for their particular interests)" (Clausewitz, 1976: 603). One might have made the same observation of the other great alliances, those of the Second World War and NATO during the height of the Cold War.

The Cold War fundamentally distorted the understanding of the nature of alliances in the international system amongst many. It prolonged a group of like-minded states in a condition of security cooperation longer than would have been natural following the close of the Second World War. Coming immediately after the cataclysm wrought by Hitler, the challenge of the Stalinist Soviet Union was a similar "extreme danger" that for a long time subordinated Western nations' calculation of their specific self-interests in favor of a collective one oriented around national survival. The slow collapse of the communist threat to the West and the ultimate disappearance of the Soviet Union has since set up reverberations within the Western alliance that have yet to resolve themselves. Still, it is readily apparent that the calculation of interest in committing to new political objectives has become more and more blatant within NATO.

The emergence of this "natural" alliance behavior will be apparent even in the actions of the US. The original American mantra during the Cold War was most clearly spelled out by the Kennedy administration, which noted that the US was willing to go anywhere and pay any price without a second's reflection. It was the doctrine of automatic, reflexive commitment, of "strategic coupling," and assured destruction. But in the current unipolar environment, America has moved more cautiously, reluctantly involving itself in commitments only after having been browbeaten into them, as in the Balkans and Africa, or having been dragged into the conflict by the pace of events, as in the Middle East or Central Asia. Vital interests, "that is [those] interests that are worth supporting militarily at the cost that must be paid" (Osgood, 1968: 5), can no longer be simply taken as a given but must be calculated anew for each confrontation.

Similarly, the interests of America's traditional allies cannot be taken for granted as they could often be during the Cold War. Alliance cohesion has become remarkably more problematic in the post Cold War environment, with each new American overseas engagement attracting more and more allied debate. With each new commitment, the ability of the Western alliance to speak with a single voice has declined, and with it, NATO's ability to make threats to its adversaries. This was readily apparent in the wrangling that occurred over Kosovo, and its impact on prolonging the war there (see especially Daalder and O'Hanlon, 2001).

Indeed, who is defined as an "adversary" has itself become increasingly problematic. As Clausewitz concluded:

> No one starts a war ... without first being clear in his mind what he intends to achieve by that war and how he intends to conduct it. The former is the political purpose; the latter its operational objective. This is the governing principle which will set its course, prescribe the scale of means and effort which is required and make its influence felt throughout down to the smallest operational detail.
>
> (1976: 574)

And yet in coalitions and alliances, because of different interpretations of the nature of the problem or threat, and the uncertainty that surrounds allied reliability, these issues are precisely the ones that become the most highly politicized. As Walt (1987: 1) notes, "The forces that bring states together and drive them apart will affect the security of individual states by determining both how large a threat they face and how much help they can expect." Some will face more threat than others, and some states will attract more support than others. In turn, operations themselves become charged with political significance rather than being conducted in the most efficient fashion possible. In other words, in alliance endeavors, unless it is an issue of pure and immediate survival, politics will always trump strict military necessity.

NCW and alliances: can there be seamless interoperability?

In many ways, the United States has been successful in finding work-around solutions to the issues of connectivity raised in the first section. While there were significant interoperability problems in the Balkans, many of these issues were resolved through the installation of technology in allied formations. Similarly, the US often devises procedural workarounds in order to facilitate greater allied cooperation. This has been most evident in Canadian participation in American carrier battle group operations and to a limited extent, the naval operations of the War on Terrorism. There would seem to be an upper limit on just how far the US is able or willing to solve some of these connectivity issues, however. This limit is defined first by the demands for information security, and second, by the nature of trust between partners.

Efficiency is the principle that animates the quest for information centralization under the NCW concept. Universal access to common databases will lead to shared awareness, and thus to the harmonization of operational goals and the elimination of inefficiencies in achieving them. As we have already seen, the animus that underlies alliances, however, is not that of efficiency but rather that of interest. Alliance operations are frequently marked by infighting and competition. NCW might be one tool for alleviating these problems in the hopes of generating a "common operating picture" or the development of a "shared awareness" between alliance partners.

However, the barrier to this is the difficulty in sharing information between partners. Information-release policies are purposefully inefficient tools in order to protect the information, the sources used to gain it, and the organizations using the information from the harm that would result from disclosure to hostile forces (McKerow, 2001: 2; Spring et al., 2000: 29–34; Chekan, 2001: 9–23). "Information release and control must be conducted in a manner that prevents damaging foreign disclosure [;] this capability must be demonstrated to information owners" before any transfer can be effected (Spring et al., 2000: 7). Information, and what it may imply about the systems that collected it, or the operational goals and capabilities of the organization that is collecting it, may be too sensitive to be entrusted to others. Further, because the long-term effect of individual disclosures can be difficult to ascertain, and because the career impact of improper disclosure is so serious, "commanders often choose stringent release rules to avoid problems" (Chekan, 2001: 11). In this way, releaseability concerns have dictated separated networks operating at different tempos. As Brigadier-General Gary Salisbury, Director of Command, Control, and Communications Systems for the US European Command, characterized the situation in September 2001:

> How do [combined planners] get these national communication and information needs and fit these into a coalition environment? The bottom line is we are generally operating two different networks at two different security levels. We run our networks at a coalition releaseability level that's basically unclassified.
>
> (Kenyon, 2001)

Dwight D. Eisenhower famously remarked, "Allied Commands depend on mutual confidence" (Spierto, 1999: 3). Like relinquishing command and control, releasing sensitive information is an act of trust between states surpassed only, perhaps, by placing troops under even the limited control of an ally; releasing closely held knowledge places technology, operations, and even personnel at risk (see, for example, Riscassi, 1993). "Trust involves a willingness to be vulnerable and to assume risk. Trust involves some form of dependency" (Chekan, 2001: 4). As we have seen, the international environment through the medium of anarchy makes trust exceedingly difficult to achieve, even in alliance contexts. Further, alliance partners generally exploit dependencies in order to enhance their control over alliance policies. Thus, we can expect that just as nations have always been unwilling to place complete control of their troops under the control of foreign nations, they will be unwilling to share completely all information they have: "As close as ... Canadian and British allies are in common interests and objectives, there will always be limits to sharing the most highly classified information with these nations" (Pope, 2001: 6). In the past, this reluctance did not typically jeopardize operations. However, with NCW information is the cornerstone of all action; the existence of separate networks operating at different speeds will have an undeniable impact on battle rhythms.

NCW, then, will have an enormous bearing on how alliances, and particularly coalitions, will conduct their operations in the future. The United States is certainly willing to share most of its information with certain partners. However, for nations with forces that don't belong to this privileged club, integration into US networks will be increasingly difficult, depending on how often they operate with the US forces and the degree of trust extended to them. Forces not permitted to take part in planning will ultimately be restricted simply to taking orders—possibly to assume high-casualty or politically distasteful roles (IDR, 2002; Kiszely, 1999; Oxendine, 2000: 19; Smith, 2001: 3). The added risk is that multinational operations will become more and more circumscribed, and that allied participation will be accepted only under the most restrictive circumstances. The US is unlikely to hamstring its own military forces or to slow its implementation of NCW given its perceptible benefits. It may decide simply to "pass" entirely on alliance participation (Carr, 1999: 15–16). Information releaseability policy would ultimately decide, then, not only the shape and nature of coalitions, but also possibly even their very existence. Finally, the unipolar nature of the current international environment will likely place additional barriers to information sharing between states, particularly between the United States and its allies. Armed as it is with the full panoply of information garnered by its worldwide intelligence services, the US will provide more than the lion's share of information to its partners and only seek highly specialized intelligence from them. Furthermore, the unipolar environment itself will generate increasing distrust amongst alliance partners as the role of independent national interests in shaping policy becomes stronger.

There are sound reasons for pursuing greater efficiency in military operations. However, much technical change is pursued for operational reasons. Often, strategic rationales for technical modernization are a secondary matter. In the present quest to maintain its technological superiority, the US is pursuing a clear strategic interest, which is enunciated in its national security strategy. As information becomes more central to this quest for military superiority, however, the shadow of unilateralism will loom heavily. States will continue to share information amongst themselves; however, perfect transparency in the form of "seamless interoperability" will be chimerical. Information will simply be too central to the competitive advantages offered by NCW to be jeopardized by automatic disclosure. It may happen on a case-by-case basis, depending on the nature of the conflict and the partners with whom the US is cooperating. But the dictates of sovereignty will ensure that seamless interoperability will remain confined to the realm of the speculative while the present international environment persists.

Notes

1   The views of the chapter are those of the author alone and do not represent those of the Department of National Defence (Canada) or the Canadian Forces College.
2   The exception here may be Sweden, which is busy implementing a mature network-centric system in its own armed forces. Still, Sweden has a long tradition of neutrality and coalition operations do primarily inform its operational ethos in the way that they inform the operations of major NATO partners.
3   Those studies that examine the issue are largely still the province of students at military staff and war colleges. There are no major works on NCW and coalition operations in the mainstream literature, despite at least six to seven years of operational experience in implementing some of these emerging concepts in Bosnia, Kosovo, Afghanistan, Iraq, and numerous naval operations in the Mediterranean and Arabian seas.
4   Disputes over strategic doctrine ultimately led to the departure of France from the integrated command structure in 1967. Similarly, differences over how relations with the Soviet Union should be handled (in the form of Germany's "*Ostpolitik*" and America's "*détente,*" the role that nuclear weapons should play in defending Western Europe, the level of commitment to self-defense by NATO members ("burden sharing")), all led to highly divisive debates between alliance members. Indeed, the debate over the "follow on to Lance," or FOTL, occurred right up to the collapse of the Soviet state.
5   Peacetime alliances generally limit themselves to defensive pacts calling for mutual support in case of attack, non-aggression treaties, or limited ententes (Kegley and Raymond, 1990: 53).

Bibliography

Alberts, D., Gartska, J., Hayes, R.E., and Signori, D.A. (2001) *Understanding Informations Age Warfare*, Mclean, VA: Command and Control Research Project (CCRP), August.

Black, M.B., Maj., USA (2000) *Coalition Command, Control, Communications, Computer and Intelligence Systems Interoperability: A Necessity or Wishful Thinking?* thesis, US Army Command and General Staff College, Fort Leavenworth, Kansas, June 2, p. 66.

Carr, J., Cdr., USN (1999) "Network Centric Coalitions: Pull, Pass, or Plug-in?" course paper, Naval War College, Newport, RI, May 15, p. 19.

Chekan, R., Col., CF (2001) "The Future Of Warfare: Clueless Coalitions?" unpublished paper, Toronto: Canadian Forces College, October, pp. 9–23.

Chernoff, F. (1995) *After Bipolarity: The Vanishing Threat, Theories of Cooperation and the Future of the Atlantic Alliance*, Ann Arbor: University of Michigan Press, p. 17.

Clausewitz, K. von (1976) *On War*, Princeton: Princeton University Press, pp. 585–586.

Collins, A. (1997) *The Security Dilemma and the End of the Cold War*, Edinburgh: Keele University Press, p. 20.

Coloumbe, R.L., Maj., USMC (2001) "Operational Art and NATO C4I: An Oxymoron?" course paper, Department of Joint Military Operations, US Naval War College, Newport, RI, February 5, pp. 17–18.

Daalder, I., and O'Hanlon, M. (2001) *Winning Ugly*, Washington: Brookings Institute.

Garnett, J. (1975) "Limited War," in John Baylis, Ken Booth, John Garnett, and Phil Williams (eds.), *Contemporary Strategy: Theories and Policies*, Beckham, UK: Croom Helm, pp. 122–124.

Gause, K. (19??) "US Navy Interoperability with its High-End Allies," unpublished paper, p. 7.

Geraghty, B.A., Cdr., USN (1999) "Will Network Centric Warfare be the Death Knell for Allied/Coalition Operations?" course paper, Department of Joint Military Operations, US Naval War College, Newport, RI, May 17, p. 15.

Gramer, G.K., Col., USA (1999) "Optimizing Intelligence Sharing in a Coalition Environment: Why US Operational Commanders have an Intelligence Dissemination Problem," course paper, Department of Joint Military Operations, US Naval War College, Newport, RI, May 17, pp. 2–3.

IDR (2002) "General Warns over Digitization Split," *International Defence Review*, January 1.

Kegley, C.W., Jr., and Raymond, G.A. (1990) *When Trust Breaks Down: Alliance Norms and World Politics*, Columbia, SC: University of South Carolina, pp. 58–59.

Kenyon, H.S. (2001) "Alliance Forces Move Toward Unified Data Infrastructure," *Signal*, September.

Keohane, R. (1984) *After Hegemony*, Princeton: Princeton University Press, p. 54.

Kissinger, H.A. (1965) *The Troubled Partnership*, New York: McGraw Hill, p. 246.

Kiszely, J. (1999) "Achieving High Tempo – New Challenges," Royal United Services Institution Journal, December 1999.

McKerow, G. (2001) "Multilevel Security Networks: An Explanation of the Problem," *SANS Information Security Reading Room*, February 5, p. 2. Available at: rr.sans.org/standards/multilevel.php,

Mearsheimer, J.J. (2001) *The Tragedy of Great Power Politics*, New York: W.W. Norton & Co., pp. 30–31.

Mitchell, P.T. (2003) "Small Navies and Network Centric Warfare: Is There a Role?" *Naval War College Review*, LVI (2): Spring.

Morgenthau, H.J. (1970) "Alliances," in Julian R. Friedman, Christopher Bladen, and Steven Rosen (eds.), *Alliance in International Politics*, Boston: Allyn & Bacon Inc., p. 84.

Osgood, R.E. (1968) *Alliances and American Foreign Policy*, Baltimore, MD: Johns Hopkins University Press, p. 18.

Oxendine, E., IV (2000) *Managing Knowledge in the Battle Group Theatre Transition Process*, student thesis, Monterey CA: Naval Postgraduate School, September, p. 19.

Pope, W.R., LTC, USA (2001) *U.S. and Coalition Command and Control Interoperability for the Future*, thesis, US Army War College, Carlisle, PA, April, p. 19.

Ravenal, E.C. (1985) *NATO: The Tides of Discontent*, Berkeley: Institute for International Studies, University of California at Berkeley, p. 23.

Riscassi, R.W. (1993) "Principles for Coalition Warfare," *Joint Forces Quarterly*, Summer.

Smith, E. (2001) "Network Centric Warfare: What's the Point?" *Naval War College Review*, 54 (1), Winter: 3.

Snyder, G.H. (1997) *Alliance Politics*, Ithaca, NY: Cornell University Press, p. 17.

Spierto, T. (1993) [Lt. Cdr Robert W. Riscassi, "Principles for Coalition Warfare," *Joint Forces Quarterly*, Summer 1993.., USN] "Compromising the Principles of War: Technological Advancements Impact Multinational Military Operations," course paper, Naval War College, Newport, RI, February 5, p. 3.

Spring, S.C., Gormley, D.M., McMahon, K.S., Smith, K., and Hobbs, D. (2000) "Information Sharing for Dynamic Coalitions," unpublished paper, Arlington, VA: Pacific Sierra Research, VPSR Report 2836, December, pp. 29–34.

Stuart, R.M., Capt., USN (2000) "Network Centric Warfare in Operation Allied Force: Future Promise or Future Peril?" course paper, Department of Joint Military Operations, US Naval War College, Newport, RI, May 16, p. 15.

Walt, S.M. (1987) *The Origins of Alliances*, Ithaca: Cornell University Press, p. 26.

Waltz, K. (1979) *Theory of International Politics*, New York: Random House, p. 88.

Waxman, M.C. (1997) "Coalitions and Limits on Coercive Diplomacy," *Strategic Review*, Winter: 40–42.

Wolfers, A. (1952) "'National Security' as an Ambiguous Symbol," *Political Science Quarterly*, 67 (4) December: 7.

8

PEACEKEEPING INTELLIGENCE AND CIVIL SOCIETY

Is civil–military cooperation the missing link?

Christopher Ankersen

Introduction

A parish priest announced to his congregation one Sunday that he had good news and bad news. The good news, he said, was that all the money needed to fund the ministries of the church was in the room at that moment. The bad news, he continued, was that it was still in the pockets of the parishioners. This situation approximates that of intelligence in peacekeeping: all the information necessary to guarantee mission success exists, the only problem is that it resides within the population. The fact that all key information (concerning the movements and intentions of belligerents, for instance) is with "*them*" rather than "*us*" is not only problematic from the point of view of where it resides, there seems also to be no easy way to acquire it. As one commentator of peacekeeping notes, "No one who has been in a recent peacekeeping operation ... can fail to recognise [the] desperation in trying to gather intelligence from local people who seem to be pathological liars"' (Bellamy, 1996: 73).

Enter civil–military cooperation (CIMIC). This is defined by the Canadian military as

> all measures undertaken between commanders and national authorities, civil, military and para-military, which concern the relationship between the Canadian Forces, the national governments and civil populations in an area where Canadian military forces are deployed or plan to be deployed, supported, or employed. Such measures would also include cooperation and co-ordination of activities between commanders and non-governmental or international agencies, organizations and authorities.
>
> (DND (Canada), 1999a: 55)

Fundamentally, CIMIC is the interface between soldiers and civilians on the battlefield and on peace support operations, and it is often viewed as the best "way in" to the local populace. Win over these "hearts and minds," so the thinking goes, and intelligence will flow readily (Boot, 2002: 297). For the purposes of this chapter, intelligence will be defined as "a term used to describe both the activities to acquire and process information and the product resulting from that process. Essentially, intelligence is information and knowledge about a belligerent obtained through observation, investigation, analysis, or understanding" (DND (Canada), 2001: 4).

It is not only strategic decision-makers who have come to the conclusion that information is the real aim of CIMIC operations; many in the so-called humanitarian space also believe that intelligence gathering is the motivating logic that underlies military CIMIC activity. Accordingly, there are concerns that CIMIC is a poisoned chalice and that it reduces the "good" that can be achieved. As Gordon notes:

> For many, [the] integration [of CIMIC] threatens to subordinate humanitarian action to political objectives with the result that humanitarian action may potentially be less able to alleviate the human suffering that is the essential heart of humanitarian action. In effect "integration" may serve to undermine humanitarian action by transforming it from a fundamental and inalienable right of those in need into simply another tool of diplomacy.
>
> (Gordon, 2004)

Further, CIMIC is not only a threat to the philosophical foundations of humanitarian action, but to the physical safety of non-governmental organizations (NGOs) and local populations. Accordingly, OXFAM has issued clear direction with regard to CIMIC and information sharing:

> Before, during and after any conflict, a clear channel of communication must be available for timely exchange between humanitarian organisations and, under the coordination of the UN, military forces. However, Oxfam will not provide any information that may endanger communities or risk the security of our staff. We will not provide information for military purposes.
>
> (Oxfam, 2003: 3)

CIMIC is not, according to this view, merely cooperation for the good of an affected population, but rather a purely instrumental pursuit, aimed not at ameliorating the condition of conflict-affected people, but merely as a means of extracting information in return for aid (Barry and Jeffreys, 2002).

The relationship between CIMIC and intelligence is somewhat more complicated than either of these perspectives might suggest. While information is elicited through the practice of CIMIC, intelligence gathering is not CIMIC's only aim. Further, rather than acting as a silver bullet solution to information acquisition, CIMIC is a subtle and indirect tool. This chapter will highlight the realities of CIMIC and intelligence on peacekeeping missions, focusing on Canadian experiences in the Balkans and Afghanistan.

While humanitarians and soldiers have long operated together on the battlefield, the emergence of CIMIC as a non-wartime activity is relatively new (Slim, 1997). The events of the 1990s throughout the Balkans and Africa were the defining moments of modern CIMIC doctrine and practice for both Western militaries and international NGOs. Because of the complex nature of the conflicts to which peacekeepers and humanitarians were responding, the nexus between conflict and development could not be ignored by either set of actors. Both groups found that a certain degree of "joint action" (either in the form of cooperation or coordination) was necessary (Duffield, 2001). Unlike war, which sees civil and military activity as either fully separate (e.g. refugee returns after combat) or completely integrated (e.g. military administration of occupied or liberated territory), peacekeeping missions necessitate far more ambiguous relations between soldiers and humanitarians (Abiew and Keating, 1999; Eriksson, 2000; Byman, 2001). Indeed, while many in either camp would like to avoid any kind of relationship with the other, there is a common factor that links them inexorably: the local population.

The local population in a post-conflict situation is a complex organism. It is a site of extreme trauma (hence the presence of the humanitarian) and an object to be protected from further harm (hence the presence of the peacekeeper). However, it is also the source of future peace or conflict. It is this latent and contingent aspect that cements aid worker and soldier together: the seeds of both success and failure are sown in the society within which they operate. For the military to achieve its mission (either in the idealized form of creating a "stable and secure" environment or in the cynical form of executing an "exit strategy"), it must work with and amongst the local populace. In a peacekeeping scenario, defeating the "bad guys" is either out of the question because of the limits of political mandates or the rules of engagement, or has been already largely accomplished, at least at the level of organized and armed military formations. What remains to be done, however, is no less daunting: domestic society must be first stabilized and then freed from those elements which pose a threat to locals and elements of the international community (including the peacekeeping force itself).

Peacekeeping operations have many military objectives, including the establishment of an armed presence, the separation of former warring parties, monitoring of disarmament activities, "direct action" against belligerent opponents, and the like. These activities are aimed at "achieving" or "keeping" the peace. In order to progress to the next level, some form of "peacebuilding" is increasingly part of the military's mandate. In Bosnia, Canadian military commanders put it thus:

> CIMIC forms [the] link between the military mission and civilian communities/public institutions. [It is] involved in political, economic, social and cultural aspects of the mission area. [It is the] primary link between military and NGOs [and it] forms the main effort for "nation building" part of the SFOR mission.[1]

CIMIC, then, allows the military to "enter" the local population and attempt to fulfill this component of their mission. Let us now turn to Canadian experiences in Bosnia and Afghanistan to see how this "entrance" was carried out and how intelligence is bound up in the process.

CIMIC as "force protection"

At its simplest, CIMIC is viewed as a means of gaining support for the peacekeeping mission. If building schools and feeding some of the hungry can reduce the amount of rock throwing, mine laying, and ambushes targeted at military forces, then that in itself is an achievement. As one Canadian commander in Bosnia put it, "CIMIC offered an opportunity to enhance force protection by demonstrating to the local population that we were there to support them." CIMIC, then, is the means by which the peacekeeping force engages with the local population in order to "tame" or "soothe" them. Humanitarian relief (in the form of emergency food and clothing) and small development projects (such as basic infrastructure reconstruction) are used to this end. In short, the logic behind "CIMIC as force protection" is that people will not bite the hands that feed them.

In this regard, the relationship between CIMIC and intelligence is quite straightforward. The primary CIMIC function is to placate the locals, and the intelligence aspect of this effort is twofold. First, information may be traded for assistance. Aid becomes conditional on "good behavior," a component of which is seen as a reliable flow of information about possible threats. Second, the process of moving amongst the population, handing out food or supervising projects, allows for opportunities for contact with locals, both the "rank and file" and the leadership. The following guidance to Canadian troops operating in southern Afghanistan in 2002 as a part of the American-led Operation Enduring Freedom illustrates this aspect of CIMIC:

> Any HA [humanitarian aid] distributed should be targeted and deliberate. No aid should be given without a deliberate intent of gaining the support of the local populace, and therefore increasing

our force protection and engendering a strong flow of HUMINT [human intelligence].

An article written for the families of soldiers serving in Afghanistan at this time expands on this point:

> Our patrols involve Canadian soldiers meeting and interacting with the local population in as friendly and non-threatening a way as possible. We voice our concerns (through interpreters), and they voice theirs. We want to preserve the security of the airfield, and we can best do that by developing a close relationship with our neighbours in the airfield vicinity.... It's in everybody's best interests to get Afghanistan back on its feet. In the short-term, we want to keep villagers on our side, so that they can help us detect Al Qaeda and Taliban elements that are still active in Kandahar province. Last week, local farmers pointed out a landmine that had been laid on a road in our sector. A few days ago, a local boy showed us to three rockets that had been fired at but missed the airfield.

The last two lines of this article highlight the mark of success in such CIMIC–intelligence operations: threats defeated because locals—through some sense of compassion, loyalty, or disdain for the belligerents—informed the peacekeepers.

As a result of its obvious focus on force protection, this kind of intelligence is most effective at the tactical level, providing early warning to deployed troops through local contacts. By 2000, this kind of low-level CIMIC-related intelligence was credited as providing 60–70 per cent of all information received at the battalion level within Canadian elements of North Atlantic Treaty Organization's Force (NATO's SFOR). However, there are suggestions that, in Afghanistan at least, the importance of CIMIC-related intelligence might extend beyond the unit level. One report credits CIMIC-based intelligence gathering with providing evidence of "active disinformation by [a foreign] intelligence [agency] about Canadian CIMIC efforts."

Despite its less than altruistic nature, CIMIC as a source of force protection has an interesting effect on the relationship between military and humanitarian actors. When information is obtained by the military that relates to the safety or security of international or local governmental or non-governmental organizations, it can be passed on. From time to time, this information is ignored, often because it must be couched in such a way as to protect the means by which it was obtained in the first place, and therefore can lack a certain "authentic" feel.

However, force-protection information also forms the core of what NGOs consider "acceptable information" that they can share, thereby adding to the volume of potentially useful intelligence available to a military peacekeeping force. A reference paper authored by the IASC following military action in Afghanistan and Iraq, stresses that, despite misgivings by humanitarian actors, there are times when certain information should be exchanged with armed forces:

> [In order] to provide protection and humanitarian assistance to populations in need, information sharing with the military forces may at times become necessary. In particular, information that might affect the security of civilians and/or humanitarian workers should be shared with appropriate entities. Information sharing between humanitarian and appropriate military actors may include:
>
> a security information;
> b humanitarian locations;
> c humanitarian activities;
> d mine-action activities;
> e population movements;
> f relief activities of the military; and
> g post-strike information.
>
> (IASC, 2004: 12)

Information that fits into these categories, and therefore can be passed on by international organizations and NGOs has immense value to military intelligence organizations for obvious reasons.

The potential of NGOs as a source of intelligence is not lost on the military; there is respect for both their "grassroots" access as well as the length of time they have spent within a country, time which allows them to get to know both the conditions and the personalities at play within a society (DND (Canada), 1999a: 102–103). NGO weariness of the military desire to "tap into" this deep well of information is best articulated in the Code of Conduct of the International Committee of the Red Cross:

> we will never knowingly—or through negligence—allow ourselves, or our employees to be used to gather information of a political, military or economically sensitive nature for governments or other bodies that may serve purposes other than those which are strictly humanitarian, nor will we act as instruments of foreign policy of donor governments.
>
> (ICRC, 1995: Art. 4)

It is evident that there is an inherent tension between sharing strictly humanitarian information and providing militaries with "useful" intelligence that cannot be resolved easily.

CIMIC as "information operations"

The CIMIC–intelligence relationship goes well beyond first-order force-protection matters. Force protection, while important, is essentially a "wait and see" defensive tactic; aid is distributed and development assisted in the hopes that information can be acquired. There is often a more active component to CIMIC, one which aims to not only protect soldiers but to change the behavior of the local population. For example, in Bosnia the Canadian commander stated that by 2002, at least, "CIMIC [was] involved in both changing the behavior of locals and influencing that behavior (carrot and stick)." Accordingly, the desired results of CIMIC "community improvement projects" were many:

1   reward reform-minded leaders/communities;
2   deter obstructionism;
3   build public confidence and long-term hope;
4   increase civic awareness and identity;
5   build inter-ethnic cooperation; and
6   improve community relations with SFOR.

In order to understand how CIMIC can be expected to accomplish all of these results, the concept of Information Operations must be explored.

When the military speaks of Information Operations, it is asserting that missions can be accomplished with more than mere raw firepower or brute force. Information is power, and that power can be harnessed to achieve objectives. While not entirely new (the work of Sun Tzu stresses these concepts) Information Operations as an integrated approach is relatively novel and its application to peacekeeping newer still. At its heart is an attempt to integrate the diverse "informational" fields of public affairs, psychological operations, intelligence, and CIMIC so that they all might assist a commander in prosecuting a battle, campaign, or war. The aim of Information Operations is "information superiority gained by the optimum exploitation of information and by denying the same capability to any adversary" (DND (Canada), 1999a: iii).

CIMIC is a two-way conduit for information, and therefore, a means to achieving information superiority: messages can be sent out to the population during the course of CIMIC activities and the effect of those messages can be monitored through the collection of intelligence. More than that though, CIMIC is not just seen as a shield, but as a lever for accomplishing the wider peacekeeping mission. This is in accordance with Canadian Information Operations doctrine, which states that

> CIMIC provides the interface with critical actors and influences in the [global information environment]. Whether in peace, conflict, or war, the conduct of a successful operation often depends on

111

CIMIC support, in some cases CIMIC may even be the main effort. Although conditions differ across the spectrum of conflict, CIMIC activities establish, maintain, influence, or exploit relations among military forces, civil authorities, and the civilian populace in an [area of operations] to facilitate operations.

(DND (Canada), 1999a: 24)

CIMIC is not only an activity undertaken to improve the lives of the local population, or as a simple source of information about threats to the peacekeeping force. As a component of a larger Information Operations campaign, CIMIC helps to gather information that a commander will need in order to make decisions. Are the locals content? What are their concerns? What needs to be done? The answers to these kinds of questions allow commanders to "fine tune" their activities, changing the emphasis from, say, deterring aggression from military elements, to addressing intimidation from organized criminal groups or reducing corruption and political thuggery. So if CIMIC as an intelligence source represents a "pull," then CIMIC as a conduit for influence represents a "push." As a commander of Canadian troops put it: "Civil military interface can provide useful intelligence [which] allows you to see the direction of the conflict, to figure out what the drivers are. The more you know, the more influence you have, the better you can push the right levers. The value of CIMIC is getting the real idea as to who's who."

The process in Afghanistan in 2002 was not dissimilar. Rather than conducting CIMIC projects in their own right, other elements were combined to achieve a synergistic effect—the holy grail of information operations. So-called "PIC Patrols" were formed, whereby elements of psychological operations, intelligence, and CIMIC were integrated into single tactical groups. These groups would travel through villages, stopping to discuss with locals topics such as the arrival or departure of young men in the area, any knowledge of upcoming para-military or terrorist activity, or the pre-occupation identity and role of key actors in the community. Often these discussions were predicated on, or revolved around, CIMIC projects (either those completed, underway, or required in the future). Patrols would visit wells or schools that had been completed in a village, and use this opportunity to gather, and disseminate, more information. As a result, it could be claimed that the intelligence non-commissioned officer that took part in these "PIC Patrols" "became the best int[elligence] source in the brigade." He was connected to the local population in a way that few intelligence personnel were, especially in an environment where HUMINT collection by Westerners is difficult. As well as the intelligence gathered, messages were disseminated, hence the "pschological operations" component of the "PIC" concept. Those messages ranged from "we are here to help you" to "keep the Taleban and Al Qaeda out of your village and all will be good."

Challenges for CIMIC

Despite the fact that the CIMIC–intelligence relationship has been successful militarily, there are also many challenges associated with it. First, getting the relationship right is extremely hard to do. While the Information Operations concept is widely acknowledged as "best practice," it has not been replicated everywhere: for instance, according to one of its own intelligence officers, the Australian Defence Force failed to integrate CIMIC fully into such a framework in their East Timor peacekeeping mission (Blaxland, 2002).

Second, while at a theoretical level having CIMIC operatives acting as "intelligence sources" seems feasible, the reality proves more difficult. CIMIC personnel are often untrained in intelligence gathering and can lack the necessary "situational awareness" of wider intelligence issues that would allow them to be of more than basic assistance. Indeed, in Bosnia, despite rhetoric from commanders to the contrary, one intelligence officer confided that he relied on CIMIC personnel only for "passive collection, which amounts to a series of requests to 'report if observed.' I don't expect a lot from them, but they do provide raw data which sometimes acts as a trigger for further investigation." This lack of skill can be exacerbated by a lack of enthusiasm. Many CIMIC personnel resent their "double role" and prefer to concentrate on what they see as the more important (and certainly more personally rewarding) job of actually helping the local population. As one CIMIC officer who worked in Kosovo exclaimed, "Why the hell else are we there?"

Third, gauging the real success of the CIMIC–intelligence interface can be extremely difficult, in either its "force-protection" or "information operations" guise. The necessary metrics for determining "lives saved due to tips from locals directly attributable to CIMIC efforts" are simply impossible to design, let alone observe. In fact, relying on CIMIC as a shield can be misleading: at the beginning of the Fallujah uprising in 2004, a CNN reporter asked a bewildered US Army captain why the Iraqis were shooting at his company. He responded by saying that he had no idea; he and his men had recently completed over 100 community improvement projects and the Iraqis should not be reacting the way they were. Nonetheless, if Western militaries are able to help reduce casualties in their peacekeeping forces, even if purely hypothetically, the price of a few humanitarian or development projects will not be seen as a burden. One life saved because of a bomb not planted will be seen as worthwhile.

Fourth, as peacekeeping continues to evolve, CIMIC and intelligence will have increasingly important roles to play. The phenomenon of Provincial Reconstruction Teams (PRTs), which will see a variety of actors, such as those involved in conflict resolution, "nation building," and humanitarian relief, working closely with military forces in the hinterland of Afghanistan, will test the already tenuous relationships in this space to their breaking point. Concepts of cooperation, coordination, and conditionality will collide and existing debates over the relationship between traditional military activities, such as intelligence gathering, and hybrid affairs such as multi-stakeholder development, will intensify (see Watkins, 2003).

Finally, it must be remembered that, just as with all aspects of peacekeeping, there is no such thing as a one-size fits all approach to CIMIC and intelligence. National differences regarding how CIMIC is to be carried out are compounded by national differences regarding how intelligence is to be gathered, analyzed, and disseminated. The resulting picture makes generalized statements and reactions inappropriate (Landon and Hayes, 2003). While this chapter has focused on Canadian operations, a similar study of American, British, or Dutch CIMIC activity (for example) may well reveal other issues.

Conclusion

There can be no doubt that the trepidation expressed by many NGOs is well founded when it comes to CIMIC's underlying objective. Gordon (2004) puts it mildly when he states that "...there is pressure to sweep civil–military co-operation (CIMIC) into military effects based planning structures; increasing the pressure on 'CIMIC' planners to achieve an operational or strategic effect linked within a strategic framework" (n.p.). CIMIC is an instrumental activity; of this there can be no doubt: "CIMIC elements support military operations by applying their skills and experience in host nation support public administration, economics, public facilities, linguistics, cultural affairs, and civil information and *by collecting information relevant to the [Commander's Critical Information Requirements]*" (DND (Canada), 1999a: 24, emphasis added).

This fact puts humanitarian organizations in a difficult position: they feel increasing pressure to cooperate with military forces, especially on peacekeeping missions, but cannot stomach any attempt to use humanitarian work for non-humanitarian purposes. In this light, the threat posed by alleged "secret" military operatives dressed in civilian clothing, handing out aid in return for information (Gordon, 2004: n.p.) becomes secondary to the overt uniformed collection of intelligence in the course of CIMIC activities. How can they be sure that any information they share will not be used for purely military purposes? How can CIMIC relief and development work be accepted and integrated into a larger humanitarian framework?

As the recent departure of Médicins sans Frontières (MSF) from Afghanistan demonstrates, some in the aid business have decided that the situation is unworkable. This poses problems not only for the military (in that it challenges the legitimacy of their activities by casting them in a negative light), but also the humanitarian community. MSF may have won the battle by refusing to work alongside the military, but they are no longer even fighting the war against real suffering in Afghanistan. In the words of their own Secretary-General Marine Buissonnière, "Ultimately, it is the sick and destitute who suffer" (MSF, 2004). In the complex emergencies that necessitate contemporary peacekeeping, there is no room for one-dimensional responses. As Pugh (1997: 192) notes, "the main challenge is to maintain the military–humanitarian link, not to ban it." For as important as the humanitarian contribution is, military CIMIC activities also make significant inroads into local communities. Military projects to restore clean water, to renovate schools, and to construct private dwellings should not be ignored. Vast sums of money and real talent are harnessed to produce tangible results, which can help to improve the lives of local populations. Further, these efforts might also contribute to the creation of sustainable peace. The military should be cautious not to jeopardize these achievements in favor of short-sighted and ham-fisted attempts to leverage information from humanitarian partners or the local populace.

Note

1   All of the primary data collected for this study was done on the basis of non-attribution, often through personal interviews. Therefore no references are made as to sources of "first-hand" information.

Bibliography

Abiew, F., and Keating, T. (1999) "NGOs and UN Peacekeeping Operations: Strange Bedfellows," International Peacekeeping 6 (2): 90–105.

Barry, J., and Jeffreys, A. (2002) A Bridge Too Far: Aid Agencies and the Military in Humanitarian Response, Humanitarian Practice Network Paper 37, London: Overseas Development Institute.

Bellamy, C. (1996) Knights in White Armour: The New Art of War and Peace, London: Pimlico.

Blaxland, J. (2002) Information-era Manoeuvre: The Australian-led Mission to East Timor, Land Warfare Studies Centre Working Paper No. 118, Canberra: Australian Defence Force.

Boot, M. (2002) The Savage Wars of Peace: Small Wars and the Rise of American Power, New York: Basic Books.

Byman, D.L. (2001) "Uncertain Partners: NGOs and the Military," Survival 43 (2): 97–114.

DND (Canada) (1999a) Information Operations in Land Operations, B-GL-300–005/FP-001, Ottawa: Department of National Defence.

—— (1999b) "Lessons Learned in Civil–Military Cooperation," Dispatches: Lessons Learned for Soldiers, 5 (3).

—— (2001) "HUMINT During Peace Support Operations," Dispatches: Lessons Learned for Soldiers, 8 (1)

Duffield, M. (2001) Global Governance and the New Wars. The Merging of Development and Security, London: Routledge.

Eriksson, P. (2000) "Civil–Military Coordination in Peace Support Operations— An Impossible Necessity," *Journal of Humanitarian Assistance*, September: n.p.

Gordon, S. (2004) "Military–Humanitarian Relationships and the Invasion of Iraq (2003): Reforging Certainties?" *The Journal of Humanitarian Assistance*.

IASC (2004) *Civil–Military Relationship in Complex Emergencies*, Reference Paper, Inter-Agency Standing Committee Working Group, Geneva: IASC/OCHA/ECHA.

ICRC (1995) *The Code of Conduct for the International Red Cross and Red Crescent Movement and NGOs in Disaster Relief*, Geneva: International Committee of the Red Cross. Available at: *http://www.icrc.org/Web/Eng/siteeng0.nsf/ html/57JMNB?OpenDocument* (accessed February 1, 2005).

Landon, J.J., and Hayes, R.E. (2003) *National Approaches to Civil–Military Coordination in Peace and Humanitarian Assistance Operations*, Washington, DC: Evidence Based Research, Inc.

Longhurst, G. (2003) "Civil Military Co-Operation—The Inukshuk," *CALL Bulletin*.

MSF (2004) "Afghanistan: MSF Leaves Country following Staff Killings and Threats," December 16. Available at: [http://www.msf.org/countries/ page.cfm?articleid=F446039F-4965–4FB0–9D21CF4C695F80C9 (accessed February 1, 2005).

NATO (2001) *Civil Military Cooperation Doctrine-Draft*, AJP-9, Brussels: North Atlantic Treaty Organization.

Oxfam (2003) *Iraq: Humanitarian Military Relations*, Briefing Paper No. 41, London: Oxfam.

Pugh, M. (1997) "From Mission Creep to Mission Cringe," in *UN, Peace, and Force*, London: Frank Cass: 191–194.

Slim, H. (1997) "The Stretcher and the Drum: Civil–Military Relations in Peace Support Operations," in J. Ginifer (ed.), *Beyond the Emergency*, London: Frank Cass, pp. 123–140.

Watkins, C. (2003) *Provincial Reconstruction Teams (PRTs): An Analysis of Their Contribution to Security in Afghanistan*, MSc thesis in Development Practice, Oxford Brookes University, September 30.

Part III

NEW ELEMENTS OF
INTELLIGENCE ANALYSIS

9

FIELD RESEARCH ON SMALL ARMS AND LIGHT WEAPONS AND THEIR IMPORTANCE FOR PEACE OPERATIONS

A practitioner's view

Context

More than ten years ago, then-United Nations (UN) Secretary-General Boutros Boutros-Ghali pledged that the UN would not make the same mistake in Mozambique as it had in Angola (UN, 1992: para. 22). Disarmament during the second UN Angola Verification Mission (UNAVEM II) had not been implemented meaningfully in the lead-up to the 1992 national elections. The União Nacional para a Independência Total de Angola (UNITA) rebel leader, Jonas Savimbi, recognizing the polls did not favor him or his party, plunged the country back into civil war. Boutros-Ghali underscored that the UN Operation in Mozambique (ONUMOZ), unlike UNAVEM II, would destroy significant quantities of arms and ammunition, and would engage the civilian population as well as the protagonists' armed forces. In the end, however, the UN made negligible progress in accounting for arms circulating throughout the country (Berman 1996). Fortunately, the Resistência Nacional Moçambicana (RENAMO) rebel leader, Afonso Dhlakama, decided to exchange his fatigues for Italian-tailored suits and gracefully accepted his electoral defeat.

In both cases, the international community failed to take full advantage of an opportunity to address the problem of small arms proliferation, in spite of the wide applicability of small arms intelligence in peace operations. This is not to say that the UN Mission in Mozambique was a failure. Subsequent economic progress and democratic elections have been encouraging. But ONUMOZ's legacy also includes a spike in lethal criminality in neighboring South Africa using weapons purchased from Mozambican caches that remained after the UN peacekeepers had withdrawn from the country.[2]

Despite widespread recognition that weapons collection efforts as part of UN peace operations leave much to be desired, the situation has not improved significantly. For example, the Report of the Panel on UN Peace Operations, commonly known as "The Brahimi Report," underscored the need to place financing of disarmament, demobilization, and reintegration (DDR) on a more stable footing (UN, 2000: paras. 42 and 47). Two years into the "Post-Brahimi Era," the UN failed to implement the report's recommendations concerning DDR when the mandate for the UN Mission in the Democratic Republic of the Congo (MONUC) was amended. The UN Mission in Liberia (UNMIL), however, did receive some funds to reha- bilitate former combatants as part of the regular peacekeeping budget (Durch et al., 2003: 28), but not in a sustainable manner.[3] The chasm between lofty rhetoric and short-term political and financial calculations of the international community—especially donor countries and members of the Security Council—has yet to be bridged.

This context is important. Any discussion of data collection on small arms and light weapons (SALW)[4] needs to acknowledge such realities. To do otherwise would give the incorrect impression that the only problem policy-makers face is a lack of good, reliable information. This is simply not the case.

Poor intelligence and analysis, however, certainly make good policies more difficult to fashion and implement. Survey information on small arms can be used for more than just weapons collection and demobiliza- tion programs. An understanding of the number, distribution, and use of weapons has important implications for such diverse concerns as force protection, mandates, rules of engagement, development programs, and humanitarian assistance.

This chapter has two parts. The first discusses the work of the Small Arms Survey (SAS or "the Survey"), a Geneva-based research institute. The second focuses on the author's personal experiences and lessons learned in undertaking field research on SALW and peace operations.

The Small Arms Survey

The Small Arms Survey, established in 1999, is an independent research project of the University of Geneva's Graduate Institute of International Studies. It serves as the principal international source of public informa- tion on all aspects of small arms, and as a resource center for governments, policy-makers, researchers, and activists. The project has an international staff with expertise in security studies, political science, international public policy, law, economics, development studies, conflict resolution, and sociology. The staff works closely with a worldwide network of researchers and partners. SAS supports independent research and publishes a yearbook as well as an *Occasional Paper* series and *Special Reports.*[5]

Through a variety of research projects and policy analysis, the Survey has helped inform the debate concerning the impact of SALW while also assisting in the design of policies to confront the threats these pose to human security. The yearbook routinely examines production, transfers, and stockpiles of small arms as well as measures to reduce their deleterious effects. The Survey's country studies and investigations of cross-cutting themes such as gender and demand have shed light on linkages between SALW and development, public health, crime, violence, and conflict. For example, the Survey has carried out and supported research and analysis that has generated a better understanding as well as improved tracking of the impacts of firearms—both direct (e.g. deaths, injury, and trauma) and indirect (e.g. economic, social, educational, and environmental). Besides undertaking baseline assessments (see below), the Survey has also participated in and helped create groundbreaking studies involving estimation techniques on weapons availability, epidemiological effects of SALW, and firearm-related violence in countries such as Bangladesh, Brazil, Colombia, Georgia, Indonesia (Aceh), Kosovo, Kyrgyzstan, Mozambique, Pakistan, Papua New Guinea, and Sri Lanka.

Over the past four years SAS has made impressive use of open-source intelligence (OSINT). It has amassed a library of books, journals, articles, official government publications, and CD-ROMs. Staff also make use of information available on the Internet as part of their desk research. The Survey has developed a number of electronic and hard-copy databases containing information on various small arms issues as well as regions and individual countries. These materials are freely shared with researchers and other interested parties. Indeed, the knowledge and insight of local researchers and institutions, in particular, represent an extremely valuable resource. The Survey is committed to sponsoring their work and furthering their capacities. In addition, the Survey has begun to develop its human intelligence (HUMINT) assets. In its first five years of operation it has established partnerships with more than fifty local and international research institutes, various civil society organizations, as well as national and international governmental agencies and bodies. Manuscripts are routinely peer-reviewed. Moreover, SAS commissions background papers on various issues of concern from people with particular expertise and privileged access to information. SAS has also created a "Baseline Assessment" framework to analyze the nature and extent of the problem that SALW pose for individual countries or particular regions. "Small Arms Baseline Assessments" (SABAs) focus on weapons acquisition, distribution, circulation, impact, attitudes, and control. The standard SABA has six specific research objectives:

1   to highlight political, economic, social, and cultural context relevant for understanding the SALW situation;

2   to assess geographic and demographic distribution, availability, possession, and use of SALW;

3   to highlight SALW circulation, trafficking, and proliferation;

4   to show the impact of SALW on society—both direct and indirect effects;

5   to outline measures established and needed to control, solve, and otherwise manage the SALW situation; and

6   to sketch implications of SALW problems based on the data gathered and analyzed.

A central component of this work includes representative household surveys. These studies assess respondents' perceptions of insecurity as well as reasons for, and attitudes toward, gun ownership. Information on interviewees' acquisition of firearms is gathered, patterns are established, and data on victimization is collated. Attitudes toward small arms control measures are also investigated.[6]

Focus groups represent a second important component. To be most effective, the examination of a focus group ought to be based on a flexible and informal discussion on a pre-determined topic to encourage maximum participation. Care must be taken to ensure that the group's composition does not inhibit a free exchange of ideas. The format facilitates the generation of insights and understandings in ways that a questionnaire alone likely would not elicit. As interaction is the key to this tool's success, the size of the group is usually limited to between eight and twelve people.

A third aspect of a successful baseline assessment is interview-based field research. SAS has undertaken several baseline assessments in Africa, Europe, and throughout the Asia–Pacific region. These typically take from 6–12 months; the major variables are the ability to identify and reach agreement with local partners to undertake the polling and which territory is to be covered. In some cases, the security environment or infrastructure of the country do not permit representative household surveys to be undertaken. In such instances, SAS has had to rely on focus groups. Interviews are also conducted with government officials, military personnel, members of armed, non-state groups, representatives of civil society organizations, among others. SAS has participated in SABAs for the Republic of the Congo, Haiti, Kosovo, Kyrgyzstan, Macedonia, Montenegro, Somaliland, Tajikistan, and several island nations throughout the South Pacific. Many of these are completed and the findings published. Most of these initiatives have received funding from the United Nations Development Program (UNDP), which explains why the list is skewed toward post-conflict settings.

Field-based research: personal insights

I continue to be surprised by the reactions when I inform people that I am undertaking a study on small arms. Many think the matter is too sensitive for respondents to give truthful answers about the state of affairs, or too dangerous to investigate effectively. Certainly, some interviewees engage in obfuscation, plead ignorance, or claim forgetfulness. As with any type of field research, a degree of caution is advisable (see, for example, Khakee 2004: 15–19). But one does not need a "cloak and dagger" approach to undertake successful field research on small arms.

By far the biggest obstacles to gaining good information are time and money. In most cases a single one- to two-week visit is too limiting to do all but a cursory job. While larger teams of researchers can partially offset time constraints, longer and multiple visits are preferred (for reasons discussed below). A credible and useful initial political–military study on SALW in a country as part of pre-mission planning can be undertaken for US$25–50,000. Ideally, a fuller SABA ought to be undertaken from the outset, which can be expected to cost an additional US$25,000 (with good local researchers). These amounts reflect what is needed for a small country or specified geographical area such as Haiti, Kosovo, or Sierra Leone. Larger countries or regional studies would cost considerably more. For example, a comprehensive national study on firearm-related violence throughout Brazil that involved considerable field-based research and sophisticated quantitative analysis cost upward of US$200,000.

In addition to adequate financing and time, successful field research on SALW requires careful planning, building trust, developing contacts, and employing solid research techniques.

Regardless of one's affiliation, successful field research requires considerable pre-visit planning. This work is not glamorous—and it is usually poorly remunerated as funders want to see the bulk of their money go toward days spent on interviews. Besides conducting the requisite desk research on the respective subject matter, one must also contact governments and organizations active in the country or region to be studied—both "in the field" as well as at headquarters and capitals. Political and logistical support from a range of governments, international agencies, private companies, and non-governmental organizations (NGOs) are extremely useful and can be obtained without granting special favors or compromising independence or objectivity.

Surveys should include visits to other countries. Obvious priorities are regional capitals and towns along borders where commerce takes place or where large numbers of people (such as refugees or internally displaced persons) congregate or cross. Diplomats and officials of foreign governments from outside the region with significant historical, political, or economic ties to the country under review also represent a potential valuable source of information and should be exploited.

An example from a recent visit to Paris for a study on the Central African Republic (CAR) underscores this concern. The government of France gave me permission to access the French army's records (*Service*

Historique de l'Armée de Terre) up to 1965. The level of detail was impressive. I was able to document the exact number and type of weapons in the inventories of CAR's armed forces and police in 1962 and 1963 as well as the number of personnel in these services. This is important because it provides a basis for evaluating a useful multiplier by which to ascertain and evaluate stockpile data—not just for CAR, but for other countries as well.

It takes time to establish contacts and more time still to establish the necessary trust to maximize a contact's value as a source of credible and useful information. Extending the length of a visit is advised, of course, but not always sufficient. Interviewees need time to check out the interviewer's credentials, read his or her work, learn about the organization he or she represents, and hear from others that he or she is trustworthy. Repeat visits also give people who are willing to help the time necessary to collate and analyze data of importance to the project.

Admittedly, there will be some people who are knowledgeable, but who never wish to divulge information, no matter how many times they are called or visited. This is a problem with field interviews in any area of research. But there are people who would be willing to provide information and who simply need to be sensitized to the project. While there continues to be some hesitancy among some members of the humanitarian aid community to discuss "security" matters, I have seen a significant change over the past five years. An ever-growing list of contacts and greater experience only partly explains the transformation. A much more significant factor is these sources' increasing willingness to share their experiences.

There are at least two reasons why aid workers are more willing to talk about SALW-related issues. Humanitarian organizations previously felt that security for their personnel would be undermined if they discussed SALW issues. And humanitarian aid workers frequently believed they had little relevant information to contribute. In recent years however they have increasingly been targeted and subjected to armed violence (Muggah, 2004).[7] And their organizations—both UN bodies and NGOs—have taken an active interest in examining the link (see, for example, Muggah and Berman 2001: vii–ix). In addition to these changes in the humanitarian field, development agencies and governments have also begun to fund studies to investigate the connection between SALW availability and use on the one hand and human rights abuses and underdevelopment on the other.[8]

Moreover, the value of information from this source is improving. There appears to be an increasing number in recent years of people with military backgrounds who have joined the ranks of humanitarian workers—many as security advisors. These people are an especially useful resource because they tend to know specifics and do not call every firearm "an AK-47" or describe every explosion as resulting from "a mortar."

Transparency is of great value and a major component of building trust, which is the cornerstone of good research. To be sure, it might be argued that the researcher should not reveal too much about his or her project to the interviewee in order to avoid bias. Yet in my own experience it has been helpful to identify myself, my affiliation, and the project and its intended audience and expected outputs before an interview. In many instances, I have offered to share my research with the interlocutor prior to publication. This requires more of a commitment on the respondent's part (and much more time on the interviewer's part). Sometimes respondents do not follow through. Though they may disagree with the analysis or findings, this additional step provides a valuable way to develop a meaningful dialogue and to expand significantly on information they have already shared.

Except in one instance, I have found my UN background to have been very useful in my work. Most interlocutors appear to treat this affiliation and experience as positive—or, at the very least, neutral. Of course, one need not have worked for the UN to be effective. Certainly, the SAS affiliation has proven helpful as well. However, a journalistic affiliation is problematic. People tend to be more wary when they think that something they say can come out in print the next day or the next week.

Other possible factors to consider when undertaking a field-based study include the prospective researcher's nationality, gender, and religion. For the most part, I have not found my American nationality to be a complicating factor. (My attempt to interview a Libyan official in Bangui was, I think, doomed from the outset.) Though I have no direct negative experiences to relate on this matter, I can imagine cultures and circumstances in which one might wish to take gender, age, and religion into consideration when selecting a research team to go to the field.

While it is necessary to schedule appointments with high-ranking officials of recipient and supplier countries to discuss small arms transfers, this is not likely to yield significant usable information, especially concerning current events. Perhaps not surprisingly, *former* government officials such as military chiefs of staff, ambassadors, and ministers can be excellent sources—though one must always pay special attention to the reasons they are no longer in government and their motivations for consenting to be interviewed. Most people are willing—even eager—to talk. Assuring anonymity is often helpful, but not always required. A proven track record of responsibility and an ability to convince the respondent that he or she is just one of many people being interviewed with similar background is a huge help. Diplomats, international civil servants, humanitarian aid workers, members of the media, former combatants, business people (such as private plane operators and truckers), religious leaders, refugees, and other members of civil society also represent potentially valuable sources of information.

125

One of the best parts of undertaking research on SALW is that it is full of surprises and each study provides new insights. For example, before my recent visits to CAR I never appreciated how valuable a source of information safari tour operators and hunters represented. Not only do they possess insights into arms trafficking and security in the hinterland, but they also represent an excellent source of information on small arms effects on development and conservation efforts. The government ministries responsible for hunting and the revenues this activity generates are also excellent sources of data and insights. Another example, again from CAR, concerns the valuable information that can be gleaned from ammunition. Normally, ammunition is not a subject that is given a lot of attention. But ammunition can tell a lot about a country's firearms and light weapons inventories as well as about small arms in circulation among the population. Data collected by the African-led peacekeeping operation, Mission interafricaine de surveillance des accords de Bangui (MISAB), shed considerable light on weapons and ammunition holdings that were not otherwise available or shared—not just via OSINT, such as in various Jane's publications, but also via HUMINT. Central African government and military officials had initially not included certain weapons in their country's arsenal that they later added when reminded of particular rounds of ammunition that MISAB reported it had recovered.

Conclusion: where do we go from here?

Good intelligence on SALW has dozens of applications in peace operations. Force protection and designing DDR and civilian weapons collection programs are but a few examples. Given the number of incidents in which peacekeepers have inadvertently been a source of weapons for protagonists in a conflict, it would be wise to assess the local ammunition supply in the area of operation. One suggestion would be that the countries participating in the operation deploy their troops with firearms for which it would be difficult to obtain ammunition through unofficial channels. This would reduce the ramifications for weapons that might be seized. Archival data can provide useful information for creating multipliers to ascertain stockpile data as a basis for better estimations of the kinds and amounts of weapons and ammunition that are in circulation and for more appropriate assessments of what is worth targeting. Black market data can provide valuable parameters as a basis for setting prices in order to ensure that buy-back initiatives do not create an unintended demand for the weapons.

Nevertheless, despite the obvious value data on SALW has for the success of a mission—both for planning and operations—and for ensuring a sustainable post-conflict transition, data collection and analysis have too often been carried out haphazardly or after the fact. As previously noted, almost all the cases in which SAS has undertaken baseline assessments have involved post-conflict scenarios. This is so in large part because of the mandates and agendas of the sources of funding. Support for SABAs from the UNDP, for example, is welcome and should be encouraged and expanded. But the UNDP is limited in that it cannot undertake and fund projects that the partner government has not supported. Thus, for example, the UNDP was unable to intervene meaningfully in Liberia in 2003 when it became increasingly clear that another peace operation was in the offing. Liberia's president, Charles Taylor, who saw himself as a victim of UN sanctions that included an arms embargo, was not going to view any proposal favorably that would shed light on arms transfers to his country.

These assessments should be performed in conjunction with planning for peace operations. The UN needs to find a way to empower and fund studies in addition to those supported by the UNDP, its Bureau for Conflict Prevention and Recovery (BCPR), and its South Eastern Europe Clearinghouse for the Control of Small Arms and Light Weapons (SEESAC). To date, studies on SALW in preparation for its various peace operations have received insufficient attention.

The good news is that a UN inter-agency working group is now looking into this issue. The UN system is undertaking a comprehensive rethink and overhaul of its approach to DDR. The Secretariat and UN agencies, funds, and programs are in the process of institutionalizing lessons learned and best practices into clear and workable policies, guidelines, and procedures for integrated programming.[9] This is a crucial step toward bridging the current gap between rhetoric and practice on the part of UN member states and the Security Council. Greater coordination concerning SALW issues among UN agencies and bodies as well as between the UN and NGOs represents a worthwhile initiative. A way must be found to ensure that lessons learned and best practices are shared with regional organizations and "ad hoc coalitions of the willing" that increasingly have shouldered the burden of undertaking peace operations in recent years. Moreover, sharing this information can only be a first step. These actors must be infused with sufficient financial resources and given the technical expertise to undertake and benefit from research and analysis.

Ideally, no study on SALW should be limited to just a politico-military analysis as a fuller SABA permits one to compare progress and to better ascertain trends over time from the outset. Post-conflict weapons collection programs would greatly benefit from a baseline assessment as a basis for comparing current attitudes and holdings, for example.

A tremendous amount of useful information can be obtained and analyzed through unclassified and non-technical means. The problem is how to fund this and how to create a structure to transmit this information to policy-makers and those tasked to implement these programs at the field level in peace operations. As noted at the chapter's outset, whether this intelligence will actually be used is an entirely different question.

Notes

1 This chapter is based on a paper presented at the international conference "Peacekeeping Intelligence: New Players, Extended Boundaries," which Carleton University and the Royal Military College of Canada sponsored in December 2003 in Ottawa, Canada. At the time the author was a Visiting Fellow at the Thomas J. Watson Jr. Institute for International Studies, Brown University, Providence, RI. He is now Managing Director of the Small Arms Survey (SAS), a project of the Graduate Institute of International Studies at the University of Geneva, Switzerland. Mr. Berman wishes to acknowledge the contributions of Anna Khakee and Anne-Kathrin Glatz of SAS who reviewed the manuscript and offered thoughtful comments.

2 ONUMOZ concluded in December 1994. For details on the changing nature of armed criminality and lethality in South Africa with weapons procured from excess Mozambican stocks—as well as Mozambican and South African efforts to combat this scourge—see Chachiua (1999). For information on "Operations Rachel," the destruction process of SALW in Mozambique, see SaferAfrica (2003). Beri (2000) provides an overview of small arms crime in South Africa and, referring to Batchelor (1996: 71–73), identifies Mozambique as "the largest single source of supply of arms to the South African domestic market."

3 The initial funds set aside for the DDR program were based on an estimate of 38,000 combatants. In the end however, 107,000 people entered the program and were eligible to receive benefits. Donors have been reluctant to make up the shortfall and the program has experienced several problems as a result. Whether the fundamental problem lies with a lax application of established and proper criteria for eligibility, or a gross underestimation of the combatants in need of assistance, the bottom line is that operational demands have once again exceeded political and financial will and resources.

4 The Survey follows the definition of Small Arms and Light Weapons provided in the UN Report of the Panel of Governmental Experts on Small Arms: "*Small Arms* are revolvers and self-loading pistols, rifles and carbines, assault rifles, sub-machine guns, and light machine guns. *Light weapons* are heavy machine guns, hand-held under-barrel and mounted grenade launchers, portable anti-tank and anti-aircraft guns, recoilless rifles, portable launchers of anti-tank and anti-aircraft missile systems, and mortars of less than 100mm calibre" (UN, 1997). See also Small Arms Survey (2004: 8).

5 Examples of these materials can be downloaded from the Small Arms Survey Web site, available at: www.smallarmssurvey.org.

6 For sample survey questions and more information, see Khakee (2004: sect. 12).

7 Muggah (2003) summarizes the findings of a victimization survey undertaken by SAS and the Geneva-based Centre for Humanitarian Dialogue (Muggah and Berman, 2001).

8 On the link between small arms and underdevelopment see Small Arms Survey (2003), in particular Chapter 4, "Obstructing Development: The Effects of Small Arms on Human Development," and Oxfam (2001a, 2001b).

9 Among other outputs, the conference "Toward a UN Approach to Disarmament, Demobilization and Reintegration" organized by the Inter-Agency Disarmament, Demobilization and Reintegration Working Group (IDDRWG) from October 28 to 30, 2004 in Geneva set up an Online Resource Centre on Disarmament, Demobilization and, Reintegration. The website is not yet available to the public. It is expected that this site will be launched in late 2005 at www.unddr.org.

Bibliography

Batchelor, P. (1996) "Disarmament, Small Arms and Intra State Conflict: The Case of Southern Africa," in C. Smith, P. Batchelor, and J. Potgieter (eds.), *Small Arms Management and Peacekeeping in Southern Africa*, New York and Geneva: UN Institute for Disarmament Research.

Beri, R. (2000) "Coping with Small Arms Threat in South Africa," *Strategic Analysis*, XXIV (1): 151–167.

Berman, E. (1996) *Managing Arms in Peace Processes: Mozambique*, Geneva: UN Institute for Disarmament Research.

Chachiua, M. (1999) *Arms Management Programme: Operations Rachel 1996–1999*, ISS Monograph Series No. 38, June.

Durch, W.J., Holt, V.K., Earle, C.R., and Shanahan, M.K. (2003) *The Brahimi Report and the Future of UN Peace Operations*, Washington, DC: The Henry L. Stimson Center.

Khakee, A. (2004) *Training and Education in Small Arms (TRESA) Module BF04A01: Basic Principles of Field Research in Small Arms Action*, Bonn: Bonn International Center for Conversion.

Muggah, R. (2003) "In the Line of Fire: Surveying the Impact of Small Arms on Civilians and Relief Workers," *Humanitarian Exchange*, December 25. Available at: http://www.odihpn.org/report.asp?ID=2584 (accessed January 11, 2005).

—— (2004) "Stop the Guns Targeting Aid Workers," *Globe and Mail* (Canada), August 11: A13.

Muggah, R. and Berman, E. (2001) "Humanitarianism Under Threat: The Humanitarian Impacts of Small Arms and Light Weapons," *Small Arms Survey*, July.

Oxfam (2001a) *Conflict's Children: The Human Cost of Small Arms in Kitgum and Kotido, Uganda*, Oxford: Oxfam GB, January.

—— (2001b) *Reaching for the Gun: The Human Cost of Small Arms in Central Mindanao, Philippines*, Oxford: Oxfam GB, February. Available at: http://www.oxfam.org.uk/what_we_do/issues/conflict_disasters/downloads/conflict_uganda.pdf

SaferAfrica (2003) *Operations Rachel*, Pretoria: SaferAfrica. Available at: http://www.saferafrica.org/DocumentsCentre/Monographs/Rachel/Rachel.pdf (accessed January 11, 2005).

Small Arms Survey (2003) *Small Arms Survey 2003: Development Denied*, Oxford: Oxford University Press.

—— (2004) *Small Arms Survey 2004: Rights at Risk*, Oxford: Oxford University Press.

UN (1992) *Report of the Secretary-General on the United Nations Operation in Mozambique (ONUMOZ)*, S/24892, New York: UN, December 3.

—— (1997) *Report of the Panel of Governmental Experts on Small Arms*, A/52/298, New York: UN, August 27.

—— (2000) *Brahimi Report: Report of the Panel on United Nations Peace Operations*, A/55/305, S/2000/809, New York: UN, August 21.

10

PEACEKEEPING INTELLIGENCE FOR THE STAKEHOLDERS

An underutilized open resource

Douglas Bond and Patrick Meier[1]

Introduction

Our work with open sources takes a participant observer approach. As such, it is distinct from most peacekeeping intelligence (PKI) activities considered at Carleton University's 2003 Peacekeeping Intelligence Conference in Ottawa. Our approach is broader than those considered in that it is not restricted to third-party intelligence activities, and it engages the community at risk as participants rather than as third parties or adversaries. In other words, our "PKI" activity seeks to inculcate a situational or security awareness within high-risk communities as it builds on local capacities to address and reduce their vulnerabilities in a sustainable way.

This approach, we suggest, nurtures a sense of ownership and control over the information collected, and to the extent that this information remains transparent and in the public domain, the approach can also encourage responsiveness by the relevant local and national governments, the at-risk communities and third parties. This approach differs from the traditionally more "remote" and "vertical" monitoring of potential adversaries. Our approach to PKI activities thus takes the *stakeholders*' perspective.

Peacekeeping experts contend that intelligence collection for current and future missions requires "a more scientific process, and greater use of technology that automate collection and dissemination" (Roach, 2003: 11). In our stakeholder approach we endorse the notion of greater scientific rigor, particularly with the integration of structured "situation" reports to complement "incident" or "event" reports. We argue that situation reporting is required to illuminate evolving situations of conflict before they escalate into violence. We also suggest that the development of timely and reliable baselines of conflict situations can help link the resultant early warnings with response options.

This move toward a more scientific field security information-collection process, like any scientific endeavor, is fundamentally a public process that must remain open to facilitate independent assessment and evaluation. Thus we argue that a rigorously implemented stakeholder approach is sorely needed in peacekeeping missions.

Field monitors

Future conflicts are likely to emerge "at the sub-state level, and peace-keepers need clear and accurate pictures of what is happening" (Svenson, 2003: 6). There is little doubt that PKI would benefit from closer engagement with local stakeholders. "Conflicts create a dynamic situation with new stakeholders as well as a whole new set of winners and losers in the political, economic, and security areas" (Musifiky Mwanasali, cited in Meier, 2003: 6). One way to engage these stake-holders is through the use of paid informants to help monitor a situation as it develops in the field.

There is an increasing acknowledgment among peacekeeping experts that "the United Nations needs a variety of informants to carry out the job of peacekeeping" (Dorn, 2003: 10). In fact, now that there is "an increased willingness to accept intelligence by the UN, there now needs to be more intelligence from the field [...] and more people capable of handing and disseminating sensitive information" (Dorn, 2003: 10). Increasingly third-party informants are hired to provide this information.

However, unlike stakeholders or victims of a conflict, third-party paid informants do not always find themselves in the "right" place at the "right" time to collect relevant information. This is because "early warning signals appear most clearly to those immediately around the disputants," and not necessarily to third-party informants (Harvard Project on Negotiation, 2004). This inevitably creates a time lag in the intelligence reports submitted by third parties: "The distribution of intelligence needs an expeditious turn-around time [...] a permanent intelligence gathering structure is needed where civil and military organizations can work together, using the same criteria and working for the same goals" (Jones, 2003: 17). Given the importance of collecting information that is timely, it is not surprising that working with stakeholder participant observers figures as one of the lessons learned in PKI (Weibes, 2003).

Thus at least two types of field monitors are potentially available to help gather information on emerging conflict at a sub-national level: paid informants and participant observers. While financial incentives may serve well to engage both constituencies, we suggest that the sense of responsi-bility and commitment by third-party informants is unlikely to match the sense of urgency felt by the stakeholders who are most immediately affected by escalating violence.

While stakeholder interests were popularized through the corporate social responsibility movement, the concept has been applied increasingly by international organizations working in development and conflict management. Harvard's Global Negotiation Project sponsors the Third Side project, an international initiative that advocates a systems approach to conflict prevention and resolution (Harvard Project on Negotiation, 2004). The Third Side is a way of looking at conflicts not just from one side or the other but also from the larger perspective of the surrounding community—from the stakeholders' perspective.

The Third Side framework maintains that, "early warning signals appear most clearly to those immediately around the disputants" (Harvard Project on Negotiation, 2004). These early warning signals are open source intelligence signals that local stakeholders are more likely privy to than outsiders. Still, we explicitly acknowledge that all informants—paid or otherwise, third-party or stakeholder—bring their own interests to a monitoring effort, and these interests may or may not be convergent with those of the local communities. Thus, to the extent that the security of the local community lies at the heart of the PKI effort, stakeholders are the third parties of choice to engage in any field monitoring effort.

In a complex situation populated with multiple stakeholders and competing interests, the distinction between third parties and stakeholders may become blurred, especially if they are drawn from the same region. Here is where the significance of transparency in PKI activities is imperative. When stakeholders are part of the monitoring effort, they expect the right to access the results of their labor, even as their effort is financially compensated. These results are embedded in the field reports they produce, which reflect their evolving security environment. Without a transparent system where this critical information can be accessed and acted upon by those most in danger, there is little reason to employ stakeholders over third parties.

An example of how a local stakeholder and field monitor can activate a response system from below may be found in the Conflict Early Warning and Response Mechanism (CEWARN) Project that monitors pastoral conflict in the Karamoja cluster along the borders of Ethiopia, Kenya, and Uganda. In July 2003 a field reporter submitted a report of a pre-raid blessing. This kind of a report is considered a signal or trigger for acute conflict in the near term, as a raid typically follows the blessing. Upon reviewing this field report, a CEWARN staff member in Addis called the country coordinator responsible for quality control in that area, and he in turn called the field monitor. Several telephone discussions later, the local police agency in the area was informed of the impending raid. The police responded by holding a previously scheduled training exercise in proximity to the two parties identified by the field reporter. The bottom line is that no raid occurred.

While we do not claim the absence of a raid in this instance as evidence of an early warning success, we do however suggest that the activation of a participant observer's interest, convergent with the peacekeeping goals of the CEWARN effort, represents a meaningful part of the processes involving CEWARN's PKI activities. Specifically, we suggest that the activation of lower-level channels of communication and rapid response goes to the heart of the stakeholders' interests. Such participation by stakeholders and system monitors facilitates and supports a more secure environment—but only when the process is open and transparent.

Thus we differentiate between a stakeholder and a third-party PKI system by access to the data as well as those constituencies engaged. Of course the distinction between third parties and stakeholders is often one of degree rather than of kind, especially in the realm of information access.

Ideally all stakeholders would have real-time access to the field baseline data that reveals the level of danger in a given situation. Such baseline data does not necessarily include the full field reports, and we are certainly not advocating the public posting of field reports that include identifying or other personal information on specific victims or alleged perpetrators. Instead we are advocating a system that makes commonsense distinctions between sensitive field report information that is to be protected and the aggregated versions of these same data used to produce baselines for public consumption.

To be clear, we are not talking about data ownership and control, which typically resides with the system (financial) sponsors, be they governments or private concerns; rather we are addressing the extent of aggregated information access available to the field monitors, be they stakeholders or third parties, and the general public. We are also suggesting that these open and transparent stakeholder efforts are more capable of facilitating rapid response to the identified crises, as evidenced in the above CEWARN example.

Field monitoring

PKI is not only beneficial to international organizations and peacekeepers,

> but also to the local population. Sound intelligence will not only save lives during the peacekeeping mission, but it will also help in the eventual transfer of power back to the host country, for these exit strategies need to ensure that countries do not fall back into chaos once the peacekeepers have left.
>
> (Laipson, 2003: 20)

Thus we argue that early warnings need to be integrated into locally based early response mechanisms in a compelling manner.

While the shift to local information networks is an improvement over remote and covert monitoring, the policy recommendations that flow from the assessments are likely to be misplaced if the field reporting and analysis functions are separated from the stakeholders. We suggest that information collection needs to be oriented toward local capacity building and toward long-term local sustainability. In this way it can best utilize the considerable local knowledge and expertise of its paid informants who are submitting the field reports.

In other words, one-way information collection efforts, even when they utilize paid local informants, represent a sub-optimal form of PKI. With such approaches, the collected field data often becomes the exclusive property of the sponsor rather than the communities from which it is derived. Even the governments, both local and national, may not be privy to the information collected in their own jurisdictions. Modifying this approach to be more inclusive and transparent is not prohibitively expensive, but it does take considerable effort and cooperation within and among the countries involved and at all levels of governance from local to national.

The challenge, then, is to collect quality stakeholder field reports in a continuous data stream while integrating the data analysis and recommendations processes with a response mechanism. In the CEWARN example, it is clear that this challenge is being met.

Based on lessons learned from designing and deploying an extensive system of local information networks, an international team of consultants and local analysts developed the CEWARN for East Africa's Inter-Governmental Authority on Development (IGAD). The IGAD–CEWARN system focuses on pastoral conflict that ravages the border regions of Ethiopia, Kenya, and Uganda within an area that is known as the Karamoja cluster. This very small area, over the course of the first nine months of data collection (August 2003 through April 2004), has posted a tragic human death toll of over 700 and livestock losses of over 32,000 head. Clearly the local communities have a stake in this conflict, and the CEWARN effort offers them a voice, even if only by bringing to the public's attention the tragic costs of the ongoing conflicts.

CEWARN's country coordinators draft their own risk assessments in collaboration with CEWARN's staff in Addis Ababa. Policy recommendations are also developed jointly, with civil and political society both participating in the effort before they are circulated among an analytic advisory group for peer review. This instills a sense of system ownership and control among stakeholders. Finally, the initial baseline reports from the field data collection effort are posted on the Internet (www.cewarn.org—as of October 21, 2004) for public access.

The inclusion of CEWARN's observers throughout the early warning and response mechanism creates incentives for activation of multiple channels of communication by the stakeholders themselves, as well as between the stakeholders and the sponsors. In this way the participant observers become stakeholders, with a "voice" to express their concerns and hopes about their evolving security environment.

Another critical issue in field reporting is the misguided notion of focusing on incidents (typically violent) or even "events" (including both cooperation and conflict) that has driven most early warning efforts to date. With this approach we notice an under-reporting of signs of local cooperation, because it is far easier to document violent incidents given their higher visibility and certainty with respect to their threshold of inclusion as an event. Thus the danger here is not fully mitigated by monitoring both conflict and cooperation incidents; the issue of conditions for, or situations of peace, and conflict is not addressed when the focus is exclusively on interactions or "events" that must be defended as significant, typically at the national level.

In addition to incident reports or "IncReps," CEWARN integrates situation reports or "SitReps" in its information-collection framework. SitReps enable observers to provide contextual information and narratives on a regular (currently weekly) basis; thus ensuring continuity in the data stream collected at the field level. More importantly, SitReps monitor precursors to conflict and cooperation. By integrating IncReps and SitReps, CEWARN observers are able to identify which precursors documented in the SitReps lead to the post facto violent incidents recorded in the IncReps. This provides the CEWARN Unit in Addis Ababa with advance warning of upcoming incidents, making conflict prevention more than a hypothetical possibility as suggested in the true story cited above about the pre-raid blessing.

SitReps monitor issues ranging from communal relations to civil society activities. These indicators place an important emphasis on peace-generating and conflict-mitigating factors that observers report on a weekly basis. Stakeholders and supporting organizations are therefore informed of peace-conducive activities happening at the local level. This facilitates the drafting of targeted response strategies. It is the inclusion of SitReps that makes CEWARN a distinctive early warning mechanism. The integration of protocols for response mechanisms lends CEWARN the capacity to actually link early warning signals with responses, and this is where the CEWARN project offers the promise of a valuable return to its stakeholders and sponsors alike.

Using both SitReps and IncReps produces more reliable baselines. Baseline analysis is a pre-requisite for effective early warning and early response. This method permits users to compare baselines over time and to anticipate behavioral change that may lead to conflict. Such changes or inflexions in behavioral baselines may signify a deviation from the "norm" which, if undesirable, may indicate a need for early response to prevent conflict.

Especially when these baselines are made available to the public in a timely way, their posting enables the community at risk to discern subtle deviations from (seasonally adjusted) "normal" values associated with ongoing conflict situations that may escalate into violence. By identifying the thresholds beyond which the situations have escalated in the past, we can then integrate a set menu of pre-defined actions for early response. For example, a list of contingency response options could be identified and relevant parties contacted automatically when one or more baselines monitoring humanitarian indicators reach a particular threshold. Users thus conduct baseline monitoring and communicate early warning alerts to relevant parties with recommended options for early response in a timely and targeted manner.

Over the next year, CEWARN plans to integrate a Geographic Information System, or GIS, component into its ongoing monitoring. Integrating spatial analysis into CEWARN's early warning analysis presents numerous advantages over other early warning mechanisms, particularly for peacekeeping operations. For example, most early warning systems are anchored by their type—structural, dynamic, or consultative—and as such they are restricted in their focus to just one element of the conflict situation. Integrating GIS into CEWARN's analysis will add structural analysis to the dynamic indicator equation, with the stakeholders providing the complementary expert regional knowledge through regular consultations.

Another major advantage of geographic displays is that they can be understood easily by anyone, regardless of language, background, or training. Maps can therefore be shared among local communities and discussed in an easier manner than tables and graphs. Maps also facilitate the formulation of local response options based on traditional, indigenous response mechanisms.

Monitoring conflict, preparing for peace

As we noted above, even an unintentional bias toward conflict indicators has important ramifications. While we do not deny the necessity of carrying out periodic *conflict* assessments, we do believe an *equal* emphasis should be placed on understanding the causes of *peace*. Indeed,

> if we are to make a difference for the majority of the people who suffer the horrible effects of civil wars, we ought to also focus our research on how ordinary people adjust their lives to cope with the constraints and opportunities brought about by civil war.
>
> (Musifiky Mwanasali, cited in Meier, 2003: 7)

Delineating the locus of peace-generating factors would provide peace-keepers with a better understanding of indigenous conflict-coping strategies employed by the locals in their operating environment (Musifiky Mwanasali, cited in Meier, 2003: 7). Peace-generating factors such as traditional conflict resolution practices could also be identified and sustained if informants adequately report these cooperative dynamics. While such activities may have been beyond the mandate of earlier peacekeeping missions, today's peacekeeping duties have changed, "[taking] on a nature that is more civilian-oriented rather than combat-oriented; peacekeepers are involved in regional development, humanitarian aid, conflict prevention, and election supervision" (Lightburn, 2003: 24).

Having reliable information on what is going right, and where, is thus of immense value to today's peacekeepers, whose responsibilities continue to expand. In addition, monitoring cooperation and conflict, and both situations and events, and then actively supporting response mechanisms in the face of an early warning signal is more compatible with the stakeholder approach described above. Instead of implementing a solution "made at headquarters," peacekeepers strengthen the existing self-help potential among crisis-threatened population groups (Musifiky Mwanasali, cited in Meier, 2003: 7)

Collaboration on peace-generating factors builds trust between peacekeepers and the local population. In return, affected groups are more likely to confide sensitive information to peacekeeping forces: "hence forces need good relationships with the local population. If the local populace is not on the side with the peacekeepers, peacekeepers will not get the intelligence from the ground that they need" (Parsons, 2003: 11).

Local stakeholders would also benefit from peacekeeping missions that adopt a more participatory approach which recognizes the worth of "all" participants in the decision-making process. At the end of the day, it is the stakeholders—the victims—who deserve the necessary support and information to address and mitigate the vulnerabilities that exist in their own communities.

Early warning for PKI

As we noted above, the distinction between third parties and stakeholders is often one of degree rather than of kind, especially in the realm of information access. Nevertheless, understanding that there is a distinction is important, particularly for early warning and PKI. Paid informants and participatory observers face different incentives and constraints, even as they both carry a bias in their observations. While the former may be driven by pecuniary rewards, participatory observers have a stake in the information they collect and in the way this information is used.

CEWARN draws on participatory observers who also are engaged stakeholders. In addition to submitting IncReps, CEWARN observers also provide weekly SitReps that monitor precursors to conflict and cooperation.

The integration of SitReps and IncReps helps to link early warning signals with early response mechanisms. This provides the CEWARN Unit in Addis Ababa with advance warning of upcoming incidents making conflict prevention more than a hypothetical possibility.

In our view, PKI in general, and early warning and response mechanisms in particular, are best conducted by and for the communities at risk. Even an early warning system that is operated for and by third-party interests is bound to conflict with local interests at some point in time, if only when they depart. Thus we seek to engage stakeholders and instill a sense of security awareness that, when combined with intensive training of local personnel, can sustain the PKI effort into the future.

The Carnegie Commission on Preventing Deadly Conflict provided compelling arguments for prioritizing conflict prevention activities over more reactive strategies. The final report published by the Commission prompted the UN system to shift away from a culture of reaction toward a culture of prevention. Almost everyone now recognizes that preventing violence before it breaks out is much easier than resolving a conflict once blood has been shed. The lesson here is drawn directly from Sun-Tzu: the best Peacekeepers never fight. They never fight because they don't need to (Harvard Project on Negotiation, 2004). The case of CEWARN demonstrates that adequate early warning makes this more than a hypothetical possibility (Harvard Project on Negotiation, 2004).

Note

1   This is a revised version of a presentation by Douglas Bond at the Peacekeeping Intelligence: New Players, Extended Boundaries Conference held in Ottawa, Canada, December 4–5, 2003.

Bibliography

Carnegie Commission on Preventing Deadly Conflict. Available at: *http://www.wilsoncenter.org/subsites/ccpdc/index.htm*

Dorn, W. (2003) "An Advanced Capability at UN Headquarters? The Information and Research (I&R) Unit of the Department of Peacekeeping Operations: 1993–1998," *Peacekeeping Intelligence: New Players, Extended Boundaries*, conference report, Carleton University, Ottawa.

Harvard Project on Negotiation (2004) *The Third Side*. Available at: http://www.thirdside.org (accessed March 1, 2005).

Jones, B. (2003) "Shaping International Intelligence Architectures to Meet Evolving Threats and Challenges," *Peacekeeping Intelligence: New Players, Extended Boundaries*, conference report, Carleton University, Ottawa.

Laipson, E. (2003) "Information Sharing in Peacekeeping Intelligence," *Peacekeeping Intelligence: New Players, Extended Boundaries*, conference report, Carleton University, Ottawa.

Lightburn, D. (2003) "Partnering: The Challenges During Complex Peace Operations," *Peacekeeping Intelligence: New Players, Extended Boundaries*, conference report, Carleton University, Ottawa.

Meier, C. (2003) "The Role of Conflict Analysis in Preventing Complex Emergencies: Integrating Conflict Assessment and Conflict Early Warning," unpublished paper, School of International and Public Affairs, Columbia University.

Parsons, R. (2003) "C4ISR," *Peacekeeping Intelligence: New Players, Extended Boundaries*, conference report, Carleton University, Ottawa.

Roach, R. (2003) "Technology to Support Tactical Intelligence," *Peacekeeping Intelligence: New Players, Extended Boundaries*, conference report, Carleton University, Ottawa.

Svenson, J.I. (2003) "Peacekeeping and Intelligence: A Swedish Perspective," *Peacekeeping Intelligence: New Players, Extended Boundaries*, conference report, Carleton University, Ottawa.

Weibes, C. (2003) "Intelligence and the War in Bosnia: 1992–1995," *Peacekeeping Intelligence: New Players, Extended Boundaries*, conference report, Carleton University, Ottawa.

11

JUST PEACEKEEPING

Managing the relationship between peacekeeping intelligence and the prevention and punishment of international crimes

Christopher K. Penny[1]

Introduction

Effective intelligence capacity[2] is an essential component of any peace-keeping mission, whether traditional truce monitoring or more robust peace support. The need for intelligence has magnified with the increasing willingness of the United Nations (UN)[3] to place peacekeepers in areas where there is, in fact, no peace to keep. Modern peacekeeping operations (PKOs) pose significant difficulties and dangers for peacekeeping forces, particularly those missions involving failed states or ongoing ethnic conflict, and there is no substitute for timely, accurate and comprehensive intelligence relating to military threats and other operational concerns.[4]

In addition to facing traditional military concerns, peacekeeping forces now frequently operate in areas of responsibility where state or non-state actors, or both, are committing international crimes against civilian populations, alongside, in lieu of, or as part of continuing belligerent military operations. This poses significant new challenges for peacekeeping intelligence (PKI). To what extent should peacekeepers collect and assess information relating to international criminal acts in addition to more traditional military concerns? Should crime prevention fall within the mandate of peacekeeping forces, acting on the resulting intelligence? In addition, whether or not active crime prevention occurs, should PKI be used to support the subsequent international[5] prosecution of individuals responsible for attempting or committing these gross human rights violations?

This chapter examines the practical and legal ramifications of these questions, focusing on the relationship between PKI and the prevention and punishment of the core international crimes of genocide, crimes against humanity, and war crimes.[6] The second section focuses on the rationale for, and implications of, using intelligence to prevent international crimes during PKOs. This is followed by a discussion of the relationship between PKI and international criminal prosecution. Summarizing this analysis, the Conclusion reiterates that the relationship between PKI and the prevention and punishment of international crimes must be limited, particularly with respect to its use in post-conflict criminal prosecution.

Mission effectiveness in robust PKOs requires the collection and analysis of information relating to the commission, or the planned commission, of international crimes by all parties to the conflict. Peacekeeping forces must be provided with the capacity to act on the resulting intelligence to prevent international crimes in their areas of operation. Failure to act, or to provide the necessary capabilities to do so, is a gross abdication of international responsibility that will not only undermine UN legitimacy, but will also threaten the ability of peacekeeping forces to consolidate peace and deter future crimes. However, while advocating the use of PKI to actively prevent the commission of international crimes, this chapter illustrates the dangers of relying on peacekeeping forces as primary investigators for the purpose of subsequent international criminal prosecution. The direct use of PKI in international criminal proceedings may have a detrimental impact on peacekeeping effectiveness or undermine the success of any resulting prosecution.

PKI and crime prevention

Comprehensive and accurate intelligence is required to inform any UN decision to authorize the establishment of a peacekeeping force. Troop contribution requests to member states should focus on actual force requirements. Resolutions, mandates, and rules of engagement must be drafted to reflect not simply political priorities but also specific operational realities.[7] Indeed, this preliminary stage is the time to determine political will and institutional capacities, not after international forces are already in-theater and facing potentially hostile belligerents.

If political support and available resources are insufficient to address the actual threat and mission requirements discerned by effective preliminary intelligence, the better course may be not to introduce a peacekeeping force at all. This must in many circumstances be better than inserting under-equipped forces with mandates insufficient to address actual threats to short-term peace and personnel safety. Either way, the decision to introduce forces should be an informed one, and adequate, timely, and effective intelligence is crucial for ensuring this result.

To a significant extent, early strategic awareness will result from third-party information, voluntarily disclosed to the UN or individual peacekeeping member states.[8] Recognizing this fact, reliance on multiple information sources will help to provide a more accurate picture of operational realities (see, e.g., Smith, 1994: 183–187). Nonetheless, independent analytical capability is also important, as without it the UN is hostage to the views of other information-providing actors, including not only third-party states but also international and non-governmental organizations, news organizations and the parties to the conflict themselves. Information from any one of these sources can be misleading and even subject to intentional abuse.

At the pre-deployment stage, accurate intelligence concerning international crimes is particularly important. The commission of genocide, crimes against humanity, and war crimes is an extremely emotive issue, and can galvanize public and institutional opinion to act. Belligerents are often keenly aware of this reality, and deliberate exaggeration or mischaracterization of crimes may be undertaken to compel international intervention, or to direct it in favor of a particular party to the conflict.[9] The UN and its troop-contributing states must be able to distinguish valid claims for just intervention from belligerent and third-party propaganda[10] (ICISS, 2001: 34; *Brahimi Report*, 2000: 12; van Kappen, 2003: 6, 8). In the international criminal context, independent, UN-authorized, fact-finding missions continue to be a significant source of impartial strategic intelligence.[11]

Once a peacekeeping mission is undertaken, intelligence remains an absolute operational necessity. Force protection alone requires situational awareness of imminent threats to personnel, to say nothing of the capability to address them. However, PKI capacity should extend to include assessment of international criminal offences, particularly for robust operations in high-risk situations. Accurate understanding of the actions and motivations of belligerents will be compromised without such information. Certainly, the commission of crimes will alter the peacekeeping environment to an extent that must be understood for mission effectiveness and conflict termination. To the extent that peacekeepers operate in areas involving the commission of widespread and systematic crimes, force protection may also be directly compromised through lack of such understanding (Aldrich, 2003: 80).

Effective gathering and assessment of information relating to international criminal acts will require specific additional training of intelligence personnel, both with respect to pre- and post-deployment phases.[12] For example, crime indicators are frequently not identical to warning signs relating to traditional military threats (Eriksson, 1997: 12). Insufficient training may also lead to the unnecessary contamination of potential evidence by peacekeeping forces, thereby undermining the strength of any future criminal prosecution.[13]

Collection and assessment of information relating to international crimes is necessary but clearly not sufficient. Modern peacekeeping forces must also act on the resulting intelligence to address major crimes when they occur within their areas of responsibility, and they must be provided with the capacity to so by the UN and contributing states. Though recognizing that logistical constraints can and will prevent action in some circumstances, failure to stem atrocities undermines the moral and political legitimacy of the UN and its peacekeeping forces, particularly when international contingents are already in-theater and face-to-face with widespread criminal activities[14] (see, e.g., Dorn and Bell, 1995: 16; *Brahimi Report*, 2000: 9–11). Such failure also jeopardizes the long-term consolidation of peace in affected areas, thus undermining the very rationale for the introduction of peacekeeping forces.

Recognizing these concerns, peacekeeping mandates, and in particular force rules of engagement, increasingly refer directly to the prevention of international criminal acts. Crime prevention by peacekeeping forces may range from establishing a deterrent presence, through indirect steps, such as jamming radio incitement of genocide,[15] all the way to direct military intervention with deadly force. In every case, timely, comprehensive and accurate intelligence is a prerequisite for effective crime prevention, whether by identifying the location for deterrent patrols, discerning the content and frequency of radio broadcasts, or estimating opposing force capabilities.

Failure to act, where feasible, when peacekeeping forces possess intelligence indicating impending atrocities will undermine both UN and force legitimacy, and their strategic and operational ability to deter future criminal acts. This is particularly true when institutional knowledge of atrocities is known to the parties to the conflict and other international actors, whether through media reports or other mechanisms. Peacekeeping force protection may also be undermined by the corresponding loss of respect and fear by belligerents, and the alienation of affected civilian populations, as well as through the collateral effect of criminal activities themselves. Even if not threatening the short-term security of peacekeeping forces, failure to suppress international crimes may serve to encourage further criminal activity, undermining the prospects for the long-term consolidation of peace and the successful accomplishment of the peacekeeping mandate (Eriksson, 1997: 3–4).

Similarly, inaction resulting from PKI failure may also strengthen belligerent willingness to commit crimes. It may even be interpreted incorrectly by the offending parties as tacit assent by the international community, based on belligerent overestimation of international intelligence capabilities (Eriksson, 1997: 3–4). Alternatively, direct admission of intelligence incapacity may lead to combatant impunity. Either way, international ignorance will clearly result in a practical inability to prevent crimes. Whether based on ignorance or lack of political will, peacekeeping inaction in the face of international crimes will have a detrimental impact on mandate achievement and long-term institutional legitimacy.

Only in very limited circumstances, if at all, will peacekeeping forces actually have a positive legal obligation to prevent international crimes occurring within their areas of responsibility, and any such duty would likely require significant territorial control exercised by the peacekeeping force. Prevention obligations are most conclusive with respect to genocide. All Parties to the Genocide Convention have a clear obligation to "prevent and punish" the commission of genocide in their own territory (Art. 1). Indeed, this obligation extends to all states as a matter of customary international law (see, e.g., *Reservations to the Genocide Convention*: 24). An argument may be advanced that this obligation protects any civilian population under the effective control of the state in question, whether or not located on national territory.[16] Otherwise, there is no generally accepted international legal obligation for states to use force to prevent genocide occurring in territory controlled by other states or sub-national actors[17] (see, e.g., Schabas, 2000: 447, 493–502). Obligations to prevent crimes against humanity, and war crimes are, if anything, less onerous than those prohibiting genocide.

Nonetheless, genocide, crimes against humanity, and war crimes are recognized internationally not only as gross violations of human rights, but also as threats to international peace and security.[18] As a result, even absent a formal legal requirement, permissive authority to act often remains. UN peacekeeping mandates now frequently refer to the prevention of criminal acts.[19] This may authorize peacekeepers to act even without an express legal obligation to do so.[20] Absent any express UN mandate, an argument may be advanced nonetheless that peacekeepers possess the international legal authority to act on intelligence indicating the ongoing or imminent occurrence of genocide, crimes against humanity, or war crimes.[21]

That said, the collection and use of PKI for crime prevention may, and often will, result in negative, short-term, operational and tactical effects. Active prevention of criminal acts will frequently place peacekeepers in dangerous situations. Not only will this threaten personnel safety, it may render other aspects of the mission more difficult by diverting limited resources. Effective peacekeeping simply cannot occur in the face of widespread and systematic crimes, though there may be circumstances in which even strong forces are powerless to act. This is an argument for greater PKI capabilities and political will supporting robust and well-equipped operations, rather than an argument against the collection of PKI and its use in crime prevention.

Active crime prevention will clearly undermine traditional understandings of impartiality, particularly in situations where belligerents are not equally responsible for gross violations of human rights. However, strict neutrality in robust PKOs has already been discredited as an effective practical strategy[22] (see, e.g., *Brahimi Report*: 9–11). Failure to act in the face of genocide, crimes against humanity, and war crimes is not laudable impartiality but rather an abdication of moral and political responsibility.

PKI and international criminal prosecution[23]

The clear argument for using PKI to support the prevention of widespread and systematic crimes against civilian populations does not necessarily equate to its further primary use for the subsequent criminal prosecution of those responsible. In fact, as this section illustrates, PKI should at best point the way for further criminal investigation by other national or international bodies. PKI is not a substitute for analysis by trained war crimes investigators, nor should it be treated as such. In fact, reliance on PKI for prosecution may threaten necessary international intelligence-sharing relationships or undermine successful conviction.

As a preliminary matter, the character of information gathering and assessment in intelligence operations differs dramatically from the requirements of criminal investigation. Military planners rely on a forward-looking sliding scale of risk assessment when acting on intelligence, and information is gathered and analyzed on this basis. While this may be consistent with intelligence needs for major crime prevention and force protection, this would not necessarily meet the burden of proof required for proving the individual responsibility of an accused beyond a reasonable doubt in criminal proceedings. Expanding the focus of intelligence operations to include establishing formal legal proof for the purpose of criminal prosecution would impose potentially significant additional burdens, changing the character of information gathering and thereby undermining the immediate availability and effectiveness of resulting intelligence.[24]

A related concern arises with respect to detainee questioning conducted by peacekeeping forces. The immediate intelligence value of such interrogations is obvious.[25] This may not be compatible with imposing a formal investigatory role on peacekeeping forces. Military interrogation of high-value detainees should not be compromised by concerns over evidence admissibility or detainee demands for legal representation.[26] This may cause unacceptable intelligence delays, undermining force protection and other pressing operational and tactical considerations, including the prevention of serious crime.

Intelligence is also not necessarily stored in the same manner as material supporting criminal investigations, if it is stored at all. In the first instance information is gathered for analysis, and intelligence is disseminated, for the purpose of aiding military decision-making, for example by establishing situational awareness and identifying threats. If it occurs at all, given the short shelf-life of most intelligence, storage will relate to this function, not to the potential future prosecution of individuals. This applies whether the intelligence in question is at the strategic, operational, or tactical level.

Should peacekeeping contingents and contributing states be required to maintain information in a format that is accessible and searchable in the context of criminal investigations, often of persons yet unknown? If so, how long should such records be maintained, and by whom? This latter question increases in importance when one considers the frequent operational rotations involved in PKOs, often not simply individual soldiers but entire national contingents. Not only may these issues place significant burdens on peacekeeping states, during and for years after the operation in question, but they may also undermine the strength and integrity of the final evidentiary product. These concerns are amplified the more reliance is placed on peacekeeping forces as primary sources of intelligence for criminal prosecutions.

Independent, centralized investigatory bodies are simply better suited than peacekeeping forces to collect evidence necessary for international criminal trials. Personnel and unit continuity may more easily be maintained,[27] along with dedicated and consistent logistic support and evidentiary chains of custody. In addition, training can be focused more directly on criminal law and evidentiary issues. That said, peacekeeping forces must be given training sufficient to not make them investigatory liabilities, particularly at the tactical level. While recognizing that military contingencies may not always permit such luxuries, where possible evidence should be preserved by peacekeeping forces for future independent investigation. This does not mean that peacekeepers need conduct such investigations themselves.

Indeed, the utility of independent criminal investigation has been demonstrated, albeit not fully, with respect to many recent conflicts involving the commission of crimes against civilians. For example, specially-trained international war crimes investigation units operated in the former Yugoslavia, collecting information and providing independent assessment of third-party intelligence to establish the basis for individual criminal prosecution before the ICTY. In East Timor, a Serious Crimes Unit conducted investigations pursuant to UN Security Council authority. Similarly, the Prosecutor of the International Criminal Court (ICC) him- or herself possesses independent investigatory authority pursuant to the *Rome Statute* (Art. 15(1)).

Independently gathered and assessed material may be provided by war crimes investigators to peacekeeping forces for the purpose of crime prevention or mission accomplishment without raising significant concerns. In the case of ongoing crimes, this will be a strong impartial source of additional information, albeit often without sufficient currency for intelligence purposes, given logistical requirements in criminal investigations. Nonetheless, information and intelligence relating to the commission of international crimes by belligerent forces must be properly secured to avoid undermining prosecution efforts, the safety of war crimes investigators, and the long-term integrity of such information-sharing arrangements.

While PKI may also establish a foundation for independent criminal investigation, serious concerns relate to its direct use in formal criminal prosecution. The catalyst for many of these issues is the threat of disclosure of intelligence content and information-collection methods in open judicial proceedings. This concern is most obvious with respect to strategic intelligence, but disclosure concerns may also arise at the operational and tactical levels. States engaged in intelligence operations, including peacekeeping contributors, have an obvious and legitimate interest in maintaining the security of information-collection and -assessment methods that may be undermined by public disclosure.[28]

Disclosure is clearly risked when a prosecution relies directly upon PKI to establish the criminal responsibility of an accused. International criminal law standards require that accused individuals be informed of the nature of the charges against them (see, e.g., *Rome Statute*: Art. 67(1)(a)). In fact, in proceedings before the ICC, the Prosecutor must:

> disclose to the defence evidence in the Prosecutor's possession or control which he or she believes shows or tends to show the innocence of the accused, or to mitigate the guilt of the accused, or which may affect the credibility of prosecution evidence.
>
> (Art. 67(2))

Though there is no international requirement for a prosecutor to provide the defense with all material relating to an accused in his or her possession, this nonetheless establishes a high disclosure obligation that threatens the security of any PKI used directly in support of criminal prosecution. The more active peacekeeping forces are in support of criminal prosecution, the less secure their information will become. In fact, to the extent that PKI is relied upon directly to establish guilt, it must be disclosed to opposing counsel and the tribunal itself.

Crucially, using PKI directly for criminal prosecution purposes may also sabotage valuable international information-sharing relationships among states and international organizations, particularly with respect to strategic intelligence. Legitimate concern over possible future disclosure may reduce national or organizational willingness to share sensitive information with peacekeeping forces, thereby undercutting mission effectiveness and force protection. This issue is of particular concern given the significant and continuing UN and state reliance on third-party strategic and operational intelligence for the conduct of PKOs, coupled with the relative absence from these missions of major information-gathering states. Indeed, for these and other reasons, most PKI literature advocates strengthening mechanisms for information security.[29]

The use of PKI solely to generate leads for independent war crimes investigation will mitigate this risk. The potential for PKI disclosure is clearly exacerbated where peacekeeping forces play a principal role in international criminal investigations, as the prosecution will have little option but to rely directly on this evidence to establish individual criminal responsibility, particularly in the absence of any independent investigation. In contrast, if the prosecution is not relying on this information to prove criminal responsibility, there is substantially less requirement to disclose it to the defense or temptation to introduce it as evidence.

The *Rome Statute* expressly recognizes the validity of such information-sharing relationships, providing that the Prosecutor may:

> Agree not to disclose, at any stage of the proceedings, documents or information that the Prosecutor obtains on the condition of confidentiality and solely for the purpose of generating new evidence, unless the provider of the information consents.
>
> (Art. 54(3)(e))

Similar provisions protect confidential information sharing between states and the two ad hoc tribunals (*ICTY Rules*: Rule 70(B); *ICTR Rules*: Rule 70(B)). When coupled with independent criminal investigation, this information could establish a solid basis for prosecution without risking disclosure.

In contrast, in the absence of confidentiality arrangements and effective independent investigation, peacekeeping states may be subject to disclosure requests relating to PKI. To the extent that disclosure is required, or even threatened, this may threaten information- and intelligence-sharing relationships between states, peacekeeping forces and the UN. On the other hand, non-disclosure may undermine the viability of successful prosecution. In either case, serious negative consequences may be expected to arise from prosecution reliance on PKI.

In fact, the ICTY and ICTR have made numerous requests for intelligence disclosure to both information-collecting and recipient states, even in cases involving significant additional independent investigation. State compliance with these requests has been limited, despite a general legal obligation for all UN member states to cooperate with the ad hoc tribunals, including with their demands for such assistance.[30] However, the ICTY itself recognized the validity of state non-compliance with disclosure requests on national security grounds, even without any express protection for such information provided in its Statute (*Blaskic*: paras. 61–69). This protection applies even where no other option exists to bring the evidence in question before the tribunal, and it has been invoked frequently by states, with some success.

The *Rome Statute* strengthens national security protections against mandatory intelligence disclosure over the judicial protections recognized in *Blaskic*. The treaty itself places dramatic limitations on the authority of the ICC to compel disclosure of material in circumstances designated by states as threats to national security.[31] Self-declared national security interests will be determinative in most cases, preventing disclosure of intelligence even where no other mechanism exists to bring comparable information before the tribunal.[32] (*Rome Statute*: Art. 72).

Further, express protection is established in the *Rome Statute* for international information-sharing relationships. The treaty provides that a state may refuse to disclose "a document of information in its custody, possession or control, which was disclosed to it in confidence by a State, intergovernmental organization or international organization" (Art. 73). Without the consent of the originator, confidential intelligence cannot be disclosed to the ICC. The UN itself has a formal agreement with the ICC that recognizes its right to refuse disclosure of information provided to it in confidence by states, other organizations, interstate and nongovernmental, and even individuals (*Negotiated Relationship Agreement*: Art. 20).

These protections are required to permit effective peacekeeping force access to necessary information and intelligence. Otherwise, the disclosure concerns outlined above would be exacerbated in the context of the ICC. Not all states are parties to the *Rome Statute*. In fact, to date the majority of states are not participants in this treaty regime, and non-parties number many of the world's major intelligence suppliers, including the United States. As a result, it is reasonable to conclude that the ICC Prosecutor will direct disclosure requests to States Parties, even if they are the intelligence recipients rather than non-party originators.[33] Whether or not disclosure actually occurs, this threat itself may jeopardize traditional intelligence-sharing relationships between States Parties and other states, potentially undermining the effectiveness of PKOs.

That said, the protection of intelligence-sharing arrangements by international tribunals must not come at the expense of an accused. While legitimate national security concerns should be upheld, resulting non-disclosure must not result in procedural unfairness or the risk of conviction on less than compelling evidence.[34] Acquittal of an accused in such circumstances is better for the long-term consolidation of international criminal standards and a just international society than is conviction, even if warranted on moral grounds.[35]

Distancing peacekeeping forces from providing direct intelligence support for criminal prosecution may mitigate these concerns both by reducing the likelihood of subsequent disclosure and limiting potentially disastrous prosecution reliance on such evidence. This course of action requires effective independent war crimes investigation.

Without such further investigatory arrangements, peacekeeping states, particularly those that are States Parties to the *Rome Statute*, may still be placed in an unpalatable position. Refusal to disclose information may lead to the acquittal of known war criminals, while consensual disclosure may undermine national security interests and potentially threaten important intelligence relationships. International peacekeeping interests are not served by forcing contributing states into such dilemmas.

In extreme cases, mechanisms exist for the international community itself to determine the weight given to each factor in this balancing process. The UN Security Council can forestall prosecution to protect national or institutional security interests, or it can require disclosure of intelligence to facilitate prosecution.[36] Indeed, the Security Council has already favored effective peacekeeping over international prosecution in other circumstances.[37]

PKI may in fact be better suited for use in the apprehension of international criminal indictees, rather than establishing an evidentiary basis for their subsequent prosecution. This role is more closely associated with the proposed peacekeeping crime prevention function, requiring training more closely related to other military activities. In fact, apprehending individuals engaged in ongoing criminal activities has a clear nexus to increased short-term security. In contrast, post-conflict apprehension carries more obviously long-term benefits and should not be as significant a focus for peacekeeping personnel. In either case, PKI will be an essential component of any apprehension operations.[38]

Conclusion

Timely, accurate, and comprehensive intelligence relating to the commission of international crimes is essential at all stages of UN PKOs. Decisions to authorize these missions must be informed and result in mandates and force compositions that reflect operational reality and permit effective mission accomplishment in accordance with the principles of fundamental justice. This must include the authorization and capability to address international crimes. Active crime prevention, where feasible, is warranted on both moral and practical grounds, as a failure to prevent genocide, crimes against humanity, and war crimes will undermine not only mandate achievement but also force security and overall UN legitimacy.

While PKI is essential for crime prevention, it should not be relied upon as the principal evidentiary base for subsequent international trials. Intelligence disclosure in criminal proceedings may undermine legitimate national security interests and international information-sharing relationships, while non-disclosure of necessary evidence on this basis may threaten the viability of dependent prosecution. Confidential sharing of PKI with independent war crimes investigators, for lead-generation only, will mitigate these risks. At a minimum, states and the UN should be encouraged to support international prosecution through such limited confidential disclosure, in addition to providing information and intelligence support to robust PKOs.

If the balance must tip one way or another, though, it must be in favor of protecting intelligence security, to provide a basis for effective peacekeeping that will include active crime prevention, even if this means a greater chance of acquittal of criminal suspects. Prosecution of individuals responsible for genocide, crimes against humanity, and war crimes is a poor substitute for forestalling their acts in the first place.

Notes

1   The author would like to thank Professors David Carment and Martin Rudner, of the Norman Paterson School of International Affairs, Carleton University for the opportunity to participate in this project, and Marla Dow, for her comprehensive and insightful comments on a preliminary draft of this chapter.

2   For the purposes of this chapter "effective intelligence capacity" refers to the ability to collect, or otherwise access and analyze, necessary information in a timely and comprehensive manner and disseminate the final product to decision-makers. "Intelligence" refers to the final, analyzed product of this process, whereas "information" is the raw, unassessed input. In contrast to this traditional military distinction, the United Nations (UN) has historically and deliberately avoided using the term intelligence to describe any part of this process, referring instead to the collection, assessment, and dissemination of "military information."

3   This chapter focuses on peacekeeping operations authorized, though not necessarily commanded, by the UN. This would include, for example, the UN Protection Force (UNPROFOR) in the former Yugoslavia, in addition to other operations in the region carried out by the North Atlantic Treaty Organization (NATO) pursuant to a UN mandate such as the Implementation Force (IFOR).

4   This chapter accepts the initial premise that effective peacekeeping cannot occur without intelligence. Indeed, in the particular context of peacekeeping, mission mandates often focus specifically on intelligence operations, albeit by different names. After all, what else are truce monitoring and disarmament verification but intelligence operations? Therefore, while this chapter advocates the further inclusion in peacekeeping mandates of intelligence capacities relating to international crimes, it considers it (now) self-evident that peacekeepers require a general intelligence capacity to be effective. (In addition to this present volume, see also Smith, 1994; Dorn and Bell, 1995; Eriksson, 1997; Johnston, 1997.)

5   This chapter focuses on the relationship between PKI and international criminal prosecution (either before ad hoc international tribunals or the International Criminal Court (ICC)). Similar issues may arise in the context of national courts or "hybrid" tribunals, however, overall conclusions may vary depending on the nationality of the court in question, rules governing the protection of evidence, and due process protections for defendants.

6   This chapter focuses on the relationship between PKI and the prevention and punishment of these three core international crimes, specifically when they are committed in a widespread and systematic manner. This narrow focus is in keeping with current international practice. For example, genocide, crimes against humanity, and war crimes are the only crimes within the effective jurisdiction of the ICC. Similar, albeit not identical, crimes found the substantive

jurisdiction of the two ad hoc international criminal tribunals established by the UN Security Council to address atrocities committed in the former Yugoslavia and in Rwanda (ICTY and ICTR, respectively). For detailed definition of these crimes, in the context of the ICC, see the *Rome Statute*, Arts. 6–8, and the related sections of *Elements of Crimes*.

7 Similarly, decisions to modify the mandate of an existing force should be informed by effective intelligence. The UN establishment of safe areas in Bosnia-Herzegovina in the early 1990s indicates the dangers of uninformed decision-making, where formal direction to peacekeeping forces did not even delineate the geographical scope of protected areas (Quiggan, 1998: 207).

8 While peacekeepers will almost certainly rely on third-party information throughout operations, this is particularly true at this early stage. The UN possesses no comprehensive strategic intelligence capability. Indeed, there are strong political and logistical arguments against establishing a general ongoing strategic intelligence capacity (see, e.g., Eriksson, 1997: 1).

9 Information flowing from Kosovo in late 1998 and early 1999 provides a key example of the emotional power of international criminal accusations and the potential for misuse by parties to the conflict. There is little doubt that armed Serb parties loyal to President Slobodan Milosevic committed atrocities against the Kosovar Albanian population. However, there are also strong indications that the insurgent Kosovo Liberation Army (KLA) exaggerated these acts, and may even have deliberately provoked them in order to garner international support in favor of intervention in support of their goals. In contrast, fear of intelligence misuse may have been a factor in non-intervention in Rwanda.

10 Even intelligence powers represented on the UN Security Council are not necessarily neutral suppliers of objective information or intelligence (Quiggan, 1998: 204). These states have their own national interests, which may and often do favor one side in a particular conflict. Whether deliberate or unconscious, this may lead to an exaggeration of accusations against other parties and the minimization of intelligence suggesting the commission of criminal offences by the favored belligerent.

Indeed, the UN Security Council states may actually provide intelligence directly to belligerents in addition to, or instead of, UN peacekeeping forces. For example, in the context of the former Yugoslavia, the US may have provided information not only to UN peacekeeping forces but also to Croatian military planners, particularly as a precursor to Operation Storm (Aldrich, 2003: 81).

11 For example, an independent fact-finding mission in the former Yugoslavia established an intelligence basis for the establishment of the ICTY. More recently, a similar investigation of atrocities in the Darfur region of Sudan may color the UN Security Council response to this ongoing tragedy. Indeed, the International Commission on Intervention and State Sovereignty (ICISS) recognizes the "particular utility" of the Secretary-General's authority pursuant to Art. 99 of the *UN Charter* to "bring to the attention of the Security Council any matter which in his opinion may threaten the maintenance of international peace and security" (2001: 35). Similarly, the Brahimi Report advocates more effective Secretary-General "information analysis roles" (ICISS, 2000: 12).

12 Indeed, PKI itself already requires assessment of factors different from traditional military requirements at the strategic, operational, and tactical levels (Eriksson, 1997: 6ff.; Quiggan, 1998: 205).

13 This argument applies whether or not peacekeeping forces are employed as principal investigators in addition to their crime prevention function. This latter issue is analyzed in detail in the conclusion to this chapter.

14 UN inaction with respect to the 1994 Rwandan genocide provides a stark illustration of this point, as does the failure of Dutch peacekeepers to react to the massacre of the Bosnian Muslim men of Srebrenica one year later.

15 However, even well-equipped and robust peacekeeping forces may not possess the electronic warfare capacity to conduct effective large-scale jamming operations. J.F. Metzl (1997) provides a detailed discussion of specific legal, political, and logistical issues relating to the 1994 US failure to jam radio incitement of genocide in Rwanda, supporting the legality and morality of the future use of radio jamming to prevent this international crime.

16 Though in many, if not most, circumstances, it may be difficult to characterize territory in which genocide is ongoing as under the effective control of a peacekeeping force.

17 The obligation under the Genocide Convention to "prevent and punish" genocide cannot reasonably be interpreted as establishing an international legal obligation for Parties to invade other states to stem criminal acts, however egregious, even where intervention is feasible. However, it may support permissive arguments for preventative action.

18 The *Rome Statute* provides that these crimes "threaten the peace, well-being and security of the world" (Preamble). Similarly, the establishment of the ICTY (and, later, the ICTR) by the UN Security Council pursuant to its Chapter VII authority under the *UN Charter* necessitated the linkage of these crimes with international peace and security (Penny, 1999: 305–309).

19 In fact, in situations where international crimes are occurring or expected, the UN should include an express reference to addressing these activities to remove any doubt, given the necessary linkage between suppression of widespread and systematic crimes against civilians and the consolidation of short- and long-term peace.

20 UN Security Council legal authority is not unlimited. Indeed, the *UN Charter* provides that absent the invocation of Chapter VII authority by the Security Council, the UN cannot intervene in the domestic affairs of a member state (Art. 2(7)). Chapter VII may only be invoked in situations where the Security Council determines the existence of a threat to or breach of the peace, or act of aggression. However, as noted above, the commission of genocide, crimes against humanity, or war crimes has been characterized by the Security Council as a threat to (international) peace and security on numerous occasions.

21 There is certainly no international right to commit these crimes that would be violated by peacekeeping force intervention. However, there may be circumstances in which the legal basis for unauthorized crime prevention remains somewhat ambiguous, particularly where the UN Security Council has not invoked its Chapter VII authority at all with respect to the peacekeeping operation, or when the crimes in question are not systematic or widespread. Nonetheless, it is difficult to refute the moral legitimacy of successful peacekeeping-force crime prevention in the face of attacks on civilians, particularly where no greater harm is caused by military action.

22 As long as prevention is directed to any party committing crimes, this is within an enlightened understanding of peacekeeping impartiality. In this regard a limited analogy with domestic police forces may be appropriate. Eriksson (1997: 3), for example, advocates the "impartiality of the police officer." However, there are dangers in taking this analogy too far. In particular, peacekeepers may be comparable to first-response units, but their role in subsequent criminal investigation should be minimized, as the following section will illustrate.

23 Prosecution is not the only mechanism to address international crimes. Though beyond the scope of this chapter, debate continues over the merits of international

prosecution relative to other methods of post-conflict reconciliation. While not necessarily the only answer, international prosecution can, at least in theory, result in many long-term positive benefits for the consolidation of peace in post-conflict societies, though these benefits do not come without a cost. Even if accepted, however, these benefits do not necessarily dictate that peacekeepers themselves must or should play a role in such prosecutions. The conclusion to this chapter addresses this latter issue, recognizing that international prosecution for crimes committed in peacekeeping areas of responsibility may, and often should, occur while not necessarily advocating this result in all such cases.

24 This is not to suggest that voluminous evidence, gathered to a lower standard, could not in some circumstances also establish individual criminal responsibility beyond a reasonable doubt. Rather, the point of this assertion is that criminal evidentiary standards should not be practical considerations for peacekeeping forces, as this will detract from intelligence resources that should be directed to crime prevention and fulfilling force mandates.

25 The UN mission in the Congo (MONUC) in the early 1960s conducted hundreds of prisoner interrogations in accordance with Geneva Convention III standards (Dorn and Bell, 1995: 22).

26 Individuals detained under the authority of Geneva Convention III as prisoners of war do not have a general right to counsel. There is no express limit on the nature of questions that may be asked during interrogation, though detainees are not required to answer questions beyond basic self-identification, and cannot be punished for any refusal to cooperate (Art. 17). However, detention by a peacekeeping force for the purpose of subsequent international criminal prosecution may give rise to a right to counsel in some circumstances, for example, if such detention results from a formal request by the ICC Prosecutor pursuant to Part 9 of the *Rome Statute* (Art. 55(2)(d)).

27 Issues may arise in this context as well however, given the frequent secondment of national police force members to such bodies.

28 Disclosure of illegality is not a legitimate concern as UN peacekeeping forces simply should not be collecting information in violation of international law. That said, international law appears to place far fewer restrictions on information gathering and assessment than do many national legal systems. In any event, while this chapter does not advocate information-gathering operations, it recognizes that states may be reluctant to disclose intelligence for many legitimate reasons including, for example, source protection for human intelligence assets and maintaining secrecy of technological capabilities, particularly with respect to signals intelligence.

29 The need for enhanced information security is a consistent theme throughout the literature on PKI. (For an early discussion of these issues see, e.g., Smith, 1994: 236; Eriksson, 1997: 10).

30 The Security Council established the ICTY and ICTR pursuant to its enforcement authority under Chapter VII of the *UN Charter*, clearly indicating in their statutes and related resolutions the requirement for state cooperation. Security Council decisions are legally binding on all states (*UN Charter*: Art. 25). Nonetheless, some states, including New Zealand and Australia, passed legislation authorizing non-cooperation with the ad hoc tribunals in cases prejudicing national security interests (*Blaskic*: para. 66.)

31 Ironically, given its absence from the resulting ICC treaty regime, American pressure was a major factor in the inclusion of significant state non-disclosure privileges during the Rome negotiations (see, e.g., Hampson, 2002: 72ff.).

32 Kittichaisaree (2001: 283) notes that this almost certainly means that the ICC will be "even more vigilant" than the ad hoc tribunals at protecting national security interests of states.

33 Indeed, practical and legal concerns remain over prosecution attempts before the ad hoc tribunals to compel state disclosure of strategic intelligence acquired from other states.

34 Nonetheless, the *Rome Statute* appears to leave room for unfairness in circumstances involving national security non-disclosure. In circumstances where facts cannot be proven as a result of non-disclosure, the Court is permitted to draw necessary factual inferences (*Rome Statute*: Art. 72(70(a)(iii)). The provision is not expressly limited to inferences in favor of an accused, instead referring to situations where "evidence is relevant and necessary for the establishment of the guilt or innocence of the accused." However, this provision must not be read to allow unproven prejudicial inferences leading to conviction, as this is simply not compatible with the presumption of innocence and the requirement for conviction of proof beyond a reasonable doubt to the contrary (see, e.g., *Rome Statute*: Art. 66).

35 Balancing national security intelligence protections and prosecution viability, while maintaining respect for the rule of law, is also an issue in many national judicial systems, particularly in the context of robust state responses to terrorist concerns in the aftermath of the September 11, 2001 attacks in, and against, the United States.

36 Realistically, the latter option is not going to occur where the information is the product of Great Power intelligence operations. The major strategic intelligence powers are permanent members of the Security Council and posses a veto over such compulsion.

37 It insured continued American support or peacekeeping missions by granting immunity from ICC jurisdiction to all peacekeepers (and other UN personnel) during the first two years after the entry-into-force of the *Rome Statute*, clearly favoring effective peacekeeping over universal international criminal prosecution (see, e.g., UN Security Council Resolution 1422 (2002)). However, all peacekeepers remained subject to potential prosecution for international crimes in other fora, both domestic and international. This jurisdictional immunity ended when the Security Council failed to renew it in June 2004.

38 However, there is a real danger that PKI can also be misused in this context. Evidence suggests that early post-conflict peacekeeping forces in the former Yugoslavia actually used intelligence to plan patrol routes that physically avoided indicted war criminals, thereby evading any possible obligation to arrest them and mitigating potential threats to personal safety (Penny, 1999: 297).

Bibliography

Primary documents

Convention on the Prevention and Punishment of the Crime of Genocide, December 9, 1948, 78 U.N.T.S. 277, in force January 12, 1951 [*Genocide Convention*].

Elements of Crimes, ICC Doc. ICC-ASP/1/3 (September 3–10, 2002).

Geneva Convention Relative to the Treatment of Prisoners of War, August 12, 1949, 75 U.N.T.S. 135, in force October 21, 1950 [*Geneva Convention III*].

International Criminal Tribunal for the Former Yugoslavia, Rules of Procedure and Evidence, March 14, 1994, UN Doc. IT/32 as am. [*ICTY Rules*].

International Criminal Tribunal for Rwanda, Rules of Procedure and Evidence, July 5, 1995, UN Doc. ITR/3/ as am. [*ICTR Rules*].

Negotiated Relationship Agreement between the International Criminal Court and the United Nations, ICC Doc. ICC-ASP/3/Res.1, concluded October 4, 2004 [*Negotiated Relationship Agreement*].

Report of the Panel on United Nations Peace Operations, UN Doc. A/55/305–S/2000/809, August 21, 2000 [*Brahimi Report*].

Statute of the International Criminal Court, July 17, 1998, UN Doc. A/CONF.183/9 (1998) 2187 U.N.T.S. 3, in force July 1, 2002 [*Rome Statute*].

UN Charter, June 26, 1945, Can. T.S. 1945 No. 7, 59 Stat. 1031, 145 U.K.F.S. 805 [*UN Charter*].

UN Security Council Resolution 1422, U.N. Doc. S/Res/1422 (July 12, 2002).

Judicial decisions

Prosecutor v. Tihomir Blaskic, Case No. IT-95–14–AR108 *bis*, judgment of October 29, 1997 on the Request of the Republic of Croatia for Review of the Decision of Trial Chamber II of July 18, 1997 [*Blaskic*].

Reservations to the Convention for the Prevention and Punishment of the Crime of Genocide, Advisory Opinion [1951] I.C.J. Rep. 14 [*Reservations to the Genocide Convention*].

Secondary sources

Aldrich, Richard J. (2003) "Intelligence Support for UK Low Intensity Operations," in B. de Jong, W. Platje, and R.D. Steele (eds.), *Peacekeeping Intelligence: Emerging Concepts for the Future*, Oakton, VA. OSS International Press, pp. 73–100.

Dorn, A.W., and Bell, J.H. (1995) "Intelligence and Peacekeeping: The UN Operation in the Congo, 1960–64," *International Peacekeeping*, 2 (1): 11–33.

Eriksson, Par (1997) "Intelligence in Peacekeeping Operations," *International Journal of Intelligence and CounterIntelligence* 10 (1): 1–18

Hampson, Fen Osler (2002) "Promoting Human Rights and the Rule of Law: The International Criminal Court," Chap. 5, *Madness in the Multitude: Human Security and World Disorder*, Oxford: Oxford University Press, pp. 62–79.

ICISS (2001) *The Responsibility to Protect*, Canada: International Development Research Centre, International Commission on Intervention and State Sovereignty.

Johnston, Paul (1997) "No Cloak and Dagger Required: Intelligence Support to UN Peacekeeping Missions," *Intelligence and National Security*, 12 (4): 102–112.

Kittichaisaree, Kriangsak (2001) *International Criminal Law*, Oxford: Oxford University Press.

Metzl, Jamie Frederic (1997) "Rwandan Genocide and the International Law of Radio Jamming," *American Journal of International Law*, 91 (4): 628–651.

Penny, Christopher K. (1999) "No Justice, No Peace?: A Political and Legal Analysis of the International Criminal Tribunal for the Former Yugoslavia," *Ottawa Law Review*, 30 (2): 259–313.

Quiggan, Thomas (1998) "Response to 'No Cloak and Dagger Required: Intelligence Support to UN Peacekeeping Missions'," *Intelligence and National Security*, 13 (4): 203–207.

Schabas, William A. (2000) "Prevention of Genocide," Chap. 10, *Genocide in International Law*, Cambridge: Cambridge University Press, pp. 447–502.

Smith, Hugh (1994) "Intelligence and UN Peacekeeping," *Survival*, 36 (3): 174–192.

Van Kappen, Frank (2003) "Strategic Intelligence and the United Nations," in B. de Jong, W. Platje, and R.D. Steele (eds.), *Peacekeeping Intelligence: Emerging Concepts for the Future*, Oakton, VA. OSS International Press, pp. 3–10.

12

THE ETHICS OF
INTELLIGENCE IN PEACE
SUPPORT OPERATIONS

Angela Gendron

Introduction

Peace support operations (PSOs) pose two problems for the ethicist: the justification for intervention and the manner in which this is conducted. While this chapter is primarily concerned with the *means*, the context cannot be ignored. If the grounds for intervention are unjust, any moral claim for the means used is hypothetical as the 2004 United Nations High Level Panel Report on Threats, Challenges and Change recognized when it recently recommended to the Secretary-General moral criteria to guide intervention decisions. Besides addressing the question of whether intelligence is an appropriate instrument of peace interventions, this chapter also looks at related issues such as the consequences of using, or failing to use, intelligence, the politicization of intelligence, and the sharing of intelligence between member states of a multilateral peace alliance.

While it is generally accepted by liberal democratic states that intelligence can be a force for good in serving their domestic and foreign policy ends, as a source of *national* power, it is not easily adapted to the needs of a multilateral peace alliance such as the United Nations (UN). The use of *force* is regarded as a necessary and appropriate tool of peace interventions, but no such consensus has been reached with respect to *intelligence*. "As the UN officially can have no secrets, peacekeeping operations are 'transparent' (Rose, 1998: 72). There are indications that this is changing, but the preference shown by the UN for the term "military information" rather than "intelligence," for example, is an indication of the political sensitivities involved.

For all but moral absolutists who prefer to change the world by the strength of moral ideals alone, some intelligence capability is both desirable and justifiable, especially for stabilization missions in hostile environments. Yet neither the UN nor the North Atlantic Treaty Organization (NATO) have a dedicated all-source intelligence unit and the ad hoc arrangements by which member states share their intelligence product with others is partial and selective. Generally speaking, opposition to the use of intelligence emanates from the headquarters of member states rather than at the operational level where good intelligence is considered essential to the effective and ethical use of force.

There are many definitions of intelligence (Davies, 2002), and differences in national perceptions abound. It has been said that "intelligence is not about secrecy but about learning what is going on by the rigorous analysis of all available information and ... by the active tasking of information collectors to confirm or deny what one thinks one knows" (Johnston, 1997: 111). But the intelligence which is the focus of this chapter, and which is of concern in a peace support context, is indeed intelligence derived from *secret* sources, which probably accounts for less than five per cent of all available information. It is collected, analyzed, assessed, and distributed under strict caveats, then selectively made available to decision-makers for action.

The value of intelligence will be less critical to the success of some intervention strategies than others. Peace alliances, just like nation states, must determine whether, and to what extent, they will allocate scarce resources to intelligence activities based on their international policy objectives and perceptions of the threat. While intelligence can be *useful* in reporting on the effectiveness of diplomatic and economic measures, it may be *indispensable* to enforcement operations in complex and hostile environments. However, given the close relationship between prevention and enforcement, this distinction is tenuous. Would-be peace-breakers might be deterred from deadly conflict if economic sanctions could be implemented effectively at an earlier stage. As the emphasis shifts from traditional observation missions to enforcement operations for humanitarian purposes, the ethical implications of *failing to use* intelligence become more of an issue.

Why do states engage in PSOs?

International policy objectives cannot be separated from the means used. For much of the twentieth century, a "realist" view of international affairs prevailed which asserted that international politics was concerned purely with the balance of power and interests. Foreign policy goals and decisions about whether and when to intervene abroad were based on a state's evaluation of its comparative power position. States defended their interests by force, unaided, or through the formation of collective security alliances with others who shared those interests. Though realists saw nothing unethical in pure self-interest, there were some who maintained that power could be used to make a better world (Schuman, 1958), and who justified interventions in the affairs of sovereign states on that basis despite the failure of Wilsonian idealism in the 1920s. Roosevelt argued that an enlightened international society could choose to act in concert to impose stability and order on the rest of the world, and it is this concept that motivates peace interventions and which became the genesis of the UN Security Council.

From the late twentieth century onward, peace has been the foreign policy goal of most postmodern states, but their preference for a peaceful environment goes beyond realism's narrow self-interest of traditional collective security, defense alliances, and a concern with the balance of power. As the effects of globalization have increased the interdependence of states, organizations, and individuals, the actions of foreigners increasingly impact on domestic policies. Individual security and the active promotion and projection of world stability are now accepted as desirable goals. In effect, postmodern states aim to export their democratic values as a means of making development assistance more effective and increasing the security of both recipients and donors. In other words, it is an inclusive self-interest writ large—a pragmatic idealism.

The extent to which states are prepared to concede or temporarily set aside their sovereign powers and cooperate with others for humanitarian purposes is an ethical decision, but the inherent tension between national interests and those of the peace alliance will depend to some extent on how narrowly states define their interests in domestic strategic terms, and how broadly they do so in conformity with the values and goals of the alliance.

Modern democracies it seems *do* have a conscience, or at least feel the need to gain support for their actions from others who share similar values. Very shortly after its election in 1997, the UK's "New Labour" government announced that, henceforth, its foreign policy would be bound by an "ethical dimension" (Cook, 1997). This seemed to signal a willingness to use power on behalf of "others," and to acknowledge that an ethical foreign policy was one which recognized that *means* are inseparable from *ends*: "To be interested in *ends* and to have contempt for the *means* which alone secure them, is the last stage of intellectual demoralization" (Dewey, 1929: 549).

Intelligence as a force for good or bad

To change the world for the better, power must be used as a force for good. Championing the cause of liberal democracy, human rights, and the rule of law without having the power or the will to enforce such ideas can be as morally bankrupt as using power purely to further self-interest. Though there is now a willingness to use *force* proactively on behalf of others—the essence of stabilization operations—there is no similar consensus about the use of *intelligence*. Unlike force, clandestine intelligence activities lack transparency, but when interventions are justified in the name of individual liberty, security, and regional stability, rather than narrow national self-interest, there is a particular need to ensure that the means are compatible with the ends and can be held to account.

Achieving consensus within an alliance about ends and means will be difficult when there are conflicting national interests and doubts about the legitimacy or the true motivation for intervening in the affairs of other sovereign states: "the humanitarian motive is one among several, even if primary rather than merely contingent" (Walzer, 1977: 101). The more complex and resource-intensive the peace mission, the more difficult consensus becomes, since the perceived interests of member states will bear upon their willingness to participate and agree on ways and means to achieve objectives.

As an instrument of domestic foreign policy, intelligence is generally accepted by liberal democratic states as a force for good but, as a source of *national* power, it is not easily adapted to the needs of *multilateral* peace alliances, which require participants to renounce temporary advantage and narrowly defined national interests in order to fulfill their international obligation to act impartially and consistently in pursuit of world peace and stability.

How states adjudicate conflicting interests and aspirations is an ethical issue that must be resolved according to their particular moral norms and values. Such ethical dilemmas are very real, but they are distinguishable from the more fundamental claim that secret intelligence gathering is an unethical instrument of peace interventions.

Does resort to secrecy and deception in the cause of peace undermine the ethical grounds for intervention? Since there is no objective moral standard, and given that the international order is premised upon the sovereignty of nations, an ethical decision to use either force or intelligence requires the articulation of rules and practices that command wide assent. While the members of a peace alliance share values and interests, they will have different practical and moral perspectives. Achieving consensus through open, inclusive, and democratic debate would be preferable to the current situation, which is one of ambivalence and ad hoc initiatives that circumvent the proscription on "intelligence" yet serve neither efficiency nor morality.

Traditional peacekeeping missions were invited to mediate between warring parties from a position of neutrality and impartiality and depended upon trust and cooperation to achieve their objectives under Chapter VI of the UN Charter. This was still the case in Bosnia in 1994 when it was said, "The erosion of UNPROFOR's perceived impartiality—a vital element in any peacekeeping mission—was one of the major causes of difficulty in finding peace in Bosnia" (Rose, 1998: 244).

It is claimed that the impartiality of interveners, or rather perceptions of their impartiality, will be compromised by the use of secret intelligence, with negative consequences for the effectiveness and safety of peace enforcers and humanitarian workers. Yet belligerents, as in the Bosnian conflict, often impugn the impartiality of intervention forces as a standard response when they fail to get their own way. Perceptions of impartiality will always be self-serving

With regard to enforcement operations, it may be that the balance of consequences lies in favor of the advantages that intelligence offers, especially since perceptions about the *credibility* of an intervention force are also important, and an intervention force must be provided with the means and the mandate to achieve its objectives. Credibility is enhanced, rather than compromised, by an intelligence capability. The "failure to project the necessary images of success greatly undermined the credibility of UNPROFOR and sapped the international will to support the mission" (Rose, 1998: 244).

Paradoxically, while intelligence may not enhance *perceptions* of impartiality, it may well serve to preserve the *substance* of it insofar as it "tells truth unto power" and can counter the local propaganda, disinformation, and biased media reporting that influences politicians and peacekeepers alike. However, it has been suggested that the increasing complexity and resource-intensiveness of humanitarian enforcement operations may require that, instead of retaining strict neutrality, specific outcomes may need *to be promoted* through the effective use of force. When lives are at stake, there may not be an option of impartiality (Carment and Rowlands, 2003).

While it is often said that intelligence is an inappropriate instrument of peace interventions and counter-productive to effectiveness in that it undermines perceptions of impartiality and neutrality, it is not clear whether such views are sincerely held or are merely a convenient means of expressing the root of the opposition which arises from the tensions and conflicting interests of asymmetric, multilateral peace alliances. The way states resolve these divergent interests and choose whether to deal with organizational inertia and bureaucracy are in themselves ethical issues, but once again are distinguishable from the claim that intelligence is unethical.

The moral continuum

How do states judge whether it is ethical to use either force or intelligence in a PSO given that it is doubtful whether the UN or any other international body could act as an international moral authority? Morality is social in its origins, sanctions, and functions, and is an instrument of society as a whole for the guidance of individuals and groups. The central question of normative ethics is what basic principles, criteria, or standards determine what is morally right or what we ought to do.

At one end of the moral continuum, extreme *idealists* such as Kant were concerned with the principles and rules of moral duty, which are derived from reason rather than experience; they guide actions and tell us what we *ought* to do, and for some—the categorical imperatives—no exceptions may be made. One of these requires us to treat others as "an end in itself," and not merely a "means" (Kant, 1997: 37). Kant condemned the use of covert intelligence techniques, even in wartime, as "intrinsically despicable." But Kant provides little practical advice for dealing with the real world. He is concerned with the principles and ideals to which we should aspire and which represent the best in mankind.

Realists or consequentialists, on the other hand, are concerned with moral values—judgments about the goodness of things based not on mere rules but on consequences. A *realist* believes in the morality of results and, at the extreme, considers *any* means that secure a desired outcome as justifiable. Machiavelli, who distinguished public from private morality, famously subscribed to the view that *raison d'état* justified any action. In the imperfect world of politics, good men intent on doing good must know how to be bad (Mansfield, 1996: 20, 33). Ruthlessness is a virtue, but not when used for mere personal advancement. It has to be in a higher cause. Given that there are no objective standards by which to determine the moral boundaries, individuals and societies must locate themselves between the two extremes. Intuitively, people accept that while ideals are important, so too are outcomes, and they adopt a pragmatic approach to morality which essentially tempers idealism with realism yet avoids a cynical calculus of self-preservation and consequences.

Postmodern states are less concerned with the ideals and principles derived from Kantian pure reasoning, than with the desire to prevent the spillover from strife-torn and failing states threatening their own peace and security. Instead of a *moral imperative* they are driven by a *strategic imperative*, which is to manage global security. But strategy, like morality, is too often the language of justification, and if we are too liberal in our interpretation of the moral rules, we might, in Machiavellian terms, condone the poisoning of princes. It is all a matter of balance; too much idealism in our choice of means may limit our ability to act ethically, or even at all: "If ethics focuses too much on the means ... it is likely to go wrong" (Cooper, 2004: 137), but too much realism and concern with outcomes risks losing the moral high ground and debasing the values which justify the intervention and the integrity of peace support missions.

An acceptable balance must be found that satisfies both the moral aspirations we have for the conduct of peace support missions and meets the practical needs and obligations of enforcement operations and force protection.

The articulation of rules governing the deployment of peace intervention forces and the methods used must, in the end, reflect a consensus among member states about what is acceptable on the basis of their shared moral values. Pragmatism, which is an ethical approach that focuses on the real, social problems of situations rather than abstract absolutes, provides an ethical alternative to the extremes of the idealist/realist dichotomy.

Just War doctrine

Pragmatism is the basis of the Just War doctrine, which seeks to temper realism—the inevitability of conflict—with idealism—the notion that the behavior of civilized societies, even in war, should adhere to certain forms of conduct which reflect shared norms and values. It recognizes the reality that war might be necessary and justifiable under certain circumstances, but nevertheless seeks to constrain the decision to wage war and regulate the way it is conducted by specifying the conditions under which a Just War may be claimed and offering moral criteria to govern the use of force. Though the doctrine was originally intended to guide the decisions by states to wage war, it is equally applicable to the actions of states in dealing with threats to domestic security that fall short of war and to the intervention decisions by coalitions of states to counter actions by others which threaten individual security and global stability. Resort to war had to pass tests of last resort, right intention, proportional means, probability of success, and discrimination to the conduct of the war.

After the Vietnam War, Walzer and others were particularly concerned to establish whether any moral basis existed for *pre-emptive and preventive* attacks and to extend Just War criteria to humanitarian and other types of interventions. The recent deliberations of the UN High Level Panel were instigated by the UN Secretary-General in an attempt to clarify the grounds for peace support and humanitarian operations and pave the way for more timely "last resort" interventions when necessary (UN, 2004).

Just War and Just Intelligence in peace support situations

No similar internationally agreed conventions or moral rules apply to the use of intelligence though in the national context, intelligence activities are subject to legislative regulation and the provisions of the UN Human Rights Convention. Only by building consensus through an inclusive and democratic process is it likely that intelligence will be accepted as a justifiable and necessary knowledge resource for peace interventions, particularly those that fall under Chapter VII Charter requirements. However, the non-transparency of intelligence activities is a cause of concern for states who fear the abuse of power by dominant members and who already suspect that decisions to intervene in the affairs of others are not primarily humanitarian but serve the strategic interests of powerful states. Kant wrote that even when morality appears to be the grounds for our actions, "it cannot be inferred with certainty that no covert impulse of self-love, under the mere pretense of 'morals, is not the real cause of our actions', for we like to flatter ourselves by falsely attributing to ourselves a nobler motive" (Kant, 1997: 19).

The ends cannot be separated from the means, but if the UN can successfully establish and win consensus about the grounds necessary to justify interventions, then the difficulties of holding the means account-able will need to be addressed. Just War criteria govern the use of force; it may be possible to devise something analogous for the use of intelli-gence (Gendron, 2005) to allay suspicion and win support for intelligence as an ethical source of power in pursuit of humanitarian objectives.

The rules which have been developed to govern the use of force—to prevent the abuse of power and ensure objectivity, fairness and account-ability—require that the decision to use force be made only after consideration has been given to the probability of success and the likely consequences; the minimal level of force which is proportional to the requirement; and to whether targets can be discriminated to avoid non-combatants and the suffering and death of innocents. Unless these conditions are met, the justification for the intervention is lost. It must be true that force commanders who have access to good intelligence are better able to comply with these requirements. Whether intelligence is "the hand-maiden of force or its master" (Keegan, 2003: 5), the two are inseparable in conflict situations.

The UN High Level Panel has proposed five Just War criteria to guide the Security Council in deciding whether to authorize the use of force—the seriousness of the threat; proper purpose; last resort; proportional means; and balance of consequences (UN, 2004). These are derived from Just War criteria. Though unlikely, if the UN or NATO were ever to establish inde-pendent and dedicated intelligence units to serve the needs of peace officials and force commanders, the decision would have to be based on the agreement and consent of member states that intelligence was a neces-sary and proportional means of countering the threats, there being no other available or sufficient means.

As the UN Panel's proposals make clear, the justification for the use of force is "as a last resort," yet this need not be interpreted to mean that force can only be used in *response* to an attack or that intelligence should not be used *proactively*.

Though the use of force and resort to secrecy and deception generate unease in liberal democratic societies, a pragmatic idealist can accept that, in defense of national interests or in furtherance of peace and humani-tarian aims, exceptional circumstance can justify their use, provided they are subject to regulation and oversight. Pragmatism might claim that to do so is to accept a lesser evil in order to avoid a greater one—"one can justify resort to it without denying that it is evil, justifiable only because other means would be insufficient or unavailable" (Ignatieff, 2004: 18).[1]

The strategic case for intelligence in the peace support context

A nation state must make decisions about whether and to what extent scarce resources are to be allocated to intelligence activities. That decision is a function of its international objectives, perceptions of the threat, and available resources. The UN, or any other collective peace alliance, must make similar decisions. Like any other organization, it must pay due regard to efficiency, but because of the nature of its work, the ethical implications of its choices will be subject to particular scrutiny. Just as efficient outcomes are not necessarily ethical, so there may be a cost in efficiency terms if actions are constrained too closely by moral considerations.

Realism is a morality of outcomes, therefore efficiency and morality are positively correlated. Idealism requires that right actions are taken regardless of the efficiency costs.

The Canadian Government among others recently called for new rules governing international actions when the governments of sovereign states fail to protect their own people from tyranny and oppression (Governor-General Adrienne Clarkson, 2004). In part the call for more clarity reflects ethical concerns and a consensus among modern states that they have a duty to intervene to protect and provide individual and regional security. But it also reflects a resource problem and the need to ensure that interventions are judicious and effective. The pressure to engage in more peace enforcement operations to deal with a growing number of intra-state conflicts has increased the urgency to identify strategies that are effective, affordable, and acceptable to the member states of peace alliances.

Military strategists have suggested that it is no longer possible to fight, let alone win wars using only military strength since the projection of force itself is dependent on tactical intelligence. Peace enforcement operations usually take place in low-intensity conflict situations where the threats tend to be diffuse and uncertain. Intelligence is required both at the pre-deployment planning stage, and in support of operations which inform decision-makers about the disposition, intentions, capabilities, and intentions of potentially hostile forces.

The increasing number of Chapter VII interventions has meant that the issue of force protection has assumed greater urgency. Since states have a primary moral duty to provide security for their citizens, when stabilization forces are working in a hostile environment, there is a moral obligation to protect them using all reasonable means. By extension, there is also a duty to protect the citizens on whose behalf the intervention has been made. These are pressing arguments for an intelligence capability and one advanced by those who are in the front line.

Secret intelligence is indispensable for filling in critical knowledge gaps and verifying open source information. It is often the only effective means of countering the activities of opponents who themselves operate clandestinely. "We need secret intelligence against secretive enemies" (Braithwaite, 2003). In hostile peace support environments, local combatants may deliberately create a "fog of war" in order to disguise their intentions, conceal humanitarian crimes, or attempt to deflect responsibility onto others. By telling "truth unto power," policy is informed by reality rather than disinformation. Two accounts of the war in Bosnia give illuminating examples of the extent to which warring parties attempted to subvert the peace process and manipulate events to their own advantage (Rose, 1998; Wiebes, 2003). Intelligence can also counter the intelligence-gathering activities of adversaries intent upon disrupting the peace process and gaining advantage over other warring factions.

In its capacity to forewarn of threats and disrupt or prevent their occurrence, intelligence has been described as the "first line of defence" (Gates, 1987: 230), which may serve to obviate or minimize the need for force. The availability of intelligence is most valuable at an earlier stage when intelligence might provide warning to the international community of growing threats and humanitarian violations. The international community might then consider a range of measures, short of force, to remedy the situation. Typically, peace support missions operate in uncertain and changing conditions where there is a constant tendency for tensions to slide into physical conflicts.

The UN Panel has recommended a peace-building commission to monitor trouble spots, offer help and advice, give warnings, and prepare for armed intervention as a last resort. If established, the commission ideally should be able to draw upon all-source assessments and indicators in order to meet its objectives.

The ability to achieve a peace settlement may depend less on military strength than on having a deep understanding of the intentions and capabilities of adversaries through a knowledge of the history, culture, and politics of a region. This goes beyond tactical intelligence in providing accurate information on the actors and issues in the conflict area, thereby enhancing the probability of achieving a just and *lasting* peace. When intervention operations do not acquire such knowledge, there will be lost opportunities in terms of winning hearts and minds and prudential information gathering among the local population. The consequent peace settlement may be superficial and temporary.

Deciding what is right

The ethic of postmodern states is to achieve outcomes through means which are consonant with liberal democratic values, but where conflicts arise there is a tendency to accept that force and deception may be necessary in dealing with states and societies where there is little respect for the rule of law and no central authority able or willing to enforce it. Exceptional circumstances, where one value must take precedence over another, can justify means which might otherwise seem inappropriate. This moral hazard has been called "the lesser evil..." and one can resort to it without denying that it is evil, justifiable only because other means would be insufficient or unavailable (Ignatieff, 2004: 18). Pragmatists would accept the need to tolerate the lesser evil in order to avoid the greater one.

Another way of looking at it is to assess the "balance of consequences." With regard to the use of force, the 2004 UN High Level Panel test was "whether military action is likely to have a better or worse result than inaction" (para. 207) A similar test could be applied to the use of intelligence, which would require that any negative effects be more than offset by the potential benefits to the safety of peace workers, their effectiveness; the UN's reputation, and its future place in the work, and the support the UN can command both from member states and the wider community to carry out humanitarian and stabilization interventions

The strategic case for the use of intelligence is strong and a realist would have no difficulty finding the balance of consequences in its favor. Whether intelligence "is the handmaiden of force or its master" (Keegan, 2003: 5), the two are inseparable in conflict situations and military strategists throughout history have sanctioned every manner of deceit necessary to gain strategic advantage and avoid war. Sun Tzu, among others, believed that ultimately good spies prevent bloodshed (Kaplan, 2002: 42). But idealists too can find some reassurance in the ethical role that intelligence can play in the initial decision to use force and in providing the information necessary to ensure that it complies with Just War criteria and Charter requirements. In trying to assess the likely consequences and probability of success, the minimal and proportional use of force necessary and the means by which the death of innocents can be avoided, it must be true that compliance is easier for commanders who have access to good intelligence. Force protection and the security of civilian populations is perhaps the strongest ethical argument for the use of intelligence.

Political sensitivities and national interests

Member states of multilateral peace alliances are required voluntarily to cooperate with others in the fulfillment of their international obligations. They must do so in an impartial and consistent manner, renouncing temporary advantage and narrowly defined national interests in favor of global peace and stability. They are not expected to *sacrifice* their vital interests for the welfare of the international community, but they are expected to set aside traditional sovereign state concerns with balance of power and *raison d'état* and identify their interests with broader cooperative, humanitarian and security aims.

Political sensitivities will dictate the decision to intervene, the scope of the mission and the means used. The political will of member states determines not only the support for its declared objectives but their levels of participation and contribution to resources. For the most part, a state's strategic interests are fulfilled by compliance with its international obligations, but when the two conflict, national interests will take precedence. The ethical issue concerns how narrowly states interpret those interests.

Peace alliances are likely to be more *multinational* in character than *multilateral*. Member states participate voluntarily but unequally and have disparate motives for so doing. Unlike the dominant "postmodern" states of whom it has been said "their vital interests are no longer vital or national" because they rely predominantly on self-regulation, mutual vulnerability and transparency for their security (Cooper, 2004: 39), those at an earlier stage of development continue to see their security in balance of power terms. These states may not themselves be fully democratic but participate in the alliance to enhance their own security and demonstrate a commitment to its values. However, the extent to which they are included in the decision-making and planning of operations will influence their perception and acceptance of its goals.

Opposition to the use of intelligence by non-aligned and less-developed states derives from the suspicion that it is the strategic interests of a few dominant members, rather than humanitarian objectives, which primarily drives the "peace" agenda. As an instrument of that policy, resort to secret intelligence would merely serve those dominant interests and in a way that might threaten or be inimical to their own. This source of opposition is waning, but inherent tensions between national and collective interests are the source of innumerable difficulties.

Intelligence sharing

Lacking any dedicated intelligence capability of its own, the UN must rely on threat assessments and other intelligence product voluntarily contributed by members. It has no power to task or dictate the priority given to its intelligence requirements and no power to force its members to share intelligence with others if members decide that it is not in their national interests to do so or if they are constrained by third-party rules or by concerns that the material would be misused or not properly protected. They may decide that the *effective* use of intelligence is best served by *not* sharing with some states, i.e. those which are known to have links with rogue states or terrorists groups.

Members of NATO similarly need only provide what they choose and the classification given will determine with whom it may be shared, some members having more privileged access than others. The greater cohesiveness and shared values of NATO members have encouraged a greater degree of sharing than in the UN, but the recent expansion is likely to lead to further compartmentalization.

Despite pressure on the ground by force commanders for the wider sharing of intelligence, problems persist because, in practice, intelligence is highly compartmentalized and sanitized to protect perceived national interests and comply with third-party agreements. Administrative rules govern the handling and processing of intelligence contributions and the military information which is collected in the field, but sharing often takes place in spite of the rules rather than because of them. Users in the field may resort to ad hoc creative and discretionary measures to compensate for the lack of formal arrangements or to circumvent rules that are seen as too restrictive.

In 1992, President George Bush committed his government to sharing intelligence with the UN in recognition that the peace support environment had changed. The pressure to engage in more enforcement operations to deal with intra-state conflict meant that there would be a requirement for:

> strategic military and political intelligence for pre-deployment planning: operational intelligence support for deployed UN forces regarding the disposition, capabilities and intentions of potentially hostile forces; and tactical intelligence to support UN forces that might themselves be engaged in sustained combat.
>
> (President George H. Bush, 1992)

Intelligence sharing is at one level an organizational issue, but the failure of peace alliances since 1992 to adjust to the changing nature and environment of PSOs and to interpret national interests more broadly is also one of policy and ethics. The essence of the problem is captured by an account of the difficulties that peace intervention forces faced in Bosnia:

> no intelligence culture within the UN; no organizational structure in the UN itself devoted to active and timely intelligence gathering and the analysis of the intelligence gathered; little intelligence contributions from outside; and finally, little willingness to cooperate among foreign intelligence services.
>
> (Wiebes, 2003: 36)

A state's failure to share relevant and timely intelligence is ethically indefensible unless there are strong grounds for supposing that the negative affects to the state or its allies outweigh the benefits. In making such a judgment, a state must take its international commitments seriously so that decisions regarding the classification and sanitization of intelligence are *biased toward* sharing and the collective need rather than against.

Classifying and continuing to review intelligence with the object of facilitating sharing may be a resource-intensive and complex procedure for organizations, but it is one which is necessary if it is to fulfill its international obligations. The September 11, 2001 attacks provided the impetus to do so in the counter-terrorism context, but despite some progress, the UN continues to receive complaints that intelligence is not shared, or that it is so censored as to be useless. If PSOs are the means by which postmodern states attempt to manage the risk of global instability posed by a range of threats, including terrorism, then intelligence sharing, particularly in the pre-conflict stage, will be vital.

Smaller states do not usually produce their own intelligence and are therefore "free riders" in that they benefit from the additional security of participating in a cooperative peace alliance while contributing relatively little if anything to its effectiveness. But they can contribute in other ways, as in the formation of regional coalitions in which intelligence is freely shared between states with a commonality of interests, values, and culture.

While theoretically it might be possible to build consensus and agree rules for the collection, processing, and dissemination of intelligence by a dedicated UN or NATO unit, it is unlikely that the agreement of member states or the required resources would be forthcoming. The current ad hoc arrangement poses less of a threat to national interests, and while not optimal, could work more effectively if protective security concerns could be managed and if the major intelligence producers demonstrated a greater commitment to the needs of the alliance and a willingness to interpret national interests more broadly.

The politicization of intelligence

Much is said in a national context about the need to "tell truth unto power," to produce objective, policy-neutral and unbiased intelligence assessments in order to avoid the dangers of politicization and the bias of experts. This danger is even greater in the context of an *international* peace alliance. Under present arrangements, neither the UN nor NATO have a dedicated and independent core of professional staff; they rely on seconded personnel from member states who in effect serve two masters and have divided loyalties.

Moreover, the intelligence product they collate is an amalgam of the contributions that member states choose to supply on a selective basis. Maintaining impartiality and objectivity under such circumstances is difficult both for member states and for the individuals whom they nominate to serve the alliance. So too is the likelihood that objective assessments may be ignored or rejected in the face of national sympathies and preferred policy options. The following example illustrates the point.

A mortar attack on the Markele market in Sarajevo in February 1994 killed 68 civilians. For a long time, the USA adhered to the view that the attacks had been executed by the Bosnian Serb forces despite a contrary and independent assessment by intelligence staff within the western intelligence community that the perpetrators were more likely to be Bosnian Muslims who had carried out the attack on their own people

(Wiebes, 2003: 68).

A member state's unwillingness to accept an assessment which ran contrary to their own preferred political position can impede operational efficiency if it leads, as it did in the Bosnian conflict, to a reduction in cooperation and intelligence sharing between alliance partners.

The unequal contributions and participation of member states and reliance on the assets and capabilities of a few dominant nations, can impair the collective alliance image. It becomes *multinational* rather than *multilateral*, and its actions, assessments and deliverances are those of a few powerful states rather than representative of a broader international consensus. This can have a negative impact on its reputation for objectivity and is likely to be destructive in terms of the cohesiveness and shared values on which alliances depend. Deploying peace enforcers from smaller member states helps to offset the hegemon image of the dominant ones, but the sophistication and costs of technical military and intelligence equipment inevitably leads to a hierarchy of states and creates further tensions.

A cosmopolitan ethic

Cosmopolitan perspectives of peace interventions, which are premised upon the intrinsic value and dignity of all human beings, have become more relevant in recent years as globalization, in bringing people and places together, combines to present the world as a single moral community. Whether the strategy adopted is guided by idealism and a moral imperative to protect fundamental human rights, or a pragmatic calculation of the costs and benefits for the wellbeing of individuals worldwide, conventional distinctions between duties to oneself (family, community, and fellow citizens) and duties to others (humanity at large) are eroded and the focus of world politics shifts from relations among states to those between people.

Though the UN Charter embodies a conception of international peace and security based on a broad idea of human welfare as survival and security, both the UN and NATO are organizations not of peoples but of states, just as international law focuses on the rights and duties of states. Pragmatists have traditionally looked beyond this top-down approach of sovereign states and their representatives to the peoples they serve. The notion of democratic inclusion is critical to their concept of ethical policies.

It is public consent which provides the "reality check," and what is real is that on which people can agree. This is as true of peace interventions as it is of other transnational activities.

Non-governmental organizations

Non-governmental organizations, or NGOs, and civil society movements have emerged as powerful participants in world politics. As people-directed rather than state-directed organizations, they facilitate consensual politics by providing a forum for discussion. They use the power of public opinion to influence the actions of states and play a key role in UN decision-making. Nevertheless, the presence of NGOs in conflict areas and the need to provide their staff with protection adds to the burden on intervention forces. Yet there may be no reciprocal benefit in terms of a willingness on the part of NGOs to share knowledge acquired in the field. NGOs maintain that remaining strictly neutral between the belligerents and the intervention forces ensures their own safety and protects their ability to provide humanitarian aid and assistance, even if ways can be devised to protect the source of the information.

In choosing not to pass on information which they acquire in the course of their work and interpreting the obligation to do so as spying for the intervention forces, NGOs are in danger of moral absolutism: of giving precedence to idealistic principles over other values, such as the safety of intervention forces. By refusing to commit the lesser evil they may open the way to a greater one.

But idealism allows for exceptions to moral rules when, in extreme circumstances, values conflict. Passing information may be justified if "other means are insufficient or unavailable" (Ignatieff, 2004: 16). In hostile peace support environments, it is unlikely that evil choices can be avoided altogether but they must be temporary and characterized by necessity and last resort. In the final analysis, it is a matter of reasoning out the consequences of various courses of action or inaction, anticipating harms, and coming to a rational judgment about the balance of consequences. They must decide what their ethical obligations are, and to whom, and how these conflicting obligations may be resolved given the means available and the consequences of doing nothing.

Just Intelligence in the postmodern era

Peace interventions are undertaken by coalitions of the willing who voluntarily take upon themselves and accept as an ethical obligation the need to act internationally for the protection of human rights and the promotion of wider security. No legal authority can force member states to fulfill their international commitments, but there is a moral obligation upon them to try. Neither absolute moral principles nor narrowly defined self-interests guide them; they are engaged less in the furtherance of some grand human-itarian plan than in managing the risks to their own and others' security.

This is an ethical pragmatism which accepts that the measured use of force may be all that protects us from a chaotic world. It reflects a realists' view of the world that in dealing with some states and societies where there is little respect for the rule of law and no central authority, force and deception may be necessary. "Working in an environment of uncertainty, dealing with situations in which one has little control, trying to reach accommodations with people that one does not always understand or trust—this leads to mistakes and unattractive compromises" (Cooper, 2004: 137).

We face a moral dilemma. Though we aspire to behave in ways that reflect all that is best in mankind, to refrain from snooping and sneaking, we must also choose those means which will enable us to be effective in imposing minimum values on states unwilling to accept them. The alterna-tive is to acknowledge that we have no right or obligation to alleviate human suffering or prevent the spread of conflict. The force of interven-tion can be used for good and for bad; it depends on the rules and practices that apply. Postmodern states may have to accept that the rules which govern their relations with each other are not necessarily those which others recognize. Neither are they rules to which no exceptions may be made. However, pragmatism is not an excuse to abnegate ideals. It requires that the extent to which intelligence (deception) and force are used be open to debate, subject to agreed rules and adopted on the basis of democratic consensus: "The future of peace interventions will depend on the articulation of rules and practices that command wider assent than at present" (Lloyd, 2002).

Note

1   The word "evil" being elsewhere defined as a moral risk.

Bibliography

Axworthy, L. (2003) *Navigating a New World*, New York: Alfred Knopf.

Braithwaite, R., Sir, GCMC (2003) "Defending British Spies: The Uses and Abuses of Intelligence," speech given to the Royal Institute for International Affairs, Chatham House, London.

Carment, D., and Rowlands, D. (2003) "Twisting One Arm: The Effects of Biased Interventions," *International Peacekeeping*, 10 (3).

Clarkson, Adrienne, Gov.-Gen. (2004) Speech from the Throne, February, Ottawa.

Cook, R. (1997) "British Foreign Policy," Opening Statement by the Foreign Secre-tary at a Press Conference on the FCO Mission Statement, London, *Daily Bulletin*, May 12.

Cooper, R. (2004) *The Breaking of Nations: Order and Chaos in the Twenty-First Century*, London: Atlantic Books.

Davies, P.H.J. (2002) "Ideas of Intelligence: Divergent National Concepts and Institutions," *Harvard International Review*, Fall 2002.

Dewey, J. (1929) *Characters and Events: Popular Essays in Social and Political Philosophy*," London: George Allen & Unwin, Vol. II.

Gates, R. (1987) "The CIA and American Foreign Policy," *Foreign Affairs*, 66, Winter.

Gendron, A. (2005) "Just War, Just Intelligence: An Ethical Framework for Foreign Espionage," *IJIC*, Summer, 17 (3).

Ignatieff, M. (2004) *The Lesser Evil. Political Ethics in an Age of Terror*, Princeton: Princeton University Press.

Johnston, P. (1997) "No Cloak and Dagger Required," *Intelligence and National Security*, 12 (4).

Kant, I. (1997) *Groundwork of the Metaphysics of Morals*, trans. Mary Gregor, New York: Cambridge University Press.

Kaplan, R.D. (2003) *Warrior Politics. Why Leadership Demands a Pagan Ethos*, Toronto: Random House of Canada Ltd.

Keegan, J. (2003) *Intelligence in War:* Knowledge of the Enemy from Napoleon to Al-Qaeda, New York: Alfred Knopf.

Lloyd, J. (2002) "The View from Across the Pond," *Financial Times*, December 28.

Mansfield, H. (1996) *Machiavelli's Virtue*, Chicago: University of Chicago Press.

Rose, M., Gen. Sir (1998) *Fighting for Peace*, London: The Harvill Press.

Schuman, F.L. (1958) *International Politics*, New York: McGraw Hill, 6th edn.

UN (2004) "A More Secure World: Our Shared Responsibility," *Report of the Secretary-General's High-Level Panel on Threats, Challenges, and Change*. New York: UN Headquarters.

Walzer, M. (1977) *Just and Unjust Wars*, New York: Basic Books, 3rd edn.

Wiebes, C. (2003) *Intelligence and the War in Bosnia 1992–1995*, Munster: Lit Verlag.

13

ENABLING INTELLIGENCE IN PEACEKEEPING

Laying the groundwork for effective education and training

Robert Heibel, Tamal Bhattacharya, and Kristan J. Wheaton

> Information and intelligence are vital to any military operation [...] When I was selected to lead the Malaysian contingent to Cambodia, I had no knowledge whatsoever of what the mission was all about. I expected some help from [the] army's intelligence organization, but that was not forthcoming. I was then invited to proceed to New York and reported myself to the UN Department of Peacekeeping Operations (UNDPKO). Unfortunately, what took center stage in my discussion with the officers at UNDPKO was logistic planning and other administrative issues.
>
> (Raii, 2001: 5–6)[1]

It is, perhaps, telling that nearly four years after Brigadier-General Raii made these comments, and nearly thirteen years after the end of the United Nations Task Force to Cambodia (UNTAC) mission, mention of intelligence and its importance to the success of peacekeeping missions is still largely absent from the UNDPKO website. There is no intelligence division in its organizational chart and it is not a topic listed in its "Best Practices" section. Further, the word "intelligence" is entirely absent from the most recent handbook on peacekeeping (UNDPKO, 2003).

Searching the UNDPKO's document library, however, tells a different story. Buried in the stacks are countless calls for better intelligence in PKOs. Virtually every after-action review of UN PKOs comments on intelligence. Successful missions praise it:

The collection and analysis of information and intelligence enhances the effectiveness of peacekeeping operations.... UNTAES senior military officials commended the critical role played by the G2 (intelligence) Cell. Its intelligence capability enabled the Mission to be proactive and kept it informed of developments. *The idea of having an intelligence capability should be welcomed* as an opportunity to bolster the effectiveness of a mission or as a pre-emptive act to potential violence or attempts to undermine the implementation of a mission's mandate.

(UN Lessons Learned Unit, 1998: 20, emphasis added)

Unsuccessful missions, however, universally regret the lack of good intelligence:

Lesson 4—There is an emerging consensus that the United Nations lacks an adequate system for information gathering and analysis ... Member States should be encouraged to share with the Secretariat and the Security Council relevant intelligence information ... the (initial survey) team, though well constituted, *was not adequately prepared for the intricacies of the political situation* in the country, a factor that contributed to the naïve optimism about the entire operation.

(UN Peacekeeping Lessons Learned Unit, 1998: 4–5, emphasis added)

Lesson 15—A military information cell should be established and integrated in the force headquarters. The cell should be part of the joint operations center ... *The lack of a well prepared "enemy assessment" to be provided to troops joining the UN force in the first months of 2000 was one of the main causes of the May crisis.*... With no knowledge of the terrain and unfamiliar with the rebels' military tactics, type of equipment or intentions, these troops were taken by surprise.

(UN Peacekeeping Best Practices Unit, 2003: 39, emphasis added)

While the UN's failure to formally embrace intelligence in support of its PKOs may seem inexplicable, there are, of course, a number of reasons for it. While the chief culprit is likely politics, the focus of this chapter is on other, less intractable, problems; those that can be solved through education and training.

According to the Global Policy Forum, a non-governmental organization (NGO) with consultative status at the UN, UN documents themselves point to the formation of "A detailed intelligence management plan" as a solution to a variety of peacekeeping intelligence (PKI) problems. This plan:

should be completed in advance of deployment. Such a plan should cover, in as much detail as possible, the mission area, the collection efforts, analysis and fusion of information, dissemination and sharing procedures, operational security and the acquisition/maintenance of intelligence products, including maps.

(Global Policy Forum, 1999)

With such a plan in hand, many of the educational hurdles and training challenges faced by a peacekeeping force become, if not trivial, then at least surmountable. A plan that outlined in some detail the basic intelligence needs and responsibilities of the participating nations would, in turn, drive education and training. A basic framework that addressed concerns such as dissemination procedures and operational security, for example, would allow commanders at all levels to prepare training plans in advance of deployment that ensured that soldiers and civilians involved in the PKO would have these procedures mastered before they arrived in the area of operations.

Is the formation of such a plan realistic, however? Given the idiosyncratic nature of PKOs, the wide variety of forces employed and missions attempted, and the hypersensitivity to anything having to do with intelligence, is there any precedent for creating an "intelligence management plan"?

The UN Security Council established the International Criminal Tribunal for the Former Yugoslavia (ICTY) with Security Council Resolution 827 in May, 1993. Entirely dependent on member states for information regarding war crimes in the former Yugoslavia as well as for apprehension of war criminals, the Tribunal rapidly established procedures for safeguarding intelligence information, whatever the source.

These procedures, memorialized in the Tribunal's Rule 70 of its *Rules of Evidence and Procedure* allow a member state to provide information and intelligence for lead and background purposes or for use at trial without having to disclose either its origin or how the member state acquired the information. The court, in turn, can take into account the source—and possible bias—of such information in rendering its decision (ICTY, 2004a). Internally, the Office of the Prosecutor for the Tribunal (the primary recipient of most Rule 70 information) has established a variety of administrative and security procedures for protecting the information from inadvertent disclosure. Rule 70 information is stored separately from other information and evidence. It is even partitioned on the Tribunal's computers. Both the Registry and the Chambers (the other two sections of the Tribunal) also have procedural and physical safeguards in place to protect Rule 70 information.

While the Tribunal is not a PKO, it has many of the attributes of such an operation. Its jurisdiction is bounded in both space (to the area of the former Yugoslavia) and in time (to the period after January 1, 1991)

178

(ICTY, 2003). It has over 1200 members of staff from 84 countries, field offices in a variety of Balkan countries, and a budget in excess of US$230 million (ICTY, 2005). Despite its large size, geographic dispersion, and complex mission, the Tribunal's security and procedural safeguards have been effective. In the nearly twelve years of the court's existence, there has never been a documented leak of Rule 70 material.

The Rule 70 process has not been without difficulties. Governments may allow access to information or witnesses for lead and background purposes but then deny the Tribunal access to these same individuals absent protective measures for the witnesses (Institute for War and Peace Reporting, June 2002). Still, intelligence information provided in this way has been crucial in convicting a number of war criminals. Jean-Rene Ruez, Senior Investigator for the ICTY's team investigating the massacre at Srebrenica clearly identified the value of this information during his testimony in the trial of General Radislav Krstic:

> I will show you an exhibit which is the Exhibit 8/1, which is an aerial imagery dated 13 July 1995, at 1400 hours [...] On this photograph, we can consider that we have a perfect implementation of the testimony of (redacted) [...] The surroundings are important, because they also enable us to check the credibility of the people who are talking about the events in that location [...] This is a good way to understand the link between aerial imagery and ground imagery.
>
> (ICTY, 2000: 618–621)

Despite the difficulties inherent in sharing intelligence information such as imagery, and with the court, hurdles have proved surmountable. For example, evidence provided by US intelligence services was used to pinpoint primary and secondary graves (Agence France Presse, 2001). General Krstic was ultimately convicted based on this and other corroborating evidence of aiding and abetting genocide and was sentenced to thirty-five years imprisonment for the crimes committed at Srebrenica (ICTY, 2004b).

With the ICTY's strong precedent as an example of how to protect intelligence in a UN operation, there is, at least, a hope that a document could be crafted that would enable intelligence sharing and related activities in PKOs. Such a document would find a natural home as an annex in the document that established the peace. Whether this document was attached to the Security Council resolution itself or, as is more likely, placed in some sort of peace agreement such as the Dayton Accords that ended the war in the former Yugoslavia, the establishment of such a document would go a long way toward laying the groundwork for a robust pre-deployment education and training program.

Negotiating an "intelligence management plan" would almost certainly not be easy. Richard Holbrooke, in his book *To End A War*, describes in detail the difficulties surrounding the discussions of just one of the nine annexes to the Dayton Peace Agreement. On the one hand he was being told by one of the Bosnian Muslim's chief consultants, Richard Perle, that the military annex to the accords was "a pathetic evasion of responsibility by the Pentagon" while, on the other, the Pentagon was responding to the Muslim position in less diplomatic tones: "Tell Perle to shove his goddamn changes up his ass" (Holbrooke, 1998: 254–258). Due to the sensitive nature of the subject matter, intelligence annexes, even among allies, are likely to engender similar strong emotions and will require delicate negotiations to implement. This is, however, no reason not to try, since evidence suggests that such efforts will succeed. Ultimately, the Dayton accords were signed and Rule 70 itself has undergone no fewer than seven revisions over the last eleven years (ICTY, 2004b).

If such a document were authorized, what would it look like? What would go into it and where would those contents come from? Peacekeeping forces commanders have at least two intelligence needs: force protection and mission accomplishment. There are at least three areas— best practices, the comparative study of doctrine and intelligence architectures, and mission-specific skills—which offer good ideas for an effective intelligence management plan that can meet both of those needs.

Best practices, either in the form of the UN's own after-action reviews or in the form of case studies, could provide a detailed list of topics for consideration. The Global Policy Forum has preserved what is probably the most comprehensive summary of the lessons learned from prior PKOs. These best practices include, in addition to the intelligence management plan discussed earlier:

1   an effective political and humanitarian early-warning system for potential conflict zones;
2   standard procedures to assure the timely sharing of intelligence;
3   a combined and well-managed civilian–military information analysis cell for political and military analysis;
4   standard operating procedures for ensuring security of information gathered and protecting source confidentiality.

(Global Policy Forum, 1999)

Case studies developed from past PKOs can also supply significant insights into what worked, what didn't work, and why. These case studies can then be used to train peacekeepers. The US Marine Corps already uses such a method for educating its officers in operations other than war, including PKOs (US Marine Corps College of Continuing Education, 2005).

The second category is a comparative study of intelligence doctrines of the participating nations. Ideally, each contributing nation to the PKO would have the same or similar intelligence doctrines. This is clearly the case in most PKOs where North Atlantic Treaty Organization (NATO) countries are involved, for example. It is also the case in PKOs where the majority of the troops supplied are from a single nation and that nation has significant intelligence capabilities (UN Peacekeeping Best Practices Unit, 2004: 13). Where such a relationship does not exist or doctrines are contradictory there can be significant problems (Nomikos, 2005). It is precisely here that a comparative study would help either craft a compromise or help decide which of the competing doctrines would be most effective in the specific operations under consideration.

The need for comparative study extends, however, beyond military doctrine. Multidimensional peacekeeping, designed to help implement a comprehensive peace agreement, requires a wider range of expertise (UNDPKO, 2003). Information about the terrain and the parties involved in the conflict will not be enough:

> There is also a need for information about less tangible matters such as opinions, perceptions, feelings, tensions and so on. Some elements of the environment are hostile, others are not. With the friendly elements good relations have to be established and the hostile ones have to be dealt with, not necessarily by the use of force. The mix of friendly and hostile elements makes the environment more complex than the one in a "warfare" scenario.
>
> (Engering, 2004: 4–5)

With this in mind, it is likely that academics might be called on to reconcile not only differing military intelligence doctrines but also military doctrines with intelligence-led policing doctrines. These, in turn, might have to be reconciled with the unique types of incidents—such as war crimes—common to PKOs. Dermot Groome, in his book, *The Handbook of Human Rights Investigations*, highlights the risks involved in taking too doctrinal an approach in a humanitarian operation:

> This book is my adaptation of generally accepted principles of criminal investigation for use by human rights workers. Not all of the procedures and techniques described in this book are appropriate in every context. The most serious of human rights violations most often occur in places of tremendous upheaval

and danger. Some of these procedures described here may be unsafe, inappropriate or impossible given your particular situation.

(Groome, 2001: 5)

Finally, the intelligence education manuals and courses developed for peacekeepers might also include the training of mission-unique skills. This could include, among other things, training in the languages and cultures of the region of operations. Since PKI operations almost always involve questioning of refugees and members of different factions or warring groups, training might also involve working with local translators of the region. Other mission-specific PKI skills, such as providing the "enemy assessment" lacking in the Sierra Leone operation or the political estimate absent as the first survey team left for Rwanda, could be developed and briefed on an as-needed basis.

It should be noted that, in all three of these sources, academics, rather than military personnel, are in the best position to play a key role. The skills necessary to compare the doctrines, write the cases, and identify the mission-specific knowledge necessary for mission success all currently lie within academia. While there may be a few military officers with the requisite skill sets and experiences to craft these types of documents, it is unlikely, given their own operational demands, that there will be enough of these military specialists in order to be able to respond effectively to a crisis. It is here that academics—specialists in peacekeeping or intelligence, perhaps—can help the commander more quickly develop the intelligence management plan in whatever form it takes. Academics also bring increasingly powerful analytic techniques to the table. These techniques, largely developed independently from the traditional intelligence community, could add a significant new dimension to PKOs. Some of the most robust of the new techniques include commercial imagery analysis, social network analysis, and predictive simulations.

Imagery analysis has long been a mainstay of the intelligence community. As little as ten years ago, there was virtually no high-resolution aerial imagery routinely available to peacekeepers. This is rapidly changing and the recent acquisition of the Keyhole software platform by Google is likely to push this technology even to remote laptops in the near future (Google, 2004). The difference that this type of commercially available analytic tool can make was nowhere more evident than during the humanitarian operations following the devastating tsunami of December 26, 2004 (see Figure 13.1). With this type of capability now available outside the formal intelligence community, it will increasingly fall to academics and NGOs to make full use of overhead imagery for peacekeeping and other humanitarian operations.

Social network analysis, or the uncovering of patterns in people's interaction, is another potentially powerful academic tool for the modern peacekeeper. Machiavelli first identified the power of networks for understanding politics in *The Prince*:

> I reply that the kingdoms known to history have been governed in two ways; either by a prince and his servants, who, as ministers by his grace and permission, assist in governing the realm; or by a prince and by barons, who hold their positions not by the favor of the ruler but by the antiquity of blood.... Whoever now considers these two states will see that it would be difficult to acquire [the first]; but having conquered it, it would be easy to hold it. In many respects, on the other hand, it would be easier to conquer [the second], but there would be great difficulty in holding it.
>
> (Machiavelli, 1952: 43–44)

Machiavelli is describing, of course, what today would be called a centralized network in the first case, and a decentralized network in the second. Tools for describing these systems have become increasingly sophisticated since the advent of the personal computer, and the software necessary to document mathematically a political, criminal, or military network is readily available.[2]

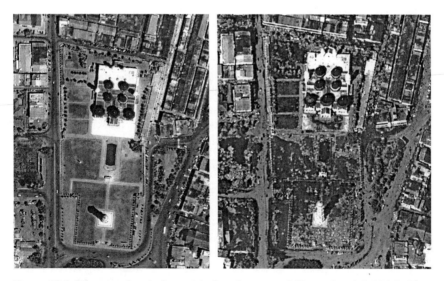

Figure 13.1 Pictures taken before and after the tsunami (December 26, 2004). The building shown is the Banda Aceh Grand Mosque on June 23, 2004 and December 28, 2004.

Source: Pictures courtesy of Digital Globe. Available at: http://www.digitalglobe.com/tsunami_gallery.html

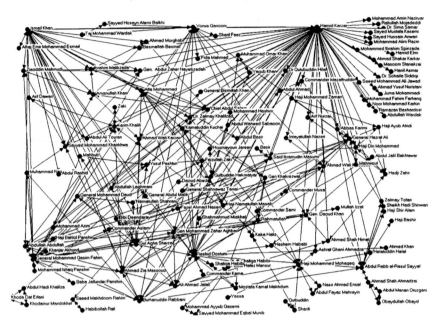

Figure 13.2 Afghan drug structure. This map displays the social structure of the Afghanistan drug trade and reveals the extent to which illegal narcotics permeate all aspects of society

Source: Courtesy Laurie Weaver

While the picture created by these networks is compelling (see Figure 13.2), the real power of the method lies in its ability to explain mathematically a network. Social network analysis can outline not only the size and type of a network; it can also be used to accurately identify key nodes by examining such factors as reachability, flow, cohesion, and influence. The technique has a well-defined language for relating the degree, closeness, and between-ness centralities of a given network (Hanneman, 2001: 60–67). While the details, definitions, and use of these variables are beyond the scope of this chapter, sociologists have been documenting the results of their studies of social networks and the uses of this method for over twenty years. These variables not only describe the network but also imply a method for strengthening or weakening the system. The knowledge necessary to create these complex but useful pictures is, like overhead imagery, available at virtually any good college or university (see Grossmann-Vermass, this volume, Chapter 14).

Beyond both imagery and social networks, peacekeeping forces of the future may also tap into the increasingly robust field of predictive simulations. As noted in Chapter 14, these simulations, based on modern political science theories but developed using the mathematics of chaos and complexity theories, might allow a peacekeeping commander to plan and predict the impact of both large- and small-scale operations. At base, these simulations would enable peacekeeping commanders rapidly to train and assimilate their troops and leaders to the conditions in a particular country or crisis (Wheaton, 1993: 77–95).

With an intelligence management plan firmly in hand, peacekeeping commanders can train contributing nation's troops to a single standard. This standard, the result of a comparative study of the various nations' intelligence doctrines, the best practices of previous missions and mission-specific intelligence tasks, would serve as a starting point for the intelligence education of the peacekeeping force. Complementing this education and training would be tools, such as social network analysis and predictive simulations, taken from the various academic disciplines that fall well outside what is "normal" inside the intelligence community. Such a combined approach will not solve the problems of politics that peace-keeping missions invariably raise, but it will go a long way toward providing the commander of the peacekeeping forces with troops trained and ready to accomplish the intelligence mission.

Notes

1 Speech (in English) by Brigadier-General (ret'd.) Mohhammed Arshad Raii, Commander, Malaysian Contingent, UN Transitional Authority in Cambodia.
2 For examples, see UCINET at http://www.analytictech.com or Analyst's Notebook at www.i2inc.com

Bibliography

Agence France Presse (2001) "Srebrenica Massacres Were Methodical, French Police Officer Says," Paris: AFP. Available at: http://folk.uio.no/toreww/srebrenica_massacres.htm (accessed January 10, 2005).

Engering, F. (2004) Keeping the Peace in a Tough Neighborhood: The Challenges Confronting Peacekeepers in Africa, Opening address, Pretoria: Centre for International Political Studies. Available at: http://www.up.ac.za/academic/cips/keepinghtepeace-conf.htm (accessed January 10, 2005).

Global Policy Forum (1999) Multidisciplinary Peacekeeping: Lessons From Recent Experience, New York: Global Policy Forum. Available at: http://www.globalpolicy.org/security/peacekpg/lessons/lesson.htm#
Intelligence (accessed January 10, 2005).

Google (2004) Google Acquires Keyhole Corp, Mountain View, California: Google. Available at: http://www.google.com/press/pressrel/keyhole.html (accessed January 10, 2005).

Groome, D. (2001) The Handbook of Human Rights Investigations, Northborough, MA: Human Rights Press.

Hanneman, R. (2001) Introduction to Social Network Methods, Riverside, CA: University of California..

Holbrooke, R. (1998) To End A War, New York: Random House.

ICTY (2000) Prosecutor vs. Radislav Krstic, The Hague: International Criminal Tribunal for the Former Yugoslavia. Available at: http://www.un.org/icty/transe33/000314ed.htm (accessed January 10, 2005).

—— (2003) Statute Of The International Criminal Tribunal For The Former Yugoslavia, The Hague: ICTY. Available at: http://www.un.org/icty/legaldoc/index.htm (accessed January 10, 2005).

—— (2004a) Rules of Evidence and Procedure, The Hague: International Criminal Tribunal for the Former Yugoslavia. Available at: http://www.un.org/icty/legaldoc/index.htm (accessed January 10, 2005).

—— (2004b) Prosecutor vs. Radislav Krstic, The Hague: International Criminal Tribunal for the Former Yugoslavia. Available at: http://www.un.org/icty/krstic/Appeal/judgement/index.htm (accessed January 10, 2005).

—— (2005) The ICTY at a Glance, The Hague: International Criminal Tribunal for the Former Yugoslavia. Available at: http://www.un.org/icty/glance/index.htm (accessed January 10, 2005).

Institute for War and Peace Reporting (IWPR) (2002) The Case of the Missing Witnesses, Washington: IWPR, June. Available at: http://www.iwpr.net/index.pl?archive/bcr2/bcr2_20020612_4_eng.txt (accessed January 10, 2005).

Machiavelli, N. (1952) The Prince, New York: Mentor.

Nomikos, J. (2005) Intelligence Requirements For Peacekeeping Operations, Athens: Research Institute for European and American Studies. Available at: http://www.rieas.gr/Papers.html (accessed January 10, 2005).

Raii, M. (2001) Peacekeeping Operations—The Malaysian Experience, Kuala Lumpur, Asia-Pacific Peacekeeping Seminar Game sponsored by the Center of Excellence in Disaster Management and Humanitarian Assistance. Available at: http://coe-dmha.org/APRI/Malaysia/PDF/LLearned.pdf (accessed January 10, 2005).

UNDPKO (United Nations Department of Peacekeeping Operations) (2003) United Nations Peacekeeping, New York: United Nations. Available at: http://www.un.org/Depts/dpko/dpko/index.asp (accessed January 10, 2005).

UN Lessons Learned Unit (1998) The United Nations Transitional Administration In Eastern Slavonia, Baranja And Western Sirmium (1998), New York: United Nations. Available at: http://www.un.org/depts/dpko/lessons/ (accessed January 10, 2005).

UN Peacekeeping Best Practices Unit (2003) Lessons Learned From United Nations Peacekeeping Experiences In Sierra Leone, New York: United Nations. Available at: http://www.un.org/depts/dpko/lessons/ (accessed January 10, 2005).

—— (2004) Operation Artemis: The Lessons Of The Interim Emergency Multinational Force, New York: United Nations. Available at: http://www.un.org/depts/dpko/lessons/ (accessed January 10, 2005).

UN Peacekeeping Lessons Learned Unit (1996) Comprehensive Report on Lessons Learned from the United Nations Assistance Mission in Rwanda, New York: United Nations. Available at: http://www.un.org/depts/dpko/lessons/ (accessed January 10, 2005).

US Marine Corps College of Continuing Education (2005) Operations Other Than War, Quantico, VA: US Marine Corps. Available at: http://www.tecom. usmc.mil/cce/students/pme/csc/stu_csc_8809.asp (accessed January 10, 2005).

Wheaton, K. (1993) Modeling and Simulating Transitions From Authoritarian Rule, Tallahassee, FL: Florida State University.

14

A BRIDGE TOO FAR?

The theory and practice of the effects-based concept and the multinational inter-agency role

Robert Grossman-Vermaas

Introduction

Conflict is no longer limited to linear battlefronts and mass maneuver. As clearly demonstrated during recent events in Afghanistan and Iraq, the historic focus on achieving military superiority at the operational or tactical levels would be better seen as perfunctory steps toward the achievement of strategic military, economic, diplomatic, and developmental aims.[1] Increasingly, conflict has become more akin to a complex and adaptive system that operates within and between the progressively more challenging environments of war, terrorism, peace support operations, and regime change. Conflict has shifted from being primarily a mechanically linear system in which military powers smash away at each other until one is far too bloodied to continue, to fluid, increasingly adaptive and often unpredictable, situations in which specialized, usually multinational, armed forces function alongside civilians in order to achieve, one would hope, shared and desired tactical and systemic effects that would lead to a shared strategic aim. Operations to attend to such threats will, therefore, require an equally adaptive approach (Grossman-Vermaas, 2004).

In multinational effects-based planning (EBP), success relies on being able to identify the desired and achievable strategic end-states that might inform campaign planning and the deployment of the optimum mix of civilian and military capabilities with which to achieve a range of long and short-term *effects*. Clearly, circumstances, not least values, will likely dictate that multinational operations include complementary diplomatic measures such as sanction, financial incentives, and trade-offs, just as easily as the deployment of an infantry brigade, wing of aircraft, or squadron of ships. Alternatively, effects-based actions may include the defense option at a level equal to or greater than the use of developmental aid and reconstruction assistance. The challenge for the effects-based concept lies with the integration, or bridging, of such efforts externally between coalition partners and internally by large, institutionally independent, military and civilian levels of government. But is this "bridging" feasible? In several states today a military "defensive" capability is but one component of a multidimensional principle of statecraft that includes diplomacy, defense, and development. In Canada, this is known as the inter-agency 3D policy.[2] But can such principles translate? This chapter explores the effects-based concept within the context of the Multinational Experimentation (MNE) series, and specifically analyzes the inter-agency "role" under the Coalition Inter-agency Coordination Group (CIACG) as it has contributed toward an experimental EBP cycle.

What is the effects-based concept?

It is important to begin with taxonomy. There are several characterizations the effects-based concept and of its "operationalized" form, effects-based operations (EBO). One definition states that EBO be considered processes for obtaining a desired outcome or effect from an adversary, friendly, or neutral through the synergistic and cumulative application of military and non-military capabilities at the tactical, operational, and strategic levels.[3] Other definitions consider EBO as operations conceived, planned and executed within a systems framework that considers the full range of direct, indirect, and additional cascading effects that may be achieved by the application of political, military, diplomatic, or psychological instruments (Davis, 2001). There are, to date, no less that two-dozen definitions of EBO. In order to encapsulate and refine, it is suggested that the following definition be considered: EBOs are:

> Operations designed to influence the long- or short-term *state of a system* through the achievement of desired physical or psychological effects. Operational objectives are sought to achieve directed policy aims using the integrated application of *all applicable* instruments of *hard or soft* power. Desired effects, and the actions required to achieve them, are concurrently and reactively planned, executed, assessed (and potentially adapted) within a *complex and adaptive system*.
> (Grossman-Vermaas, 2004: Classified, emphasis in original)

The effects-based concept is still immature. EBP has demonstrated some potential, but has not yet progressed to a mature experimentation or prototype phase.[4] Prototyping the concept will require the maturation of the appropriate theoretical and analytical frameworks, both of which

189

consider conflict as a holistic spectrum of political, military, economic, social, legal, and ethical and infrastructure and information segments. This framework (or frameworks) and associated methodologies will enable decision-makers to plan for operations more effectively and then to adapt plans as situations evolve. That said, future operations that reflect the principles of the effects-based approach will, by their very nature, require political and military leadership to both *anticipate and understand* the consequences of actions. Ultimately, decision-makers will require a framework that integrates processes that link strategic aims to operational effects; effects to networks and nodal relationships; actions to resources and organizational mandates and accountabilities; resources to the appropriate actions required to achieve the desired effect(s); and resources to supporting processes and capabilities.

The achievement of a long-term strategic aim necessitates that EBO planners develop a better appreciation of increasingly complex human networks and the dependency linkages that connect communities of interest (see Figure 14.1). It also requires a significantly more sophisticated understanding of culture and human values over time and space as well as a multidimensional analysis of primary, secondary, and follow-on actionable "nodes," "targets," networks, or dependency relationships between nodes, that are to be influenced during the course of operations (Smith, 1995; Guastello, 1995).

It is worth underscoring that EBO are outcome-focused and involve a broad range of activities, of which military action is only a subset. For example, if a state or coalition has, as one of its strategic aims, the establishment of a democratic regime within a failed state, there may be an infinite or permutated number of possible actions and resources available to produce the necessary desired effects, including diplomatic, developmental, international organization (IO), inter-governmental organization (IGO), and non-governmental organizations (NGO) ways and means.[5] Unfortunately, as will be seen below, conventional military planning staffs have made little more than superficial gestures to incorporate the so-called "other" instruments of power into multinational planning and command and control processes. Moreover, there has been little attempt made to integrate these levels of influence into a prototypical EBO headquarters. If indeed EBO are to include the combined direct and indirect administration of *any* means at the nation's disposal applied in a synergistic manner in order to elicit a desired strategic outcome based on the achievement of cumulative effects, then there is a long way to go before operationalization of the concept. It is imperative that planners think rigorously about how best to synchronize and orchestrate effects and the proposed actions and resources needed to achieve them. This involves a strong, and ultimately transparent, civilian and military information sharing and knowledge management process that reacts to the potential propagation of effects.

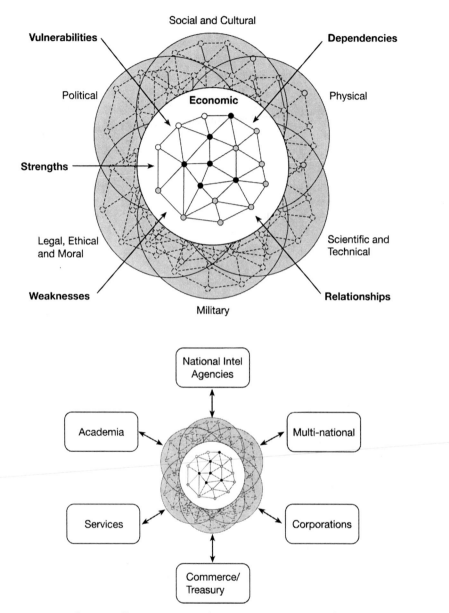

Figure 14.1: Theoretically, an operational net assessment (ONA) for EBO requires inputs from a wide range of political, economic, social, intelligence, technological, infrastructure specialists in order to make an assessment of strengths and vulnerabilities within a "system of systems." The weaknesses and vulnerabilities within the system are then exploited to induce effects.

Source: USJFCOM, Rock Drill Draft, *Concept of Operations for Multinational Experiment 3*, November.3, 2003b.

191

EBO, MNE 3 and the inter-agency role

The evolving international security environment and subsequent changing role of armed forces is an essential backdrop to our discussion. Understanding this environment is key to the effective civil–military implementation of EBP and execution. This understanding also reflects the desire to move away from the traditional realist view of war as a tool of state to the desire to view conflict's entirety—pre-crisis, crisis, and post-crisis—inclusive of a civil–military domain. There are historical precedents of the shift in civil–military relationships. During and immediately following the first Gulf War, there was a marked shift in civil–military relationships. This was most evident during operations under the UN flag in Cambodia and the former Yugoslavia and the North Atlantic Treaty Organization (NATO) war in Kosovo. Peacekeeping operations emerged from the new security environment of the post Cold War era reflecting these new demands and new challenges. Between 1989 and 1999 there were well over forty instances of UN-sponsored intervention around the globe (Durch, 1997; Freedman, 1994). Significantly, during this period, not only did multinational missions multiply, they were complex, innovative and multileveled.

The Centre for Defence Studies at King's College London recently identified five communities whose participation is critical to the successful resolution of future international crises. These are, in no particular order: donor governments; armed forces; multilateral agencies; NGOs; and private industry (Hippel, 1999; Duffield, 2001). As the operational net assessment (ONA) concept has demonstrated, this list might benefit from the addition of academia and national and international intelligence agencies—these communities have become significant players in the pursuit of regional and global stability through trend analysis and indicator measurement. However, this union of several seemingly disparate players has had a long and turbulent history. As Mike Duffield argues, in adapting to the new security environment of the post-Cold War era, each of these communities was in turn driven to revisit fresh issues such as how and in what manner they would be involved in multinational military operations (Duffield, 2001: 52). This acclimatization to new geopolitical realities underwent several iterations, impacting organization, process, and, above all, policy. In the 1990s, the integration of development and security, along with the privatization of these responsibilities gradually produced more effective ways and means to achieve a common objective. Parties that were autonomous throughout the Cold War era now found new forms of "synergy, overlap and mutual interest" (Duffield, 2001: 52). However, the question remains as to whether this integration can translate effectively to a transformational EBP concept and doctrine.

The following sections will explore the integration of military and non-military organizations (NMOs) in the conduct of EBP and operations. It will introduce MNE 3 as a case study on coalition EBP. The analysis is critical, but it is not intended to denigrate the efficacy of multinational experimentation as it relates to the effects-based approach; on the contrary, it is designed to explore gaps in our collective understanding of what components are required for the practical application of the conceptual issues related to the effects-based approach, and to explore avenues for further exploration.

Multinational representation and association with US Joint Forces Command (USJFCOM) has expanded since the command's inception. From the outset, the joint experimentation plan at USJFCOM was intended to provide the transformation framework for inter-service (and multinational) conceptual, experimentation and doctrinal development, interoperability and integration. USJFCOM Joint Experimentation Directorate (J9) thus sought (and still seeks) to envisage, develop, explore, test and then validate twenty-first-century warfighting concepts such as rapid decisive operations, operational net assessment (ONA) and the effects-based concepts of EBP and EBO. These concepts are seen as transformational, driving both thought and technology, with prior civil–military demarcations less visible. Further, the experimentation process sought (and still seeks) to provide a way to ensure that the US, and its allies could operate effectively and inter-operably in the complex security environment of the future. To this end, J9 has initiated several experiments since 2001. There are four scheduled transformational MNE series events that include the Multinational Interoperability Council (MIC) nations. The first, Limited Objective Experiments (LOE) 1 (November 2001), investigated coalition military planning. The second, LOE 2 (February 2002), explored the development of the ONA. MNE 3 will be discussed below and MNE 4 will occur in 2006.

MNE 3 was a US-directed and -sponsored exploratory experiment that attempted to examine the processes, organization(s), and technologies required for an ad hoc coalition to plan an EBO within a representative complex system. The third in a series of four experiments related to coalition planning, information sharing, and the effects-based approach, MNE 3 was a "virtual," i.e., internationally dispersed yet technologically networked, experiment on a series of concepts under the general mantle of EBP. These "sub-concepts" included, amongst many others, the CIACG in the EBP process, a construct designed, in part, to explore the necessary coordination and integration of the defense and development communities.

The US experiment design team intentionally opted to explore the EBP concept within the construct of a Coalition Task Force (CTF) headquarters, which mirrored the US Standing Joint Forces Headquarters (SJFHQ) organizational structure. There were several persuasive, and some not so persuasive, reasons for the inclusion of the SJFHQ component into the experiment design. The most important for this discussion, however, was that it afforded the six MIC participants (Australia, Canada, France, Germany, the UK, and the US), as well as the nascent NATO Response Force (NRF), the opportunity to observe and evaluate the efficacy of the US C2 SJFHQ (and CTFHQ) prototype within an experimental EBP framework. It also offered USJFCOM proponents the opportunity to observe the multinational reception of the SJFHQ core element within a controlled and documented experiment.

The experiment operated within a collaborative information environment (CIE). The CIE involves the establishment of a multinational information-sharing domain; hardware and software tools enabling information exchange across a classified network; and an, as yet, relatively immature knowledge management process that would allow for the posting and exchange of relevant operational information. MNE 3 was successful in providing the CIE medium by which national planners could share information while refining the EBP process and drawing on information within an ONA database in order to plan operations.

The SJFHQ construct, or core element, is now entering the prototype phase in the US. The model consists of a small team (Â±58 people) of operational planners and information command and control specialists attached to and complementing a Regional Combatant Command (RCC) headquarters.[6] These specialists form the core for the Joint Task Force (JTF) command structure. (USJFCOM, 2003a) The construct envisages four specialist teams (Knowledge Management, Plans, Operations, Information Superiority) working collaboratively toward the development of an operational EBP for the commander. Though guided and under the leadership of the Commander, JTF (or in the case of MNE 3 a CTF), the four specialist teams are detached from the traditional hierarchical C2 relationship in order to provide the commander with, what is hoped to be, fully comprehensive operational plans. In early 2005, the SJFHQ construct will be fielded, augmenting several RCCs by developing pre-crises knowledge bases and providing guidance.

The SJFHQ is expected to provide each (US) geographic commander with an informed C2 capability and enhanced appreciation of the operational environment, thereby facilitating a more efficient ONA and EBP process capable of delivering "a rapid, decisive operation" (USJFCOM, 2003a). Theoretically, the expertise provided by the SJFHQ affords the commander better pre-crisis planning, more timely situational awareness, and, one would hope, a more holistic understanding of the operational "system of systems" that would thereby enable decision superiority. Using the CIE (or some comparable portal), the SJFHQ is expected to develop and maintain knowledge of the crisis environment through the establishment of habitual working relationships with inter-agency colleagues. In practical, or at least in experimental, terms the hopes for a coalition-friendly SJFHQ construct are equally high. The experiment design for

MNE 3 envisaged each national participant being involved (or in some cases embedded) in the SJFHQ experiment equivalent: a CTFHQ.

But perhaps the most ambitious assertion by proponents of the construct is that it could maintain "established habitual relationships through the combatant commanders to the inter-agency community" (USJFCOM 2003a). The justification for this is two-fold. A link with agencies other than the military could assist the operational HQ in making appropriate decisions based on a more strategic civil–military understanding of an evolving and adaptive crisis environment. Second, it could provide to SJFHQ analysts source material on the crisis environment that would enable the mitigation of potential unwanted second- and third-order effects.

NMOs, the CIACG, and MNE 3

At the outset, the injection of a functional inter-agency planning group into the experiment design for MNE 3 was considered fundamental conceptual priority (USJFCOM, 2003c). This would help to integrate, coordinate, and facilitate military and non-military components in the development of effects-based plans. It was also essential for validation of the effects-based concept at its most holistic level.

The CIACG "sub-concept" was incorporated into the design and play of MNE 3 and, as it turned out, was one of the more stimulating aspects to be played. The CIACG construct had its genesis in USJFCOM discussion papers and concept evaluations related to the SJFHQ, though each national participant presented issues related to its own historical understanding of the multinational inter-agency approach to pre-crisis and crisis decision-making. But for USJFCOM, the construct originated as a quasi-integrated, though unfortunately not integral, advisory facility for the commander and planners in the course of campaign planning. Known as the Joint Inter-agency Coordination Group, or JIACG, the concept aimed to "establish operational connections between civilian and military departments and agencies that will improve planning and coordination within the government" (USJFCOM, 2003c: 5). At the national, or JIACG, level the group was envisaged as a "multi-functional, advisory element that represents the civilian departments and agencies and facilitates information sharing across the inter-agency community" (USJFCOM, 2003c: Version 2.6, 6). In sum, it was expected to serve as a liaison between civilian and military actors and support the SJFHQ planners by advising on civilian agency operations and plans. It was also to provide a so-called "third-party" perspective on civilian agency approaches, capabilities and limitations that would inform the development of an effects-based approach and enable the coordination of national instruments of power. Presumably, when a JTF is formed and deployed, a JIACG would extend this support to the commander's staff through the JFHQ political-military planning staff. This would become the mechanism to optimize planning and ensure the best use of capabilities to achieve the desired effects that would include the range of diplomatic, information, military, and economic (DIME) inter-agency activities. This is the conceptual basis for the CIACG.

Throughout 2002 and 2003, the issue of disjointed operational planning amongst agencies was addressed through the Joint Chiefs of Staff (JCS) initiative, which was designed to establish a JIACG directorate for crisis intervention within the RCCs. Still, and in hindsight, prior to implementation the JIACG concept would have benefited from further refinement, certainly at the national level, and, ideally, at the multinational level. Granted, this was new ground. It must be stated that, to date, no model exists. There is no existing coherent operational planning structure that is multi-agency in nature or one that extends planning and coordination into the multilateral spheres that are involved in complex crisis response and action. The attempt to address this challenge within MNE 3 through the inclusion of the JIACG concept was certainly legitimate and timely.

The concept was expanded to include civilian agency representatives of the participating coalition countries. In accordance with the Concept of Operations (CONOPS), the emergent CIACG was to focus on coordinating and harmonizing operational planning between the coalition military planners and the relevant civilian agencies or departments of their respective governments (USJFCOM, 2003d). Thus, in both theory and practice, any difficulties envisaged for the establishment of a national inter-agency model were now magnified.

Present-day Afghanistan (2003–05) provided the experimental scenario for MNE 3. The scenario included, in its pre-experiment stages, a UN request for CTF intervention in order to stabilize a volatile situation in southern Afghanistan. Injects posited to MNE 3 players required the establishment of a CTFHQ that was prepared to conduct a pre-crisis EBP procedure in coordination with a CIACG. The CTF was to proceed through specific, albeit conceptual, EBP steps, culminating in an effects tasking order (ETO). The ETO would flow from and reflect the previous steps in the EBP process and would outline the effects-based ways and means to enable the EBO.

Theoretically, the EBP process steps replicate the operational "steps" required to perform EBP within a "real world" coalition environment (Figure 14.2).

The process begins with the CTF gaining an understanding of the strategic context, aims, and direction. This emerges from the operational level Focused ONA, which incorporates national and multinational information and intelligence related to the environment (in the case of MNE 3,

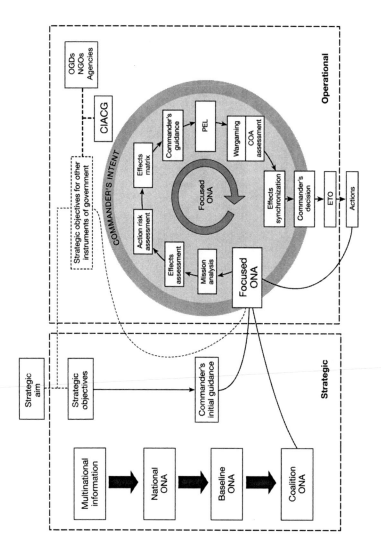

Figure 14.2: The EBP process steps for MNE 3. The CTF participants were to proceed through the operational steps (right side) in order to consider the appropriate effects, nodes, actions, and resources that would sufficiently enable the coalition's strategic aim. This process was to include several points where assistance, guidance, or advice could be offered by the CIACG, though this was not successfully achieved.

Afghanistan). Collation, in turn, enriches the analysis and contributes to the derivation of a multinational appreciation of threats and opportunities. During MNE 3, this was replicated in slow time, i.e., the experiment steps were designated into specific time slots. CTFHQ would then proceed through a series of EBP steps toward producing an ETO. In MNE 3, these steps were replicated, but with limited success.[7] What is particularly significant for our purposes was the "role" of the CIACG. The MNE 3 multinational EBP CONOPS clearly underscored the relative importance of the CIACG in the EBP process and, particularly, in the penultimate steps (USJFCOM, 2003c). However, the experiment also highlighted the conceptual frailties of the concept itself.

MNE 3 and the CIACG: more questions than answers

MNE 3 confirmed that the CIACG is a potentially useful and evolving concept in need of further refinement. If anything, the CIACG piece highlighted the requirement to integrate, coordinate, and facilitate the activities and capabilities of multinational military, other government departments (OGDs), and other non-military, non-national governmental organizations and humanitarian, developmental and relief agencies, with that of the CTF. It also highlighted the necessity to incorporate military and non-military perspectives, sensitivities and support requirements, and insofar as possible, to reconcile competing demands. Indeed, the CONOPS for MNE 3 suggested aspirations for a more holistic crisis planning process than had previously been the case in multinational operations with a military strategic bias, and these expectations were given a greater weighting by the choice of the Afghan stability operation scenario.

Still, portions of the CIACG CONOPS for MNE 3 reflected inconsistencies attributable to its genesis in national concept development and this affected the experimental EBP process. At first glance, the CIACG appeared to emulate the role of the JIACG, for the Commander, RCC. For a national commitment, and in particular a US national commitment, this approach may have been satisfactory. However, MNE 3 was specifically designed as a discovery experiment relating to a coalition planning process. During play, it became clear that the role of CIACG was more complicated than the US-derived complement, the JIACG, and its links to the CTFHQ more intricate.

Conceptually, EBP prescribes a level of adaptability that mitigates some of the complexities of conflict. It also demands a cognitive shift from linear, or sequential, plans and operations, to adaptive and distributed plans and operations to keep pace with (if not anticipate) both contextual changes and the tempo of operations. This necessitates a dynamic EBP process. The CIACG is not a mature "enabling" concept. As such, there was a natural tendency for the CIACG (and its several multinational components) to react strongly to immediate military circumstances in order to better define its own relationship with the CTF as planner, guide, liaison, or otherwise. At this stage of conceptual development, a more rigorous review and analysis of CIACG integration into CTFHQ activities may be required. On one level the CIACG provided liaison between OGDs, IOs, IGOs and the CTF; on another level the CIACG offered specific guidance to the Commander, CTF during phases of the EBP process; at yet another level, the CIACG provided planning and assistance through subject matter experts (SMEs). This latter "role" was perhaps the most contentious during the experiment, the specific issue being: at what stage does a multinational inter-agency group limit its "coordination" activities to that of advice rather than assistance? Perhaps NMO and inter-agency roles need refinement for each CTF contingency. However, core functions should be identified in common doctrine with the assumption that additional functions could be added as required.

Other questions to emerge from the experiment were: should some or all multinational military commands and NMOs be fully integrated into the CTFHQ to provide EBP advice and/or contingency options? If it is the former, what criteria should be used in selecting representation? Should multinational NMOs always be present during CTF planning phases in order to provide "another" perspective, offering external advice and expert guidance on the probabilities of cascading effects and, therefore, on the success of the mission?

During MNE 3, it became obvious that a CIACG was required to operate at a much higher level than anticipated—both strategically and temporally. This was not appreciated in either the EBP or SJFHQ CONOPS. Similar to interactions associated with Allison's organizational process model, the Group perceived itself as a conduit, or, often times, as a translator or champion of higher strategic objectives (Allison, 1971: 4–5, 10–11). This being the case, the Group felt particularly responsible for developing perspectives on how best to achieve the desired strategic end-states for the coalition. Discussion and debate often ensued regarding the direction and longevity of the stability operation, e.g., was it to end after a sixty-day combat operation? Was it to include developmental activities, humanitarian efforts, and the so-called "soft" objectives that may take years to achieve? Prior to and during stability operations, such issues are routinely considered by NMOs. However, during EBP and EBO, any incertitude as to civil–military options and end-states may actually be counter-productive. For example, the decision to avoid the pursuit of immediate combat tactical effects because they might damage physical infrastructure may actually preclude their use as "enabling effects" requisite for the more long-term "soft" operational and strategic aims, such as stability.

Finally, a concept that integrates multinational military organizations and NMOs in a construct such as the CIACG presumably reflects the values of the nation, or nations, that develop it. National, cultural, socio-logical, organizational, and even psychological, issues will be reflected in the composition, roles, and even proposed actions of the CIACG. This is a delicate balancing act, particularly at the multinational level. If the CIACG is to be a true coalition construct, and therefore a reflection of many national and international inter-agency relationships strung together, there is a need for a rigorous (and lengthy) examination of these relationships prior to further experimentation.

The effects-based concept, NMOS, and MNE 3: conceptual observations

The EBP process, both as theoretically conceived and as developed for MNE 3, requires the establishment of a coalition military and NMO group for planning EBOs. Future concept development and refinement is strongly recommended. The CIACG played a considerable role in MNE 3. Indeed, the experiment design and process steps were augmented throughout the two-week experiment to reflect the increasing import of the CIACG sub-concept. The impact of the CIACG on EBP was most apparent during the following process steps (see Figure 14.2):

- *Commander's Initial Guidance*: The aim of the CIACG was to provide specific advice to the Commander, CTF, in order to frame his guidance in acceptable terms for multinational NMO and inter-agency sensitivities and coordination. This is an important insight (albeit slightly manufactured, given the artificiality of the experiment). One conclusion drawn from the experimental CIACG After Action Report is that integration of the CIACG in all planning developments should be initiated prior to the outset of the EBP process. There should be a clear role established for the CIACG and a clear relationship to the commander outlined in full. How this is to be achieved requires further investigation.
- *Effects Assessment; Actions Assessment and Priority Effects List (PEL)*: The CIACG played an active role in the assessment phases. During these phases CTFHQ planners consider what effects would prove most valuable and what Actions would be required to enable these desired effects. The CIACG played an integral part in establishing the causal links and weighing the relative priority of one effect and/or action over another. This sort of injection is essential to 3D policy projection and the integration of DIME instruments: Why kill when you can create? Alternatively, why aid when you can degrade, damage, or depose? These questions are critical to the conduct of EBP and EBO in a complex environment and yet they are not easily resolved without some associated risk.

- *Wargaming/COA/Synchronization*: Ideally, these steps would require active coordination and reach-back through the CIACG. This was not successfully achieved during MNE 3. In order to maximize the synchronization of effects, however, CIACG SME is critical. Effect "blowback", or at least the consideration of probable cascading, unwanted, or unintended effects, can only be determined with CIACG involvement in the planning process.

If the effects-based concept is to prove practicable, the CTF (and the coalition) must appreciate fully the status and authority of each associate member of the inter-agency group assigned to it. In practice, it may be that governments choose to issue their members with credentials formally outlining their authority bounds—within the CTF and between members of the CTF. Similarly, suitable arrangements are required to ensure that NMO advice, coordination, and guidance are commensurate with the allocated role of the CIACG. Military and NMO injects into a CTFHQ are essential; equally, they too must be held accountable for their input to planning decisions.

The MNE 3 CIACG was designed in part to stimulate thought and act as a catalyst for effects-based dialogue and knowledge management. It was envisaged that the CIACG should and would eventually assume the same sort of role with respect to non-official entities, e.g., NGOs and the media, which, for example, are a major source of information and a major source of influence in theater. This is a sticking point. In a volatile military theater, perceptions of overt NMO influence on specifically military operations may seriously cripple command and control relationships. On the other hand, perceptions of military influence on IOs and NGOs operating in theater for long-term developmental planning must also be avoided. During MNE 3, this relationship was strained several times. This is a topical issue that remains to be addressed.

In a complex conflict environment, multinational military and NMO roles are likely to remain situationally dependent. The ad hoc nature of the CIACG offers both advantages and disadvantages. Clearly, coalition civil–military and inter-agency coordination mechanisms for regions frequently in crisis will be further developed and better maintained than arising areas of interest. NMO roles will need to be clarified for each operation. However, emergent, minimum-core functions could be entrenched in common doctrine with the assumption that additional functions could be added as required. Several national MNE 3 CIACG After Action Reports tabled options regarding the role of the CIACG.

In MNE 3, the CIACG role was designed to meet experimental demands for EBP that do not envisage NMO control and/or direction over a stability operation. Indeed, the US concept developers for the MNE 3 CIACG construct have stated that the primary role of a CIACG is to provide civilian advice and subject matter expertise to the CTF commander and effects-based planners regarding civilian agency operational-level activities during the planning stages of an operation. Naturally, this advisory role could evolve over time, as requirements and circumstances demand. This begs the question: at what point in EBP and execution process is the decision made to forego routine multinational civil–military liaison in favor of a CIACG complement?

Several issues regarding roles remain unanswered and require exploration within the context of the effect-based concept:

- What should the operating relationships between the inter-agency or NMO group(s) and their respective national governments be? Is there such a thing as one CIACG that operates within, or amongst, the CTFHQ? Should it maintain the higher (or strategic) level of interest? If so, how should this translate to the operational level? How best are communities of interest represented, established, and sustained?
- Assuming that there is an agreed upon end, ways and means strategy for EBO between the civil–military actors, what ethical issues need consideration? Clearly, should an NMO lead group be tasked as liaison between the CTF and NGOs, IGOs, and IOs in the area of concentration, there is the potential for an ethical dilemma. At what point does the NMO lead risk inciting a conflict of interest when it acts as a conduit between humanitarian and relief organizations and the armed forces tasked by the commander to pursue tactical effects? Does the NMO lead recommend and then coordinate relief and humanitarian activities under the helm of the CTF? Presumably not.
- What, then, should the composition of a CTF inter-agency, or NMO, group look like? During MNE 3, several debates on the composition of the CIACG were initiated. Clearly, civilian SMEs should be involved in EBP, and for MNE 3 they were chosen from a wide range of OGDs, foreign offices, and departments of state. However, inclusion of members for the purposes of "human intelligence" from IGOs and NGOs may also be necessary in practice. As mentioned above, this raises both practical and ethical challenges. Where and how does one receive, evaluate, and use expert advice in an area of concern? How can immediate tactical, and possibly physical, effects be reconciled with long-term strategic, and possibly psychological, end-states?

Finally, if NMOs are expected to make a strong contribution to the development of the effects-based approach, then a strong identifiable civilian champion is needed for whatever form the inter-agency group takes. This leader would presumably come from the lead nation, though there is a strong argument to be made that this leader should come from another coalition nation because this would provide greater legitimacy.

The above recommendations would imply some balance to effects-based decision-making:

- The relative value of the NMO group is greatly increased if members can readily reach-back to national networks. This is not easily realized, however, as current security and information-sharing practices may preclude secure national communications systems from operating in both the NMO and CTF area.
- During operations, it may be appropriate to transfer CTF subordinate leads from military to civilian command. Conceptually, an EBO will eventually require the transition of authority to a civilian lead. Effects, if properly chosen, will require a civilian administration to ensure action taken is directed properly and considers all humanitarian, social, economic, political, cascading effects.
- Should EBP be restricted to focusing on a military objective, it is recommended that a military liaison officer be posted as a permanent member of the generic NMO coordination group, or, CIACG.

These points challenge the extant SJFHQ (or CTFHQ) model and open for discussion the proposed civil–military EBO C2 structure illustrated in Figure 14.3:

- Analysis of MNE 3 suggests that concept development and experimentation efforts recognize and accept the primacy of coalitions as the most probable paradigm within which nations may participate. These efforts should therefore be willing to explore alternative C2 processes and organizations, some of which include the injection of a truly multinational NMO into the EBP planning structure. Should it be the case that a CTF is required, a complementary, coordinated, multinational NMO, or, Inter-Agency Command Group, should be available to provide strategic and operational advice (and not guidance) to the Commander, CTF. To adapt to each contingency, the composition of this Command Group should be ad hoc; however, members could be national representatives at the ambassadorial level chosen by their respective states. This approach has recently been explored by the US Pacific Command (PACOM) (NATO, 2003).
- The Commander, CTF, could be augmented by a civilian equivalent, capable both of serving to achieve the strategic objective through an effects-based plan, as well as providing the military commander with rational and objective advice *and* planning guidance. The civilian would not provide military operational advice; rather he or she would provide guidance on the area of operations; operations and coalition unity of effort; diplomatic and inter-agency feedback to contingent nations; and would provide NMO liaison services.

- An NMO liaison would act between the Deputy Commander and the four collaborative subject matter areas in order to provide feedback to the Inter-agency Command Group, as well as to maintain the fluidity of options available to the SJFHQ.
- Each of the four SJFHQ areas would also have the inclusion of one NMO liaison to ensure that long-term strategic objectives are being met once military EBO commence

Conclusions and challenges

The above discussion on the theoretical requirements for inter-agency participation in EBOs, as well as experimental observations on coalition EBP, have provided some support for the notion that future effects-based processes and structures will utilize both military and NMO components. Indeed, strategic and operational errors may result from the failure to inte-

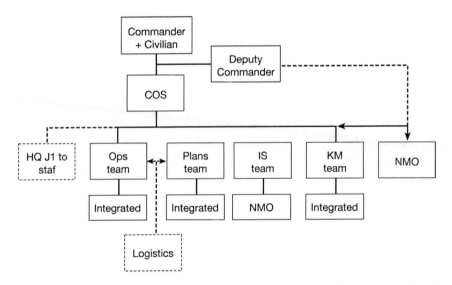

Figure 14.3: This figure shows a proposed CTFHQ conceptual organization based on the more holistic inclusion of multinational military and non-military organizations and inter-agency components. Each of the four pillars—Operations, Plans, Information Superiority (IS) and Knowledge Management (KM)—are augmented by an NMO liaison; there is an added NMO component attached to the IS cell; there is a distinctly separate NMO component for advice to the CTFHQ; and, most importantly, there is a civilian equivalent to the CTF Commander embedded within the command chain, who may act as a guide, liaison with civilian agency counterparts, or as an advisor.

Note
COS: Chief of Staff

grate, or at the very least coordinate, military, non-military and inter-agency roles, perspectives, and obligations. This is a very real challenge.

Evidence thus far has indicated that in the days and months following the coalition military invasion of Iraq, actions were not driven from an inter-agency effects-based plan that might have included a civil–military outcome-based mission analysis, effects and action assessment, and an effects-based course of action requirements. There was also scant attention paid to potential cascading short- and long-term effects, or what Chalmers Johnson terms "blowback," that might result following the use of over-whelming military force (Johnson 2000) (Johnson, 2000). One suspects that there was little integrated civil–military thought of the Iraqi theater as a complex adaptive system of systems with interacting nodal behavior. As experienced at the experimental level, there also existed little practical evidence of the inclusion of NMOs in the operational decision-making processes and organizations that cultivated the war in Iraq (Fallows, 2004: 52–74). Indeed, months before the invasion, the Office of the Secretary of Defense (OSD) and Pentagon planning staffs repeatedly dismissed inter-agency efforts to prepare plans for the combat and post-conflict phases in Iraq. The US Agency for International Development (USAID) and several NGOs were rebuffed alongside the more traditional Central Intelligence Agency (CIA) and the National War College. Hastily formed to explore post-war reconstruction and social efforts, the inter-agency Iraq Working Group was successively resisted by Donald Rumsfeld and his deputy, Paul Wolfowitz, because, they were told, "the President has already spent an hour on the humanitarian issues" (Fallows, 2004: 69). As Dayton Maxwell, Special Advisor to the Administrator of USAID and former advisor to the Coalition Provisional Authority (CPA), has recently claimed, in the context of the Global War on Terror, NMOs have been virtually absent from the planning and execution of events (Maxwell, 2004).

At the beginning of military operations in Iraq, there were over eighty non-military organizations operating alongside thousands of military personnel from several nations. Five independent groups formed the Joint NGO Emergency Preparedness Initiative (JNEPI) to serve as a "command post" for NGOs (NATO, 2003). JNEPI activities were focused and adapt-able and included planning, pre-positioning of equipment and supplies, coordination and information sharing. Interestingly, significant sources of funding for JNEPI included USAID. However, one of the five groups, the International Medical Corps, warned its members and other NGOs to avoid the appearance of being "with the occupiers" (IMC, 2003).

Successive combat operations in Afghanistan and Iraq, while tactically successful, appear to have been temporally short-sighted (Diamond, 2004: 34–56, *Economist*, 2004: 13). In some way they have suffered what some civil–military professionals have termed "the tyranny of the immediate," in which short-term tactical objectives are sought (and approved) over the more difficult long-term end-states (Maxwell, 2004). During the Global War on Terror and the subsequent war in Iraq, the symbiosis between military- and NMO-outcome planning diminished. Why this occurred has yet to be sufficiently analyzed and is beyond the scope of this study; suffice it to say that civil–military planning by RCCs may, in fact, be anathema to the very conceptual pillars of the effects-based concept and its inter-agency "role." This form of military governance also does not translate easily to coalition partners.[8]

These operational challenges mirror those identified during MNE 3. At what point do NMOs and military organizations agree that cooperation and collaboration might be more effective at producing a shared, desired, operational effect than segregation and disagreement? At what point do NMOs and military organizations agree that collaboration is, instead, not applicable at all and that unity of effort would be tantamount to an ethical schism? This is an important ethical issue that cannot be resolved here. There is, however, a compelling need for effects-based planners—both civilian and military—to consider these questions. Alternatively, there are arguments for recommending that RCCs include liaisons to the NMO community and vice versa. This parallels some of the recommendations made above in Figure 14.3, as well as examples explored within PACOM Multinational Planning Augmentation Team (MPAT) on-line "exercises." This latter group focuses on short-term planning for operations other than war (MOOTW) and includes in test-case multinational crisis planning efforts NGOs and ad hoc civil–military networks (MPAT, 2004).

Presumably, the end-state of an effects-based plan is one that is holistic in all respects, one that promotes the integration and realization of the 3D principle. That being the case, EBO planners must resolve the failures in communication and coordination that stand to jeopardize the achievement of shared strategic outcomes. There is, as yet, little effective means (or desire) to communicate through the EBP process. The addition of liaisons, specific to the tasks (or end-states), could enable a faster and more effective transition to a stable post-conflict environment. The opportunity for coordination through liaisons should not, however, infer control.

The "interventionist years" of the immediate post-Cold War era were notable for the widespread inclusion of developmental, social and humanitarian affairs into defense policy, not to mention the widespread inclusion of security issues in the planning stages of regional development and reconstruction efforts. This phenomenon may provide us with some guidance as we refine the effects-based concept. It is now generally accepted that IOs and national or international OGDs should not only be made aware of conflict and its effects, they should be party to the pursuit of objectives designed to promote regional and global security.

Based on results from MNE 3 and consideration of the past, present and future security environments, this chapter contends that national and international NMOs and inter-agency partners should be directly involved in the operational planning and execution stages of a coalition effects-based effort. IOs and NGOs need to be aware of the potential effects of military intervention, and, if possible, align capabilities and efforts toward stability, development, and resolution. Ironically, the ultimate outcome of intervention, then, would be to avert future violence and post-conflict instability (Read, 2004). These sentiments are well expressed in the policy statements of several leading IOs, UN agencies, non-partisan think-tanks, NGOs, and financial institutions.[9] Indeed, NMOs have expanded their mandates to include working directly with national and international armed forces. Interestingly, following recent events in Afghanistan and Iraq, there have been strong calls within the US legislature for the establishment of a Civilian Reconstruction Service (CRS) that works closely with military elements toward an EBO objective. Ideally, this would occur within an integrated strategic planning environment that takes into consideration conflict and post-conflict planning sources (Maxwell, 2004). This form of planning cell, however, requires more study and experimentation prior to implementation (Maxwell, 2004).

Conflict is complex in nature and armed forces must adapt to the environment(s) with which they are faced. Security and stability operations today require concepts, processes and tools. The means to perpetuate conflict—child soldiers, eco-terror, computers, weapons of mass effect, and terror against civilians—demand that one must be prepared to explore all necessary ways in which crises are addressed, including the integration of civilian and military roles, functions, and processes. Threats emanate from everywhere and the armed forces tasked with their address are collecting intelligence from civilians; delivering humanitarian aid, protecting NGOs, and eliminating funding sources. They are killing and protecting, destroying and rebuilding. Information and intelligence to aid forces comes from a variety of indicators: population; religion; economic spending; resource allocation. Obscure indicators such as the cost of weapons, the price of brides, and the nature of tribal blessings can also foreshadow conflict. The sources of knowledge about these indicators, or nodes, are most assuredly not the armed forces, but rather NMOs and inter-agency partners. Finally, cultural, social, economic and NMO and inter-agency awareness by the military is not simply a case of generic civil–military training. Our experience with MNE highlighted that these areas require legitimate "bridging" between civilian and military values and perspectives before any possible implementation of the effects-based concept.

Notes

1 This chapter does not necessarily represent the views of the Canadian Department of National Defence. The threat of asymmetric retaliation and guerrilla warfare (slowly) persuaded coalition forces to reassess strategic options in Iraq in the spring of 2003 (see Andrews and Tyler, 2003: A8).

2   The 3D approach is a recognized approach endorsed by the Canadian Defence (DND/CF), Diplomacy (DFAIT), and Development (CIDA) sectors. See the CIDA website at www.canada-afghanistan.gc.ca/menu-en.asp (accessed July 15, 2004).
3   US J9 Experimentation, US Joint Forces Command (USJFCOM), working defi-nition, 2002. See also the draft of the EBP concept for MNE 3, a joint concept between the UK Joint Doctrine and Concepts Centre (JDCC), the Canadian Forces Experimentation Centre (CFEC), the German Bundeswehr, France, NATO ACT, Australian Defence Science and Technology Organization (DSTO), and the US Joint Forces Command, August 2003.
4   It should be noted that while the EBO concept requires further refinement, there are a number of multinational and Canadian initiatives in place that are investigating the "sub-concepts" involved in the effects-based approach. Canada has been involved in the conceptual development, analysis, technolog-ical development, experiment design, and participatory phases of Limited Objective Experiment 2 (LOE 2) and MNE 3. The former experiment was conducted in February 2002 and addressed multinational information sharing in "real time" over a secure collaborative information environment (CIE) and the development of a multinational operational net assessment (ONA) database; the latter, which took place in February 2003, explores the techno-logical, organizational, and process requirements for multinational EBP and coalition development of a robust ONA database. MNE 4 is scheduled for Spring 2006 and will be an experiment on the conduct of EBO in a stability operation environment.
5   An example of an international organization (IO) is the UN; an example of an intergovernmental organization (IGO) is the Association of South East Asian Nations (ASEAN); an example of an NGO is Amnesty International. The distinction between an IO and an IGO are sometimes blurred.
6   The RCC construct is unique to US C2 structure and regional military command. In future this anomaly may create difficulties for multinational part-ners who wish to integrate into the SJFHQ construct.
7   The analysis for MNE 3 was released in two forms: a Canadian national contingent report and a full USJFCOM report. Both are unclassified.
8   As of mid-2004, there are some indications from within the US Department of Defense recognizing the need for further changes to its "way of war" (see Costa, 2004: 1; Ricks, 2004: A10).
9   These, for example, include the Organization for Security and Cooperation in Europe; the European Union; the World Bank; the UN Development Program; the UN High Commission for Refugees; and the Carnegie Commission.

Bibliography

Allison, G.T. (1971) *Essence of Decision: Explaining the Cuban Missile Crisis*, New York: Little, Brown & Company.

Andrews, E.L., and Tyler, P.E. (2003) "As Iraqis' disaffection grows, U.S. offers them a greater political role," *New York Times*, June 7.

Canadian International Development Agency (CIDA) (2004) Available at: http://www.canada-afghanistan.gc.ca/menu-en.asp (accessed July 15, 2004).

Costa, K. (2004) "Pentagon kicks off effort to re-examine the basic principles of war," *Inside the Pentagon*, July 1.

Davis, P.K. (2001) *Effects-Based Operations: A Grand Challenge for the Analytical Community*, RAND MR-1477-USJFCOM/AF, Santa Monica, CA: RAND.

Diamond, L. (2004) "What went wrong in Iraq?" *Foreign Affairs*, 9/10: 34–56.

Duffield, M. (2001) *Global Governance and the New Wars*, London: Zed Books.

Durch, W. (1997) *UN Peacekeeping, American Policy, and the Uncivil Wars of the 1990s*, London: Macmillan.

Economist (2004) "The right plan for Iraq," September 25.

Fallows, J. (2004) "Blind into Baghdad," *The Atlantic Monthly*, 1/2: 52–74.

Freedman, L. (1994) *Military Intervention in European Conflicts*, Oxford: Blackwell.

Grossman-Vermaas, R. (2004) *Action Group 10 Operational Briefing*, Dalhgren, VA: The Technical Cooperation Program (TTCP) Joint Systems Analysis Group, Joint Warfare Analysis Center, April 29.

—— (forthcoming) *(Dis)course of Action*, PhD dissertation, London, University of London.

Guastello, S. (1995) *Chaos, Catastrophe, and Human Affairs: Application of Nonlinear Dynamics to Work, Organizations, and Social Evolution*, Mahwah, NJ: Lawrence Erlbaum Associates.

Hippel, K. von (1999) *Democracy by Force: US Military Intervention of the Post-Cold War World*, Cambridge: Cambridge University Press.

IMC (2003) Press release, 12 March 2003, International Medical Corps. Available at: http://www.imc-la.com (accessed March 24, 2004).

Johnson, C. (2000) *Blowback*, New York: Henry Holt & Company.

Maxwell, D. (2004) Keynote address to NATO ACT/USJFCOM CD&E Annual Conference, November 3, 2004.

MNE 3 Concept Development Team (Australian Defence Science and Technology Organisation (DSTO); Canadian Forces Experimentation Centre (CFEC); French Ministry of Defence; German Bundeswehr; NATO Allied Command Transformation (ACT); UK Joint Doctrine and Concepts Centre (JDCC); US Joint Forces Command) (2003) Draft of Effects-based Planning Concept for Multinational Experiment 3, August.

MPAT (2004) Multinational Planning Augmentation Team. Available at: http://www2.apan-info.net/mpat (accessed November 7, 2004).

NATO (2003) Draft NATO White Paper, Coalition Warfare: Coordination and Planning Options, unclassified.

Read, R., US Col. (ret'd.) (2004) Address to NATO ACT/USJFCOM CD&E annual conference, November 3, 2004.

Ricks, T. (2004) "US army changed by Iraq, but for better or worse," *Washington Post*, July 6.

Smith, R.D. (1995) "The inapplicability of principle: what chaos means for social science," *Behavioral Science*, 40: 22.

USJFCOM (2003a) *Standing Joint Forces Headquarters*. Available at: http://www.jfcom.mil/about/fact_sjfhq.htm (accessed March 24, 2004).

—— (2003b) *Rock Drill Draft, Concept of Operations for Multinational Experiment 3*, November 3, unclassified, for official use only.

—— (2003c) *MNE 3 Experiment Directive*, version 2.6, unclassified, for official use only.

—— (2003d) *DRAFT Combined Inter-agency Coordination Group (CIACG) Concept of Operation for MNE 3, Revision 1.1, 04 Sep 03, Improving Cooperation Among US and Coalition Military and Civilian Operational Planners in Crisis Intervention*, unclassified, for official use only.

INDEX

CPSIA information can be obtained at www.ICGtesting.com
Printed in the USA
LVOW100531100812

293717LV00002B/61/P